Gay Fatherhood

Gay Fatherhood

Narratives of Family and Citizenship in America

ELLEN LEWIN

THE UNIVERSITY OF CHICAGO PRESS   CHICAGO AND LONDON

ELLEN LEWIN is professor of women's studies and anthropology at the University of Iowa. She is the author or editor of several books, most recently *Feminist Anthropology*.

The University of Chicago Press, Chicago 60637
The University of Chicago Press, Ltd., London
© 2009 by The University of Chicago
All rights reserved. Published 2009
Printed in the United States of America

16 15 14 13 12 11 10 09   1 2 3 4 5

ISBN-13: 978-0-226-47656-8 (cloth)
ISBN-13: 978-0-226-47658-2 (paper)
ISBN-10: 0-226-47656-1 (cloth)
ISBN-10: 0-226-47658-8 (paper)

Library of Congress Cataloging-in-Publication Data
Lewin, Ellen.
  Gay fatherhood : narratives of family and citizenship in America / Ellen Lewin.
     p. cm.
  Includes bibliographical references and index.
  ISBN-13: 978-0-226-47656-8 (cloth : alk. paper)
  ISBN-13: 978-0-226-47658-2 (pbk. : alk. paper)
  ISBN-10: 0-226-47656-1 (cloth : alk. paper)
  ISBN-10: 0-226-47658-8 (pbk. : alk. paper) 1. Gay fathers—United States
—Case studies. I. Title.
  HQ76.13 .L49 2009
  306.874'2086640973—dc22

                                                              2008055271

FOR VIRGINIA OLESEN —

mentor, colleague, and friend

Contents

Acknowledgments

My journey into the worlds of gay fathers has been one I never anticipated I would undertake. I found my way to this topic one night in 1999 when I sat down to read *The Velveteen Father* by Jesse Green, a new book that according to reviews had at least two irresistible elements—parenthood and gay identity—so once I acquired it I was eager to dive in.

I ended up staying up far into the night, not going to bed until I had finished the book. What moved me most was the urgency and intensity of Green's desire to be a father. In a world that gave his desires little support, and even actively discouraged him, he was determined to have a child—somehow. Unavoidably, the book made me think about the lesbian mothers I had worked with some twenty years earlier, women who consciously had to carve out a space in the world to be both lesbians *and* mothers, since most people couldn't imagine that a person could belong to both categories. I was struck, as well, by the many ways that other gay people acted to enforce the boundaries between parenthood and being gay, and by the fact that the pressures Green faced in choosing fatherhood were even more intense than those experienced by women. Lesbians had access to cultural constructions of "woman" that enabled motherhood, making it seem natural, if incompatible with lesbianism. Gay men had no such images to draw upon. They were simply faced with conventions that told them it wasn't appropriate for them to want to have children.

I realized that night that I wanted to use what I'd learned about lesbian mothers to understand how gay men manage the conflicting cultural demands of being gay and being fathers. This was not a topic I could have imagined embracing in the earlier years of my career, when feminist anthropology and feminist scholarship meant studying "women" (narrowly defined) and no one else. In trying to give voice to women's experiences, many of us thought at the time that we knew entirely too much about men's experience. After all, hadn't men monopolized all forms of discourse, and silenced women? And wasn't it our job to compensate for these erasures?

But it had become clear to me by the time I began this project that a feminist intellectual stance is one that focuses on the interplay of gender with many different elements of social life and culture. That indexical womanly activity—reproduction—has turned out to loom large across a spectrum of human endeavor, and to be central not only to defining the lives of women but also of men. Comprehending that means letting go of notions of reproduction that are already fully implicated with femininity even before inquiry begins, that is, forcing ourselves to ask questions about masculinity and men that don't assume that everything's been said before.

So this has been a very rich and fulfilling research experience. I undertook a series of interviews in the Bay Area and in the Los Angeles area as an initial leap into the research. But having moved to Iowa only a couple of years before launching the project, I realized that San Francisco could no longer serve as "my village." And so I moved my focus to Chicago and its environs, which enabled me to immerse myself in a very different sort of place than San Francisco, one with a more down-to-earth sense of itself, though still having a large and diverse gay population. Exploring the enormous and varied faces of Chicago has been an extra reward that came to me from this work, which I undertook incrementally, beginning with a spring-break sojourn in Oak Park in 2000, and eventually completed during a nine-month period of fieldwork in 2002–2003.

Like all books, this one owes a debt to many different people. I want first to thank the nearly one hundred men who gave generously of their time to share their experiences and ideas with me. In keeping with anthropological conventions, I cannot name them, but they know who they are and I hope they are aware of how much I appreciate their collaboration in this venture. I particularly value their willingness to embark on this project without a clear idea of exactly where it was going, or whether it would benefit them in any way, other than having a chance to articulate their ideas and reflect on their lives. I hope they can recognize matters that are important to them in these pages.

A number of people helped me frame this project and meet fathers and others connected with them. Jay Ruby introduced me to a network of Oak Park residents who were the key to everything I did from then on; in particular, Bob Trezevant was a wonderfully engaging and self-reflexive interlocutor. Following my instinct that members of the clergy would offer good connections to fathers, I met with a number of such community figures in Chicago, and I particularly want to express my appreciation for their willingness to welcome me into their congregations and to introduce me to gay parents. The reverends Greg Dell, Paul Koch, Brad Mickelson, Perry Wiggins, Jacki Balile, and Rabbi Suzanne Griffel were all very supportive. The reverends Alma Crawford and Karen Hutt welcomed me to the Church of the Open Door, and at the Praise Center I was fortunate to get to know pastors Kevin Tindall and Phyllis Pennese. Attending services at the Church of the Open Door and Praise Center gave me some needed spiritual grounding during the research and connected me with members of the African American gay community in Chicago. Rabbi Yoel Kahn's perspective, as a rabbi, a gay father, and someone who thinks about the changing shape of the gay community with uncommon originality was, as always, a person I relied on as I tried to frame an early understanding of the issues. Conversations with filmmaker Johnny Symons also helped clarify the project and his 2002 film *Daddy and Papa* inspired my efforts to give voice to gay dads through ethnography.

A number of staff members at Horizons, a gay community services center in Chicago, were generous with their time, as were Patricia Logue and Rosemary Mulryan, attorneys located in Chicago. Margaret Fleming at Adoption Link in Oak Park unraveled some of the mysteries of adoption for me. Members of Rainbow Families invited me to join them at a number of events, as did Lambda Kids and Families. Bruce Koff, a psychotherapist in Chicago, offered many useful insights.

John D'Emilio deserves special thanks for helping me to feel at home in Chicago and particularly for finding me two temporary "homes"—house-sitting arrangements in Chicago and Oak Park—for the time I was doing my fieldwork. It was great to not feel like a vagabond while in the field. I joined Leni Silverstein for the High Holidays my first fall in Chicago; she hosted me often at her home, and attended enthusiastically to the feeding of my body and spirit throughout the year.

I was fortunate to obtain financial support for this project from more than one source. The Arts and Humanities Initiative (AHI) at the University of Iowa provided funds that permitted me to launch the work in San Francisco and Chicago, beginning in 1999. My work was supported by two other AHI grants at crucial times in the research—during the major period of fieldwork in 2002–3 and in 2006–7, when I was working intensively on this book. A grant from the National Endowment for the Humanities, albeit not approved until my second application (when I took the word "gay" out of the title), enabled me to take a year off from my teaching responsibilities and to focus on the analysis. During that time, I was housed at the Obermann Center for Advanced Study at the University of Iowa, a blissful refuge from the commotion of the university. And though it didn't involve any funds, an honorable mention in the rigorous competition for the Martin Duberman Prize given by the Center for Lesbian and Gay Studies at the City University of New York offered a sign that I was on to something.

I have presented portions of this work at a variety of conferences over the years, including at the American Anthropological Association, the Society for the Anthropology of North America (SANA), the American Ethnological Society, and the Trans/positions conference at Purdue University. I was particularly honored to be invited to an inspiring conference held in Paris in December 2006, "What Gay Marriage Does to Norms," sponsored by the Institut National des Études Démographiques and the École Normale Superieure, organized by the amazing "Gang of Four," Virginie Descoutures, Marie Digoix, Eric Fassin, and Wilfried Rault. I also presented material from this project in invited presentations at several different institutions—the College of Wooster, the University of Kansas, and Iowa State University. Audiences at each of these events asked challenging questions that enabled me to sharpen my reasoning.

A panel at the American Sociological Association connected me to a number of scholars working on lesbian/gay family issues—most notably Mignon Moore and Suzanne Pelka—who have become valued colleagues. I also presented work at the 2008 Lavender Languages and Linguistics Conference in Washington, DC, to an especially energetic audience. Roger Lancaster, a fellow panelist at the SANA conference in Mérida, Mexico, challenged my every point and thereby helped me figure out what I really wanted to say.

Members of two different writing groups made up of University of Iowa colleagues offered cogent critiques that helped keep me from wandering away from my argument. Particular thanks go to Nanette Barkey, Susan Birrell, Jennifer Glass, Lisa Heineman, Catherine Komisaruk, Tina Parrott, and Johanna Schoen. Other friends and colleagues read portions of the manuscript and had wonderfully helpful suggestions. I am grateful to Lee Badgett, Cymene Howe, Bill Leap, Suzanne Pelka, and Leni Silverstein for the careful attention they gave to many pages of manuscript with which I burdened them. Tom Boellstorff was a particularly generous reader, offering some of the most penetrating but also supportive comments I have ever received from a reader. Bill Leap, Elijah Edelman, and Brett Williams came to a small seminar I gave at American University and helped me work through one of the most troublesome parts of an early draft, which helped set the whole project in the right direction. At the very end, Misha Quill very ably produced the index. As always, my life partner Liz Good-man kept me focused and was the final judge of everything I wrote. While I was in the field, Liz took care of our cats and dogs, shoveled the sidewalk, battled ice storms, and endured other adversities on her own with (almost) no complaints.

I am also grateful to the two anonymous readers for the University of Chicago Press, whose comments on the final draft of the manuscript were invaluable as I tried to clarify my argument, but who also made clear that they expected the book to make an important contribution to the field. Many other staff members also eased the transformation of the manu-script into a book, but Kate Frentzel's graceful copyediting was a particu-larly critical part of the process. Doug Mitchell, my editor at the Press, has been incredibly encouraging through the whole process, making me feel that every word I produced was precious. I can't imagine working with a finer editor, or with one who is a more accomplished jazz drummer!

"How Can You Study Such Yucky People?"

S ome years ago I gave a presentation as part of an interdisciplinary panel on marriage presented at the American Studies Association annual meeting. My comments concerned the kinds of unexpected transformations that can follow from same-sex commitment ceremonies, even when they are undertaken in the complete absence of claims to legal legitimacy. I told the story of an upper-middle-class lesbian couple whose public behavior epitomized discretion and who had struggled to craft a ceremony that would avoid all forms of confrontation and would assure their continued privacy. After the ceremony, however, the couple found themselves taking relatively dramatic public stands in support of gay rights and "outing" themselves in a number of locations, a shift most evocatively represented by the changing meaning they attached to the rings they had exchanged in the ceremony (see Lewin, 1998, 109–12, 206–8, for more detail on this story). During the Q&A period that followed the panel, a well-known scholar of queer cultural studies stood and addressed me. "How can you study such yucky people?" she said, abruptly sitting down to signal that no discussion of this comment could follow.

There are a lot of points that could be made about this story, but I'd like to focus on two in particular. The first can be framed in terms of the aversion to "real life" that was implied by her statement. The second is more complex, but directly connected to the first. It assumes that queerness unquestionably resides in visible and intentional subversions of cultural norms and the related expectation that explicit and visible resistance is the only sort of queerness worthy of the name. If one is in the business of queer scholarship or activism, this sort of queerness counts as transgressive and therefore almost automatically worthy of admiration. By extension, all behaviors and styles that are coded as *not* achieving these standards of transgression or "queerness" fall into the complicated category my interlocutor technically defined as "yuckiness," disparaged as not queer, dismissed as accommodationist, and thus not deemed worthy of respectful investigation.

The Real World

Let me start with the troubling matter of the "real world." The scholars and activists who have most doggedly rejected taking the objectives of ordinary lesbians and gay men seriously have tended to engage in something anthropologist Sherry Ortner has aptly called "ethnographic refusal." Beginning with a basic understanding of ethnography as "the attempt to understand another life world using the self . . . as the instrument of knowing," she makes clear that ethnography is not just a set of practices, most typically involving fieldwork, but a stance that yields "an intellectual (and moral) positionality . . . an interpretive mode" (Ortner 1995, 42). Its hallmark is what Clifford Geertz called "thickness," a term that no longer calls for exhaustiveness or holism so much as a kind of contextualization (Ortner 1995, 43). In these terms, ethnographic refusal is found in work that fails to consider the complexity of a situation that might be revealed by fuller engagement with the multiple lived realities of subjects. It is in work that rests too comfortably on preordained accounts of how people end up on particular paths, what Marlene Mackie (1977) has called "congenial truths." Such complexity might be contained not only in the wider society, where differing positions in terms of gender, race, class, or other status markers influence the range of choice people have, but at the level of the individual, where consciousness, intentionality, and identities are rarely stable or internally consistent. I read Ortner as calling for scholarly and political practices that take full account of the diverse motives and meanings that real people use in going about their lives. Such a position requires faith in the authenticity of people's behaviors and beliefs and a repudiation of a reflexive tendency to dismiss what is unappealing to the analyst as corrupt or malicious.

Kath Weston's short essay "Theory, Theory, Who's Got the Theory?" engages a similar issue, addressing two domains she calls "straight theorizing" and "street theorizing." Straight theorizing is what most people recognize as theory, adorned with footnotes and jargon that are both seductive and intimidating. In contrast, street theorizing is "the activity that engages people as they go about their business," sometimes indistinguishable from "everyday wisdom" (Weston 1998, 145). Weston notes that queer studies has tended to privilege straight theorizing at the expense of street theorizing, often dismissing the latter as merely "raw data." She urges a fuller engagement with that theorizing that most of us do as we go about our daily lives and urges us to use it more explicitly as we attempt to craft straight theories.

In the absence of a serious engagement with the feelings and aspirations of ordinary people, queer theorists and activists assert what they think things *should* mean, relying on idealized notions about what the world ought to be like to understand whatever takes place around them. Because of this disengagement from everyday experience, queer theory has tended to glorify cultural and social phenomena interpreted as subversive and to disparage behaviors it codes as complying with mainstream agendas. While some of the exhortations of queer theory might inspire acts of defiance in its adherents, I see it as leading both to empirically untenable positions and, perhaps paradoxically, to strikingly conservative conclusions, eerily channeling positions taken by the religious right and other passionate opponents of gay rights.

Binary Sexualities

The notion that homosexual and heterosexual are non-overlapping, deeply different categories isn't new, any more than binary categorizations of gender are. Historically, narratives of gay life long framed "family" and "gay" as mutually exclusive (Newton 1993). Along the same lines, the existence of lesbian mothers and gay fathers was long understood as an unavoidable legacy of the kind of homophobia that drove gay people into heterosexual marriages, evidence of the monstrous obstacles that prevented persons who were "really" lesbian or gay from living as such openly. Gay and lesbian parents thus were seen as an artifact of the preliberation days of the closet, with the related, but unspoken, assumption that they would cease to exist once conditions permitted lesbians and gay men to come out while still young. In the individualist discourse that has long permeated gay liberation thinking, once homophobia had been defeated, lesbian and gay people would be free to live as "who they really are," and those essential identities were not imagined to include parenthood. In the meanwhile, lesbians who did choose to become mothers were often suspected of capitulating to "a key element of women's subordination—compulsory motherhood" (Calhoun 2000, 135).

The fact is, nevertheless, that some lesbians and gay men invested heavily in their families even during these times—whether these consisted of parents and siblings or children added to households under various conditions. This reality, however, didn't shake the power of images that framed "gay" and "family" as oxymoronic. But as the gay and lesbian rights movement began to make all aspects of our lives more public, other forms of family formation became visible. Starting with the "lesbian baby boom"—later dubbed the "gayby boom," in both the lesbian and gay and mainstream press (Kolata 1989; Steckel 1985; Weeks, Heaphy, and Donovan 2001)—and extending into debates over domestic-partner benefits, civil unions, and same-sex marriage, demands for gay and lesbian family entitlements simply became too insistent to ignore.

By the turn of the twenty-first century two dynamics concerning the demands of lesbians and gay men for various insignia of family recognition had taken shape. On the one hand, a steady stream of legal challenges to existing statutory and policy obstacles, the passage of new laws extending marriage rights to same-sex couples in nations as diverse as the Netherlands, Spain, Canada, and South Africa, and, largely in response to these developments, civil disobedience—notably the flurry of same-sex weddings that occurred not only in San Francisco, but in less obvious locations like New Paltz, NY, Asbury Park, NJ, and Bernalillo, NM, in 2004—all brought the issue of such rights into debate across the political spectrum. More recently, judicial decisions have made same-sex marriage legal in Massachusetts and Connecticut (as of this writing), and other states have either outlawed such unions or, in the case of New York, have agreed to recognize marriages performed in other jurisdictions.

Gay and lesbian parenting became more visible during these years as well; for example, the publicity received by such celebrity lesbian moms as Rosie O'Donnell and Mary Cheney made the image of purposeful lesbian motherhood far more concrete in the public imagination than it had ever been. Press coverage made it seem that all gays and lesbians wanted was the right to share in the benefits of marriage and family. Even as the 1996

Defense of Marriage Act (DOMA) made legal recognition more difficult, many gay people began to believe that obstacles to same-sex marriage would inevitably fall, much as analogous barriers to interracial marriage had in 1967 (Wolfson 2004).

At the same time, however, opposition to such developments intensified, drawing on two basic positions, but in both cases, I contend, reflecting essentialist readings of lesbian and gay identities. First, there was the predictable hostility of conservatives and members of the religious right. In their calculus, being gay or lesbian stands as an absolute contradiction to their understandings of parenthood and family, both practically and morally. Conservative and religious-right antipathy to all divergences from nuclear-family forms reputed to have prevailed throughout human history have remained intense, even as public demands to legitimize lesbian and gay families and couples have grown more insistent. Conservative opponents of lesbian and gay family rights voice a number of concerns, depending on their location in the culture. Some join their hostility to non-heterosexual families to wider anxieties about the future of the American family, frequently invoking catastrophic images of the impending collapse of all that morally upright citizens might hold sacred.

It is not uncommon for their denunciations of gay and lesbian families to bleed into comments about out-of-wedlock births, deadbeat dads, divorce, and other ailments they offer as evidence of the collapse of "family values," in what might appear to displace anxieties about *heterosexual* family stability (Calhoun 2000). These lamentations often include denunciations of cultural relativism, political correctness, abortion, and other perceived affronts to the survival of male-female monogamous marriage, taken to be natural, ancient, and unchanging throughout human history (Coontz 1992, 1997). What is important for the present discussion is that conservative opposition to gay and lesbian families is rooted in a conviction that homosexuality and family life are categorically and morally contradictory.

Queer Fundamentalism

Perhaps surprisingly, vigorous opposition to movements for family rights also has coalesced among queer scholars and activists who are intent on celebrating what they consider inescapable differences between queer people and the rest of the culture. This opposition takes a number of forms, some relatively generous, some superficially celebratory, and others intensely acrimonious. Some simply disregard the existence of lesbian and gay family forms, either naming them as outside the boundaries of queerness or simply ignoring them even when they are plainly visible. Others consider the struggle for marriage, in particular, to be a distraction from more urgent issues facing the larger LGBT collectivity (Ettelbrick 1992). Let me review some of these views briefly and make some comments on what these positions have in common. This will lay the foundation for what I have set as my task in this volume, and indeed, in the rest of my scholarly work.

As I write this book, hostility to same-sex domesticity and a culture war over the future of all such social forms have continued to be central to the thinking of gay/lesbian/queer scholars who represent a number of positions. Paradoxically, this has meant that even as increased media attention to same-sex families has raised awareness about their existence, these very same families often feel distant from lesbian/gay communities and identities. Queer commentators vilify the struggle for family legitimacy as an attempt to assimilate to mainstream, middle-class values, which they view as intrinsically distinctive from what it means to be lesbian or gay. They understand queerness to be the foundation of a distinctive culture, and frame the family aspirations of some gay people as a repudiation of that culture's essential attributes and as a threat to its continuity. Much as homophobic opponents of same-sex families fear them as destructive of what they see as foundational cultural values, queer activists make strikingly analogous claims. Queer culture, in this reading, is intrinsically oppositional and subversive, so any effort to acquire what are defined as the indexical features of heterosexual life is excoriated as a fundamental betrayal of the very essence of queerness.

The particular emphases of commentators who have taken these positions vary, but all depend on a belief in a revealed truth about what queerness "is" or "should be." In an early statement, activist Michael Bronski looked to sexuality as the foundation of queers' difference from others: "Not engendering new life, divorced from the social and economic structures of heterosexual marriage, and apparently employing sexuality as the primary form of self-definition, homosexuality represents sex incarnate" (Bronski 1984, 191). This repudiation of parenthood emerges more recently in the vision of queerness articulated by literary critic Lee Edelman in his diatribe against the "reproductive futurism" he sees as inherent to having children and his largely unintelligible glorification of what he calls the "death drive" essential to queerness. "Queerness," he tells us, "names the side of those *not* 'fighting for the children' " (Edelman 2004, 3; emphasis in original).

Cultural-studies scholar Michael Warner's argument against "the normal" also depends on a basic conviction about what gayness is: "If there is such a thing as a gay way of life, it consists in . . . a welter of intimacies outside the framework of professions and institutions and ordinary social obligations" (Warner 1999, 116). Warner's definition of gay or queer existence is monolithic; those homosexual persons who conceive of their relationships or their position in the wider social universe in other terms would seem to be axiomatically not gay, though what they would be instead is unclear. This position centers queer identity in unspecified but nonetheless non-normative sexual behavior; gays that seem to crave "respectability" then must distance themselves from the taboos that entangle real queers. Warner is not blind to the diversity of gay life. He gestures at what he calls "defensive and apologetic" queers when he acknowledges that "it is true enough that many gay men and lesbians have had little to do with the extremes of queer sexual culture. They might be happily coupled veterinarians in a suburban tract home with nothing more scandalous on their minds than wearing white linen after Labor Day. Well, bully for them" (Warner 1999, 48–49).

Other formulations, though less saturated in hostility, also focus on resistance and subversion as lying at the heart of queer existence. Judith Halberstam, for example, uses an oppositional image of family and queerness as the opening definition in her recent book: "Queer uses of time and space develop, at least in part, in opposition to the institutions of family, heterosexuality, and reproduction" (Halberstam 2005, 1). Others worry that marriage would domesticate lesbians and gays, and that the most problematic aspect of this process would be their withdrawal from a fundamental resistance to heteronormativity seen as the proper hallmark of queer cultural sensibilities. For example, cultural critic Suzanna Danuta Walters argues that "gay marriage might grant visibility and acceptance to gay marrieds, but it will not necessarily challenge homophobia (or the nuclear family) itself; indeed it might simply demonize nonmarried gays as the 'bad gays' (uncivilized, promiscuous, irresponsible) while it reluctantly embrace the 'good gays' who settle down and get married" (Walters 2001, 349).

In other cases, authors like legal scholar Ruthann Robson deplore what she sees as a tendency of feminist and lesbian legal theory to abandon "previous critiques of the oppressive and political nature of the family in favor of advocating recognition for 'our' families." Robson argues that "the celebration of the family accompanies a general depoliticization and privatization of lesbianism," and laments the shift from theorizing "lesbian community, tribe, and perhaps even 'nation'" to a preoccupation with family (Robson 1994, 977).[1] She rejects the conviction of many who seek the recognition of gay and lesbian families on functional grounds—that their domestic units provide all the usual benefits expected of families—as a stance that reifies particular configurations at the expense of others and reduces relationships to mere instrumentality. Her recommendation is that theorists take up a strategy of "unnaming"—refusing to adopt the terminology and analogy provided by family—as "the most conceptually radical form of resistance to the family's power to domesticate lesbianism" (Robson 1994, 992). Another legal scholar, Nancy Polikoff, has argued that "an effort to legalize lesbian and gay marriage would make public critique of the institution of marriage impossible . . . [and that] the limitations of marriage, and of a social system valuing one form of human relationship above all others, would be downplayed" (Polikoff 1993, 1546; see also Polikoff 2008; Vaid 1995).

In an effort to situate all of these trends in larger political-economic realities, particularly those engendered by neoliberalism, historian Lisa Duggan has coined the term *homonormativity* to describe "a politics that does not contest dominant heteronormative assumptions and institutions, but upholds and sustains them, while promising the possibility of a demobilized gay constituency and a privatized, depoliticized gay culture anchored in domesticity and consumption" (Duggan 2003, 50). She positions all gay and lesbian struggles for mainstream entitlements as part of a larger-scale process by which queer politics is stripped of its intrinsically progressive potential, rendered featureless and insipid, positioned in a consumerist model that turns political demands into nothing more than illusory choices.

Even some scholars who have recognized the existence of gay families seem to have difficulty disengaging from the conviction that queer difference is incontestable. Sociologist Judith Stacey interviewed gay men in Los Angeles, focusing in large part on their views of family and their own desires to be (or not to be) parents. Although these interviews revealed that the desire of some gay men for parenthood "beckons to many hungering for lasting love, intimacy, and kinship—for that elusive 'haven in a heartless world'" (Stacey 2006, 29), ideas consistent with rather mainstream American notions of what families are all about, Stacey trained her sights on a conclusion she apparently had drawn before even beginning her research: that "gay male parenthood . . . occupies terrain even more avant-garde than do gay cultures of adult eros and intimacy" (2006, 29). But she doesn't question her narrators about the extent to which they understand themselves to be gender radicals. Rather, Stacey begins by asserting that gay sexualities are manifestly "avant-garde," and so moves easily to casting gays and lesbian as "postmodern family pioneers" (2006, 28–29). Her research captures the intense yearning that underlies gay fathers' struggle to achieve parenthood, but her assumptions about how gay and lesbian subjectivities are "obviously" positioned interfere with the ability of her narrators to have their own accounts heard.[2]

In a similar vein, other scholars leap easily from the claim that since gays and lesbians are fundamentally subversive, their families must therefore constitute revolutionary forms capable of overthrowing the evils of patriarchal family formations (Agigian 2004; J. Thompson 2002). Political scientist Valerie Lehr agrees, but worries that queer families will too easily seize on normative family values and denigrate their own unique contributions to social change (Lehr 1999).

Some other researchers are similarly crippled by their reliance on a priori categories that sabotage their avowed efforts to document the lives of real gay people. In his 2003 book on gay men in suburbia, for example, sociologist Wayne H. Brekhus described men who lived in suburban areas near New York City. Some of those he interviewed felt that their gayness was not the leading component of their identity, seeing it as an accidental trait that didn't speak to their preferences and accomplishments. Brekhus categorizes these men as "integrators" who, he explains, are hybrids of "gay and suburban attributes that are manifested at the same time." He continues, "The suburban gay integrator is an identity centaur whose suburban and gay sides mix to create a worldview that is neither exclusively suburban nor exclusively gay" (Brekhus 2003, 75). In this formulation, "gay" and "suburban" are understood as fundamentally contradictory, virtually by definition, with "suburban" implying some bundle of characteristics inconsistent with "gayness." So completely does Brekhus segregate gayness from the sorts of mainstream values that might influence gay men to live in the suburbs that he fails to take note of any evidence of gay fatherhood or of gay men who hoped to become fathers in the suburban locales where he worked.[3]

Even among scholars who seem to be giving serious attention to the growing importance of "family" in the lives of lesbians and gay men, there

is sometimes only fleeting concern with the parental aspirations and experiences nonheterosexuals may actually have. In his important book *Telling Sexual Stories,* for example, British sociologist Ken Plummer devotes
considerable attention to the kinds of accounts his narrators give about
family and intimacy, particularly their concern with "families we choose"
(Plummer 1995). But unlike Kath Weston, whose pioneering work on both
"chosen" and "biological" lesbian and gay kinship informs his discussion
(Weston 1991), Plummer assumes that the significance of gay kinship lies
solely in its difference from conventional understandings of family. "Gays
and lesbians," he tells us, "may provide mutual networks of support,
care and friendship that are as strong as any family, and maybe stron-
ger because they are chosen rather than simply given. . . . New personal
stories have emerged around 'families we choose or create' rather than
'biological/blood families'" (Plummer 1995, 154). Plummer's focus here,
while gesturing toward gay men and lesbians who ask "how am I to be
involved with children[?]," subsumes the importance of such formations
under what is more interesting to him: the ways that gays and lesbians *by
definition* create new and diverse social forms, challenging convention and
contesting "the very concepts of kinship and family" (Plummer 1995, 154;
see also Giddens 1993, 2002).

Along similar lines, and also echoing Weston's terminology, Peter
Nardi's study of gay men's friendships celebrates the cultural creativity revealed by gay men's characterization of friendship circles as "family," but
gives no attention to the family bonds gay men can create through fatherhood (Nardi 1999). I would suggest that both Plummer and Nardi have
some difficulty imagining that gay and lesbian people could participate in
seemingly mainstream family institutions without being swallowed up and
culturally erased. The possibility that gay/lesbian identities might persist
even as lesbians and gay men move out into the "real world" has received
scant attention, leaving us with little understanding of how (or whether)
those identities might be reconfigured under such conditions.

These works reflect a preoccupation in scholarship of lesbian and gay
life with those practices and cultural formations that situate queerness as
a distinct and intrinsically oppositional ethos. Scholars and the general
public continue to assume that there is something different—and defi-
nitionally subversive—that is necessarily imbedded in the daily business
of being lesbian, gay, or queer. Even as the foundation of lesbian and gay
identity continues to elude investigation—is it specific sexual practices,
stigma and marginality, banishment from one's family, a particular esthetic

sensibility?—scholars bury themselves in the confrontations some queer people present to the mainstream, choosing either to ignore or to belittle other kinds of sensibilities.

Nor does the avowed concern with "diversity" some queer scholars have expressed materialize in serious examination of nonwhite gays and lesbians or those located in lower socioeconomic groups. In the context of this lapse, gay and lesbian family is taken to be nothing more than symbolic, the very real economic ramifications of family legitimacy deemed too trivial to mention. Family bonds that particularly flourish in low-income communities of color, such as the informal fostering that has historically been central to African American communities, are left out of analyses that, despite their expressed suspicion of identity politics, insist that transgressive sexuality constitutes the only identity gay and lesbian people can legitimately possess (Badgett 2001; Carrington 1999; Hawkeswood 1996; Maskovsky 2002; Meeks 2006).

Allan Bérubé (2001) has suggested a link between the presumed whiteness of all gay people and political strategies some activists employed in an effort to gain the attention of powerful political figures. While gay movement leaders have made extensive use of an analogy between racial discrimination and prejudice against gays and lesbians, Bérubé contends that many of their strategies have depended on allowing the assumption that gayness is white to remain in place. In the meanwhile, popular assumptions that gay men are both white and affluent make the experience of nonwhite, non-affluent gays and lesbians simply illegible. While many have seen the surge of marketing to gay populations as a sign of inclusion and political power, Katherine Sender points out that gay marketing and media practices make "people of color, older people, poor and working-class people, and a host of other less privileged sectors of society . . . underrepresented or invisible." The ideal, and visible, gay consumer "risk[s] producing a gay version of the 'model minority' stereotype" (Sender 2004, 237).

It's not surprising that same-sex marriage and related efforts to secure full rights for families have become a magnet for acrimonious debate on both the right and the left. Marriage, after all, is commonly understood to be an institution with such a long history that it seems to somehow exist outside of time, a claim that, indeed, is often made by those who consider themselves the guardians of its traditions. Its normativity is enshrined in many different reminders, some more visible than others. There are the material indicators of its importance such as weddings, rings, newspaper announcements, honeymoons, name changes, and extravagant gifts, to mention but a few. And there are the legal and social entitlements that mostly assume visibility when they are absent: tax benefits, the right to make medical decisions for a spouse, pension and survivor benefits, assumptions about parenthood, and over a thousand other items, small and large, that accrue to couples whose marriages are legally recognized. But most basically, the struggle for access to the family stands as part of a process of claiming the right to exercise citizenship on the same basis as others in the society (Bell and Binnie 2000; Calhoun 2000; Cott 2000; Evans 1993; Kaplan 1997).

Perhaps paradoxically, both queer critics of demands for family-related entitlements and opponents who ground their positions in conservative political and religious rhetorics draw on substantially the same images of lesbian and gay people as profoundly different from the mainstream in ways that embody subversion, disorder, and license. If being gay or lesbian is assumed to always be defined as self-conscious resistance against the mainstream, as a daring challenge to the status quo, then both conservative and queer critiques of family desires can be seen to be rooted in the same set of ideas. "Putting same-sex marriage, lesbian motherhood, and the formation of lesbian and gay families off at the margins of a lesbian and gay political agenda," says philosopher Cheshire Calhoun, "looks suspiciously like a concession to the view of lesbians and gay men as family outlaws" (2000, 154).[4]

Debates about *how* the family or marriage should be studied in gay communities have tended to turn on deeper controversies about *whether* either family or marriage should be advocated for lesbian and gay men. Some commentators seem to regard any effort to describe the family values held by (some) lesbians and gay men as a headlong retreat from resistance to all forms of heterocentrism, homophobia, and oppression, a craven capitulation to hegemonic forces. What might be called the assimilation debates, however, are not merely matters of doctrine, but reflect markedly different approaches to empirical research, a fundamental difference between an interest in what should exist and what actually animates real people's lives. Those who disparage the lives of gays and lesbians whom they judge as failing to achieve some predetermined subversion quotient essentially claim a very restrictive reading of queerness, one limited to particular geographies and only acceptable when manifested in particular stylistic statements. As much as some scholars have repudiated the basic dichotomy between resistance and accommodation, the intensity of the debate persists, growing ever more antagonistic even as particular efforts to gain rights for lesbians and gay men seem to be succeeding. Ultimately, as sociologists Amy Hequembourg and Jorge Arditi (1999) point out, they represent contradictory positions on basic questions of agency, and thus offer sharply divergent approaches to formulating political strategies.

Gay fathers are merely the latest entrants into this contentious arena. They are challenged by homophobic forces that would erase their ability to form families. They are subjected to the sexist assumptions of a public that cannot conceptualize how a man, let alone a gay man, could be, or could want to be, a primary parent. At the same time that they must manage these assaults, they are at least rhetorically buffeted by queer ideologies that question their motives, their values, and their politics. But they are also valued by some segments of the various constituencies with which they interact—by lesbians and gay men who are inspired by their familial aspirations, by straight people who see them as asexual and domesticated and thus not threatening, by social service providers who seek them out as placements for unwanted children, by agents who profit from mediating between them and birth mothers, egg donors, and surrogates. Their particular realities, their negotiation of these varying terrains, are the subject of this book.

CHAPTER ONE

Family Values

New Questions about Lesbian and Gay Peoples in the U.S.

In 2002, both mainstream and gay media featured stories on a gay couple from Lexington, Kentucky, that had fathered quadruplets with the aid of a surrogate. Thomas Dysarz and Michael Meehan told their story on television shows, in newspapers and magazines, and were everywhere presented as heroic and admirably family-oriented; a tableau that appeared on a network morning news show pictured them sitting side-by-side with a baby on each of their four knees. Their status as minor celebrities recalled the media treatment typically extended to large-order multiple births, such as that of the McCaughey septuplets in Iowa (Duquaine-Watson 2005), a heady combination of shock and disbelief. Some of the images deployed in these accounts depend on the same fascination with the "gee-whiz" elements of new reproductive technologies that have driven coverage of other reproductive oddities—postmenopausal women who succeed in gestating and delivering babies, and women who serve as surrogates for their daughters and give birth to their genetic grandchildren.[1]

An article in the gay magazine *The Advocate* quoted Dysarz as he described their lives since the birth of the babies: "Everything is focused on the children, and with multiples it's just so much of everything. . . . We make our formula by the gallon. We'll probably go through 30,000 diapers between now and the time they're out of diapers" (DeLaMar 2003). Meehan (the sperm donor for the quads) was the only legal parent, a condition unlikely to change given Kentucky's hostility to second-parent adoption.

But at the time *The Advocate* article was written, the same surrogate was pregnant again, this time with Dysarz acting as the biological father. The emphasis on the heroic logistics the men had to undertake to manage quadruplets, and their desire to have even more children, suggested an intense commitment to family that eclipsed their homosexuality. The coverage went on to detail the baptism held for the infants at Lexington's Cathedral of Christ the King, an event picketed by the peripatetic antigay Kansas minister Fred Phelps, but an event that also gave rise to a counterdemonstration, Rally for a Hate-Free Lexington.

Mainstream media coverage of the couple stressed the seeming paradox between their conservative "family values" and their unusual family constellation. A February 2004 ABC News *Primetime* program, for example, described the men's family—Meehan and Dysarz, the surrogate, the five children she carried for them, and the three children she'd had previously (in her marriage)—as constituting "uncharted territory" that would turn conventional notions of family "upside down." But at the same time, the program made much of the two men's personal conservatism: "They moved from Los Angeles [to Lexington, Kentucky] because they wanted more traditional Middle American values around them. The couple may be challenging convention, but they are decidedly conservative. Dysarz is anti–abortion rights, against divorce, devoutly Catholic, Republican. He and his partner are gay" (ABC 2004).

What fascinated journalists from both mainstream and gay media were the apparent contradictions between the challenge the two men seemed to pose to traditional families and their commitment to extremely conservative social and religious positions. Still later in 2004 the story of Meehan and Dysarz became further sensationalized by their separation. According to an article in the *Lexington Herald-Leader*, each man retained custody of the children he had biologically fathered, but a dispute erupted after Meehan accused Dysarz of domestic violence and attempted to secure a court order restricting his contact with the quadruplets.[2] A judge dismissed the domestic violence allegations, but other local courts refused to allow the surrogate, Brooke Verity, to terminate her parental rights, following a report by an attorney appointed by the court to represent the children that emphasized the importance of a mother and father to growing children (Spears 2004).

Popular media's attention to gay fathers like Dysarz and Meehan play on the contradictions between formulaic expectations for gay "lifestyles" and fatherhood. These representations challenge expectations that gay men are necessarily unconventional in all aspects of their lives with the discovery that some gay men may value the mundane rewards of family, marriage, children, and religion, offering a capsule representation of the distance gay people's demands for families have traveled in recent years. As we have seen, however, the praise the two men garnered was hardly unanimous. They also drew the attention of homophobic activists and received shabby treatment in Kentucky courts. In many ways, their story parallels the larger story of gay fatherhood in the United States.

Family Wars

Only about two decades have passed since "family values" emerged as an ideologically weighted phrase fueling a culture war between commentators who positioned themselves as defenders of tradition and those who supported expanded definitions of what families could be. Self-appointed guardians of heterosexual nuclear families focused on a diverse set of adversaries—out-of-wedlock motherhood, divorce, and abortion figure especially prominently—but nothing has galvanized anxieties over cultural relativism, changes in norms related to gender and sexuality, and the moral decay thought to be related to these shifts like homosexuality. Homosexuality itself, of course, is not so much the actual target of conservative activism as its increasing visibility and legitimacy. And few aspects of homosexuality have excited as much distress as ever more vocal demands to claim the right to establish publicly acknowledged marriages and families.

The existence of varied domestic, sexual, and reproductive configurations is nothing new, nor is the periodic explosion of panic from various quarters over the impending collapse of civilization. Historians have documented the patterns of domestic life that have emerged under particular social conditions, showing how such arrangements have been shaped by economic pressures and opportunities, by social constraints, and by cultural preferences; anthropologists have produced similar findings that reveal wide variations in kinship arrangements across cultural boundaries.[3]

Probably almost no one who charted the origins of the movement for lesbian and gay civil rights in the 1970s would have predicted that by the beginning of the twenty-first century demands for access to visible insignia of marriage and family would emerge as among the most contentious issues the movement would raise. Both academic and popular writings on lesbians and gay men have long rested on foundational assumptions of difference and separation that defined gay and lesbian life almost exclusively in terms of indexical sexual behaviors. This emphasis has meant that there has been little attention to how homosexuality might overlap with and merge into other kinds of social and cultural formations, as well as to how gay and lesbian identities might be more contingent than has been generally assumed. Regardless of its specific focus, lesbian and gay activism for many years tended to seek tolerance in hopes that tolerance would erase criminal sanctions for same-sex erotic practices and would allow gay people some measure of personal safety. This focus on tolerance often highlighted claims that homosexuals were no different from heterosexuals, but these claims usually had to do with notions of psychological or moral equivalence rather than literal sameness. Such claims still assumed difference, but tried to moderate notions that sexual difference was equivalent to moral deviance, mental illness, or crime (D'Emilio 1983).

In this chapter, I will examine the events that have fostered the emergence of gay fathers as a visible (if still numerically small) constituency and have facilitated their participation in the worlds of adoption and assisted reproduction. I will provide basic demographic data, review the legal impediments that have challenged gay fathers, and offer some examples of how they have been portrayed in popular media. In addition, I will seek to situate gay fathers in the larger context of cultural readings of fatherhood that predominate in the U.S., and describe the processes by which gay men are able to achieve fatherhood in the current climate. These discussions, and a review of methods I used in my research, provide the backdrop to the study of gay fathers' narratives that will follow in subsequent chapters.

As many commentators have noted, the lesbian and gay rights movement was directly inspired by the civil rights and feminist movements that preceded it. Controversy about difference and equality has, of course, resonated throughout both civil rights and feminist movements, fueling debates about tactics, strategies, and basic objectives. But demands for family-related rights for gays and lesbians didn't typically emerge as explicit political objectives, or as the center of an organized plan for gaining rights, but rather exploded out of individual cases and personal stories that were sometimes viewed as distracting from broader and more pressing agendas. As I noted in the prologue, supporting the rights of lesbian and gay parents was at best a side issue in the early days of gay liberation, as most activists assumed that such parenthood was a relic of past oppression.[4]

Given the weight of sexual behavior as the defining attribute of gays and lesbians, procreation and family formation hardly seemed like central problems for homosexuals.

Perhaps even less predictable than the rise of the family as a focus of gay and lesbian activism has been the emergence of a singularly unlikely protagonist in that struggle—the gay father. Prior to the late 1980s and early 1990s, the few public debates about gay families virtually always revolved around lesbian mothers, shifting in emphasis over time with changing legal and social conditions. These emphases reflected, of course, the larger numbers of families with children that were headed by mothers—heterosexual or lesbian—but they also spoke to deeply held, normative assumptions that men are naturally disengaged from child rearing, even when they are members of intact, heterosexual families.

Gender stereotypes about women as innately nurturing, irresistibly drawn to parenting were as apt to be held by lesbians themselves as by the general public (Lewin 1993). Such normative gender expectations—notions that intense commitment to parenthood is (and should be) a feminine preoccupation—turn up in a variety of discursive contexts that have nothing to do with sexual orientation, most notably in discussions surrounding infertility and assisted reproduction (Greil 1991), but also in a variety of feminist-inspired discourses on shared parenting and egalitarian marriage (Ehrensaft 1987). They are also, of course, a mainstay of conservative and religious right discourse, incorporating ideas about what constitutes "good" mothering that find their way into policy (e.g., so-called welfare reform) and that shape the organization of the workplace and the economic disparities that continue to follow gender lines (see, for example, Hays 1996; Stone 2007).

Given this context, the increasing visibility of gay fathers has been an unexpected development. These men burst on the scene through a number of avenues, but in most cases, they have been distinctive in their particular insistence on becoming parents, or on being recognized as gay men who are also fathers. The passion with which gay fathers have pursued both the actual goal—becoming parents—and matters of representation is the characteristic that is most marked in this process. In other words, these men do not just happen to be fathers. Their visibility derives from their insisting upon the right to bring children into their lives, to organize their time around the exigencies of childrearing, and to constitute their identities in a manner that resembles neither popular images of men in general nor of gay men more specifically.

How common is gay fatherhood? As is the case for any demographic question about gay and lesbian (or other stigmatized) populations, it's hard to say. Economist Lee Badgett draws on a number of surveys in an effort to clarify the involvement of gay men and lesbians (as compared with heterosexuals) in parenting. Some of her sources indicate that some 15 percent of gay men report having children living with them. Others put the percentage at over 20 percent, while still others distinguish between gay men who are parents (regardless of where their children reside) at 27 percent, and gay men who have children in their households at 15 percent (Badgett 2001; Simmons and O'Connell 2003). Other estimates put the number of children living with either lesbian mothers or gay fathers in the U.S. at somewhere between four and six million (Castells 2004, 285). Demographers Gary Gates and Jason Ost (2004) note that states in the Midwest have seen the most rapid growth in the numbers of gay households willing to identify themselves to the Census Bureau. Like heterosexual families, "gays who have children . . . gravitate toward [the suburbs and the heartland] for the same reasons that straight parents do: better schools, bigger gardens, peace and quiet" (*Economist* 2007, 58).[5]

None of these figures clarify how these children came to live with gay fathers, nor do they reveal situations under which gay men might be involved with children who do not reside in their homes on a fulltime basis or might be noncustodial parents. In other words, these figures do not help us to distinguish gay men who became fathers in previous heterosexual marriages or other arrangements from those we might call "intentional" gay fathers—those who have purposefully sought and achieved parenthood in the context of their lives as gay men.

Gay Fathers Come on the Scene

Around the time that the same-sex marriage debates began to take a major place in public discourse, in the 1990s, gay fathers began to make an appearance in popular culture. Early representations of and writings about gay fathers focused on men who had children in heterosexual marriages and who later left those marriages. Since fathers were less likely than mothers to seek custody of their children after divorce, the kinds of legal conflicts that arose with former wives typically coalesced around questions of whether the children should be told about their fathers' homosexuality and what sorts of visitation arrangements would be approved.

Many of these cases turned on issues that echo earlier challenges to lesbian mothers. The foundation of most of the objections to fathers' involvement with their children, whether custody or visitation was the issue, was a diffuse moral approbation and a related assumption that gay identity would necessarily be associated with scandalous and exhibitionistic sexual behavior. In a 1998 North Carolina case, *Pulliam v. Smith*, for example, the court terminated the custody of a father who had raised his two sons since birth and also ordered that he be permitted one month of visitation in the summer as long as his sons were kept out of the home he shared with his male partner. Although all the evidence presented to the court showed that the man was an exceptional parent, the court found that his private sexual behavior and expression of affection "will likely create emotional difficulties for the two minor children." The state supreme court upheld the ruling, but said that its decision was not based on the man's identity— that of "practicing homosexual"—but on the presumption that he "was regularly engaging in sexual acts," even if such behavior occurred in the privacy of his bedroom (Cain 2000, 250).

In another case, argued in Mississippi in 1999, a father was denied custody of his son even after the mother had married a man who had beaten her and threatened to kill the son. Despite a host of supporting evidence—the son's calls to the police during violent episodes, the mother's problematic employment situation, and the gay father's stable job in California—the trial court reacted as follows: "The conscience of the Court is shocked by the audacity and brashness of an individual to come into court, openly and freely admit to engaging in felonious conduct on a regular basis and expect the Court to find such conduct acceptable, particularly with regard to the custody of a minor child. The parties are not in Kansas anymore [the state where the family had previously resided], nor are they in California" (Cain 2000, 251). Since this case was brought prior to *Lawrence v. Texas*, the 2003 case in which the Supreme Court invalidated sodomy statutes, the "felony" in question consisted in assumed acts of sodomy. The state supreme court later modified the ruling slightly, reversing the order that the father's partner move out of the home during the son's summer visits (Cain 2000, 251).

As was the case earlier for lesbian mothers, the questions raised in custody and visitation disputes have generated scholarship that uses small comparative studies to demonstrate the ability of gay men to be good parents. Most of this research focuses on the mental health of the family members, the gender-related behaviors of the children, and sometimes touches on the anxieties experienced by formerly married gay men as they struggle to make sense of the contradictions that seem to characterize their new situation (Bozett 1987). This literature proceeds from one small clinically oriented study to another, each demonstrating that formerly married gay fathers are "no different" from their heterosexual counterparts in such areas as parenting attitudes, involvement and intimacy with their children, sex-role orientations, self-esteem, and other psychological measures (Patterson 1995).

When the focus is on the children of these men, as well, studies consistently show that outcomes are roughly comparable to those among children of heterosexuals. The entire corpus of research, of course, is based on relatively few studies, and often depends on self-report, laboratory findings, or other data that may not inspire complete confidence (Stacey and Biblarz 2001). But regardless of whether such comparisons offer tools appropriate to understanding the gay fathers' general level of parental competence, their overall consistency does point broadly to the likelihood that families with gay fathers can meet the basic needs of children as adequately as other families. When added to the fact that no scandals alleging neglect or abuse have surfaced during the years that gay fathers have become visible actors on the national scene, the data seem to support those fathers who wish to play a significant role in their children's lives.

The situation of formerly married gay fathers has not been completely comparable to that of lesbian mothers. Beyond the fact that it is more often visitation rather than custody that has preoccupied those charged with evaluating gay fathers, with the emergence of the HIV/AIDS epidemic in the 1980s, gay men found themselves stigmatized not only because of their sexual identities but as possible carriers of a dread disease (Benkov 1994).[6] In cases where fathers are HIV-positive, challenges to their involvement with their children are often based on anxieties about their spreading the infection, with judges sometimes requiring men to wear gloves or other protective garb when interacting with their children (Zaslow 1994). Elsewhere, opponents to paternal custody or visitation have argued that the stigma associated with AIDS would be detrimental to the child—an argument reminiscent of claims made about homosexuality itself in earlier lesbian mother custody cases—while others have cited the likelihood that an HIV-infected parent would have a shortened life expectancy, thus exposing the child to a range of stressful circumstances related to illness and death (Mahon 1988). In other cases, the gay father's HIV status has seemed to enter arguments over custody and visitation as evidence of moral corruption that should disqualify his desire to be an active parent, though in some of these instances it has been difficult to distinguish the judicial response to HIV from bias against homosexuality itself (Cooper 1992; Zaslow 1994).

Even when custody or visitation agreements are not in contention, the epidemic has meant that some children whose fathers have come out as gay might not only have to absorb and make sense of that information, but might also have to experience the loss of their fathers to the disease. The shame and secrecy that often accompany such losses only exacerbate their impact (Benkov 1994). Gay men who fathered children in past marriages, of course, have been as likely as other formerly married fathers to view their parental obligations as more material than affective, making them less apt to contest biases that relegate them to a marginal position in their children's lives.

It should be noted that the advent of HIV/AIDS may have had another kind of influence on gay men's involvement in parenting. The epidemic, or more precisely, the catastrophic losses it generated in gay men's social circles, seems to have fostered a new interest in monogamy, domesticity, and the arguably safer pleasures such activities would be expected to yield. Some observers have noted that interest in parenthood seems to be a response some gay men have made to the existential challenges posed by years of loss. For example, in a book chronicling the impact of HIV/AIDS on gay life in America, policy analyst John-Manuel Andriote quotes community activists and service providers on this point. One psychiatrist spoke of his growing desire "to leave a legacy in the world" by adopting a child. Torie Osborn, a leading gay/lesbian activist, referred to the "gayby boom" she had witnessed in the 1980s: "There's a huge transformation of values, a huge resurgence of spirituality and of connecting to kids. If I look at my friends across the country, gay and gay-identified, the people who are coping the best with the epidemic are the ones who have kids in their lives and straight people in their lives" (Andriote 1999, 403). It is worth noting that the shift Osborn mentions not only involves parenthood but also expanding connections outside gay/lesbian communities. Indicators of gay men's moves toward a less ghettoized existence and a broader definition of themselves as citizens abound in comments on the post-AIDS scene, and are themes I will return to later. Of course, such moves cannot be made by gay men acting independently; the extent to which the wider community welcomes gay people is a major determinant of how such changes are implemented.

Along similar lines, others who track social trends among gay men have documented the growth of social institutions not centered on bars, clubs, and baths, including hiking groups, sports teams, religious organizations, and many others (Bull and Gallagher 1996). In a related development, Twelve Step programs grew rapidly in the gay community in the 1980s, indicating a widespread desire to jettison the behaviors associated with a bar-centered social scene (Newton 1993). Whether such activities are completely new or merely more visible than in the past, they do seem to have achieved greater cultural centrality in the years immediately following the first period of the epidemic in the 1980s. Anecdotal evidence from lesbian mothers points to greater receptivity to the presence of children in contexts that include both lesbians and gay men, with men showing a new willingness to support such family-friendly services as child care. The entrance of children and families into gay spaces may not be uniformly celebrated (Green 1999; Newton 1993), but their presence continues and increasingly has been normalized.

As is implied by these accounts, particularly those that focus on the transformative potential of children, a new kind of gay father gained visibility on the national stage during the 1990s: the intentional gay father. These are fathers who break the mold in a number of ways. Despite being gay men, they prioritize parenthood seemingly at the expense of stereotypically gay male preoccupations with entertainment, sexual adventure, and other forms of pleasure-oriented consumption that assume relative affluence. While various sources indicate that gay male couples are less likely to be raising children than are either lesbians or heterosexual couples, the number of men who have become parents after coming out as gay is not insubstantial.

Gay Fathers in the News

Recent media treatments have documented particular instances of injustice suffered by gay fathers and their families. For example, a widely distributed documentary film on gay fathers, *Daddy and Papa*, profiles several families that formed under various circumstances. It gives a detailed account of the case of a Florida man, Doug Houghton, a nurse at a local hospital, who became the legal guardian of Oscar Williams after the boy's father, a troubled man without a stable home, simply left his child with Houghton at the hospital. He later joined with a group of gay foster fathers in Florida in a suit over the state's policy banning adoption (but not fostering) by gay men. The film highlights the bond that developed between Houghton and his son over the years, particularly noting the ways in which his parenting helped to resolve the serious health problems the child had when he first arrived. It also includes an interview with the boy's biological grandparents, who strongly support Houghton's efforts to adopt (Symons 2002).

Other plaintiffs in the Florida case have also had their stories appear in the media. Wayne LaRue Smith and Daniel Skahen of Key West, both of whom are white, sought to adopt two boys, ages five and six, who were their foster children for over two years. One boy is white and the other biracial and both have developmental problems that improved steadily after they were placed with the two men. Because the older of the two boys made such marked progress after his placement with the two men, the state threatened to actively pursue a permanent placement with a heterosexual family. An article that details the case in the *New York Times* captures the two men's fears that their children might be suddenly removed from their home, largely because they had done such a good job with them. The article quotes one of the fathers:

> Mr. Smith said their best hope for keeping their family intact was that the older boy was, like many of the children in foster care in Florida, not quite what prospective parents were looking for. "Nobody wants to adopt a 6-year-old with developmental problems who is biracial," he said, bitterness tinged with hope.
>
> He paused, because he had been too sweeping.
>
> "I do," he said. (Liptak 2003)

Notwithstanding the sympathetic treatment these families have received in some forums, in January 2005 the U.S. Supreme Court refused to review Florida's ban on adoptions by gay men and lesbians. Although state regulations permit adoptions by persons who might not seem like optimal candidates for parenthood, "those who have failed at previous adoptions and those with a history of drug abuse or domestic violence," the Supreme Court let stand a decision by the 11th Circuit Court of Appeals that stated that "the accumulated wisdom of several millennia of human experience ... [showed that the] optimal family structure" for raising children was one with a married mother and father (Greenhouse 2005).

Cases such as these captured the attention of a wider public when television personality Rosie O'Donnell championed their cause on national

TV, coming out as a lesbian mother in the course of publicizing their plight. The fact that gay fathers who wish to adopt may be matched with children unlikely to be chosen by heterosexual families who (presumably) have more attractive options generates an image of heroism and selflessness that contrasts dramatically with more usual representations of gay men as pleasure-seeking, self-indulgent, and culturally situated at some distance from their families. A plot line in the HBO series *Six Feet Under*, for example, offered a realistic, if somewhat parodic, representation of how David Fisher, a white gay man who works in the family funeral parlor, and his African American partner Keith sought to form a family. Over the course of several episodes, beginning in 2002 and finally culminating in 2005, they move through investigating numerous options, including attempting a private adoption with a birth mother who turns out to be unreliable. They finally adopt two troubled but appealing black teenage boys through the foster care system. As they move fitfully toward parenthood their relationship has its ups and downs, and they often question whether they should continue their efforts to become parents. Interestingly, the story line is embedded in the ongoing saga of the entire family, presented as no odder than the other plot elements that made up the quirky series narrative.

Thinking about Fathers

Given these accounts, we might wonder about the relative invisibility of gay fathers in gender-studies scholarship across the disciplines, and particularly about their general omission from the work of scholars of gay life. In the U.S. context, fatherhood is a status that is manifestly tied to underlying ideologies of masculinity conceptualized as achievement, financial provisioning, striving, and strength, but rarely in terms of nurturance or caretaking. That these ideologies are dominant and hegemonic is so obvious that it seems superfluous to even mention them. But a review of the contours of these ideas is called for here.

Fatherhood is, of course, not a monolithic condition, but rather consists of a bundle of meanings that have shifted with other historical developments around the world as well as in the American context. In early nineteenth-century New England, for example, fatherhood was understood in terms of familial authority whereby "the man at the head of the family . . . embodied God's authority in the daily life of each person" (Rotundo 1993, 11). This was a period, importantly, when the family was more than an affective domestic arrangement: it provided the primary setting for economic production and located men in terms of their ancestors and descendants, thereby anchoring individuals' social and political position. As industrialization took hold, however, the location in which men could enact masculinity began to shift from the family to the workplace, a development that inevitably made paternal involvement in the family more abstract and more economically measurable.[7]

As sociologist Ralph LaRossa argues, there is no single history of fatherhood. Ethnicity, region, class, race, and a host of other social, cultural, economic, and ecological variables mean different things for families and fathers in different places and at different historical moments. These variations share one attribute even as they differ: they are intimately tied to gender politics, to normative conceptions of masculinity and femininity, regardless of what specific behaviors might characterize actual mothers and fathers as they go about their ordinary activities (La Rossa 1997, 15). In other words, gender—the division of human beings into men and women—is typically conceived of as the expression of "natural" differences in reproductive roles between persons who become fathers and mothers, and such conceptions tend to be framed in the language of nature—of idealized versions of maternal and paternal behavior—wherever they occur. For example, at different times in the U.S. context fathers have been viewed as primarily economic actors, as political or moral authorities, as distant objects of respect, or as intimate sources of affection ("dads") (La Rossa 1997, 137). While these varied articulations of fatherhood demonstrate the malleability of the institution, at any given time they are enshrined as universal and immutable. In the current U.S. context, a single type of family has come to assume cultural dominance, what sociologist Dorothy Smith (1993) has dubbed the "Standard North American Family" or SNAF. This is the unit also known as the "nuclear family," in recent times invoked as the essence of healthy social life by social conservatives, even as it has been denounced by feminists, advocates for cultural diversity, gays and lesbians, single mothers, and others who don't fit comfortably within its boundaries. Three decades of feminist critiques of the nuclear family as the institution that most palpably solidifies traditional gender expectations and the inequality of women have led to calls for men to become more directly involved in the daily business of caring for children.[8] These critiques have received a lot of visibility in the media and elsewhere, and are often blamed by social conservatives for having sparked a radical reconfiguration of the family.[9]

Despite feminist attention over the past three decades to the importance of changing paternal behavior, those who have had to assess attempts to reconfigure the role of the father have reported mixed results at best. Psychologist Diane Ehrensaft, for example, describes couples that have committed to share parenting equally, but for whom such sharing generally amounts to gendering specific tasks and then declaring them "separate but equal" (Ehrensaft 1987). She notes that even in families that have tried to equalize the contributions of mothers and fathers, assumptions about mothers being more innately emotionally tuned-in or fathers having a greater commitment to success in the workplace remain largely intact, with domestic life still being coded as "feminine" even when men participate in it actively (Ehrensaft 1987).[10]

These studies reiterate a long history of similar findings about families that might be expected to adopt egalitarian domestic arrangements. Although the various research ventures in this area conceive of equality in a number of different ways, and use diverse samples and methods for their investigations, it seems that fairness and equity prove to be moral judgments that are mired in gender expectations more often than descriptions of actual domestic workloads (Ehrensaft 1987; Hertz 1986; Risman 1998). Even for men claiming to be practitioners of "the new fatherhood," a style of parenting that involves men directly in the daily activities of their children, changes characterize attitudes more than behaviors, and often are found among older, relatively privileged men who may no longer need to focus on employment. These men also usually select "the more pleasurable aspects of childcare, such as playing with children or taking them out" (Segal 1990, 35), but leave the more routine obligations to mothers. In other words, caretaking and domesticity continue to be coded as feminine even in maverick families that seek to overturn gender conventions. This is not to say that men have no interest in the development of their children, but rather that their responsibilities for their success rest more on providing the conditions under which their children can develop than on involvement in quotidian details.

Anthropologist Nicholas Townsend has written evocatively of what he calls "the package deal," the meanings that American men attribute to their marital and paternal obligations. Townsend makes clear that fatherhood is important to the men he studied, but that they associate successful performance as a father with marriage, employment, and home ownership, interacting achievements that enable men to be fathers to their children. Success in fatherhood demands, in particular, employment that not only facilitates material wellbeing and home ownership, but also enables mothers to stay home and directly meet children's emotional needs (Townsend 2002).[11]

Regardless of the ideology of either fatherhood or motherhood that might be espoused in particular settings, it is useful to understand actual parental behavior as a set of practices that are imbued with gendered meanings as they are performed. The sentiments and complex web of associations that attach to these practices, particularly insofar as they are performed in the home—a site replete with emotional associations— might be said to constitute the active process of being a family. These are concrete practices as well as acts coded for gender—such activities as preparing food, tending to children, cleaning the house—that can be carried out by anyone, but are nonetheless nearly always interpreted as being the characteristic work of women (DeVault 1991).

If these varied approaches to fatherhood underscore one consistent theme, it is that fathers are conventionally imagined to be relatively marginal to the daily business of parenting, both in terms of their routine practices and their emotional investment in these practices. Even with the voices of feminist critics exerting some force on the formation of new expectations for paternal involvement, fathers continue to be conceptualized as persons who facilitate the formation of families but who stand outside the ordinary operations of these units. While motherhood is on many levels the defining attribute of womanhood, the single activity that most definitely makes gender what it is, fatherhood is not conventionally mandatory for the formation of manhood in American culture. Nor is fatherhood expected to be the focus of passionate yearning, an achievement that men consider essential to their emotional survival as women are thought to do with respect to motherhood. As sociologist William Marsiglio puts it, "What is clear is that men's direct physiological contribution and experience in procreation, particularly in western societies, is restricted to their sperm" (Marsiglio 1998, 54).

But research on how single fathers manage their parental duties suggests that fathers' stories may be more complicated. Barbara Risman (1986) and Andrea Doucet (2006) have examined the organization of caretaking in single-father households, that is, under conditions when the possibility of delegating the daily routines of childcare and domestic responsibility is absent because there is no woman available to shoulder these tasks. Both scholars are drawn to the question of whether and under what conditions men can accomplish such tasks, or, as Doucet poses the question, "Do men mother?" Risman shows that fathers report little difficulty assuming responsibility for homemaking responsibilities and other hands-on dimensions of parenthood that seem so challenging for fathers in homes with mothers. She concludes that the ability to "do" mothering is neither psychologically nor structurally predetermined, but is rather the outcome of particular conditions that call for men to assume the practical and expressive tasks (at least among the relatively affluent, disproportionately white respondents who completed her survey).

Doucet's work largely confirms these findings. Her study of single and stay-at-home fathers (including some gay men) particularly focuses on fathers' encounters with female-dominated parental activities in such settings as playground play groups. The men describe being highly conscious that their position as primary caregivers is perceived as anomalous and requires explanation. They are keenly aware that their parental roles are not what they themselves anticipated for their lives, and that they need to constantly assess how to do what they do.

Doucet worries that constructions of mothering as *work* rather than *identity* (as framed by such feminist theorists as Sara Ruddick) establish an untenable distinction between practice and identity. "In everyday practices, there is often a blurred line between who people think they *are* and what they *do*" (2006, 223; emphasis in original). Doucet goes on to conclude that material assessments of gender equity fail to capture the complicated dynamics by which both fathers and others organize their expectations and generate meanings. Doing mothering work is only part of the story; framing that work in terms of gender is another that may proceed relatively independently.

Even as the gendering of caregiving and domesticity has become somewhat more flexible in recent years, these domains remain devalued as "women's work" in the wider society; the resiliency of these patterns helps to shape the experience of mothers (as has been well documented) and fathers, as well. But since these activities also represent the most important locus of power that women possess, women may themselves resist efforts to allow men to partake of the pleasures, as well as the disadvantages, of primary caretaking. Doucet is careful to make clear that "the fathering stories recounted in this book are marginal ones; they sit quietly on the borders of most men's lives in more contemporary societies" (250). That is, even as some men do the things that mothers do, the larger system of gender stratification remains intact.

As we have seen, most researchers are concerned with how women *do* mothering, or with whether and how men might also *do* mothering or

fathering, or other gendered work. In other words, the focus of most scholarship has been on performance. Some scholars of gender have looked
at how the meanings associated with motherhood shape women's perceptions of themselves and their ways of interacting with the world around
them (Hays 1996). But there have been few analogous considerations of
fatherhood, perhaps because scholars believe that fathering is only rarely
at the heart of men's identities. Studies of men who are primary or even
fulltime parents usually position their situation as reactive: the fathers
being examined have gained custody of their children through divorce,
death, or economic exigencies, and they rise to the occasion and do what
needs to be done. The conventions of custody law, which usually assume
that the mother is the most appropriate custodial parent, reinforce these
ideologies.[12]

But what makes fatherhood important to men whose involvement in
this domain is not generally reactive? What about men who don't have
to be fathers but actively seek the burdens of parenthood? Those who do
parenting work may experience it as rewarding, but what makes men want
to do this work in the first place? And how do they go about becoming
fathers?

Becoming a Father

What does it take for gay men who have not had children in marriages
to achieve fatherhood? The first thing to be noted about the quest for
parenthood is that nothing about it is easy or straightforward. Since gay
men do not even have the options available to (some) lesbians to become
pregnant through donor insemination or some other mechanism, becoming a parent requires either fostering, adoption, or surrogacy, or making
a shared-parenting arrangement with a woman or a lesbian couple. None
of these paths is easy to negotiate, and many of them require a substantial
financial investment. I will discuss these options more fully in chapter 2;
here I offer a general overview of the choices available to gay men who
wish to become fathers.

Official Channels

As is the case for all persons hoping to become parents through foster care
or adoption, single gay men and couples must navigate a virtual minefield

of regulations. But unlike heterosexuals, gay men (and lesbians) may find themselves legally excluded from some adoption pathways or impeded from pursuing options for which they seem to be technically eligible (Mallon 2004). Moreover, the regulatory climate in each jurisdiction varies, so that strategies that have proved effective in one location may not be accessible in another. As of this writing, Florida and Mississippi are the only states that have enacted an outright ban on adoptions by gay men and lesbians, but in other states a variety of obstacles confront nonheterosexuals who seek to adopt.[13] In a number of states, married couples or unmarried individuals may be permitted to adopt, but regulations may be interpreted to bar adoptions by "unmarried" gay or lesbian couples. In Utah, for example, a state law enacted in 2000 seemingly permits any adult to adopt but also says that "a child may not be adopted by a person who is cohabiting in a relationship that is not a legally valid and binding marriage," which rules out unmarried heterosexuals as well as homosexuals (Lambda 2004). In 2008, Arkansas passed a citizen-initiated statute, the Unmarried Couple Adoption Ban. Though supporters of the measure admitted that is was aimed at gay and lesbian couples, it banned anyone except heterosexual married couples from fostering or adopting children (Kellam 2007). Most commonly, no explicit mention of homosexuality appears in state laws, and cases are handled on an individual basis, a situation that can sometimes lead to different results in urban and rural parts of the same state, or even results that vary between specific judges or local agencies. Nor is the information needed to select appropriate judges, agencies, or other resources readily available, so particular personal networks or connections drawn from chance encounters can determine the success of gay couples' efforts to break into the adoption system.

Like lesbian mothers, gay fathers in couples may hope to complete a second-parent adoption—a procedure that makes both partners the legal parents of the child—when only one member of the couple has been able to undertake the initial adoption process. But like other laws that affect family formation for gay men, regulations governing such adoptions vary depending on jurisdiction and can even be differently implemented by different judges. As of this writing, resistance to second-parent adoptions continues to be widespread as many courts apparently are unable to grasp the idea that a child might have two mothers or two fathers.

Even in states where gay men can adopt, the path to placement may be littered with impediments. Social workers either may not consider them suitable placements, regardless of regulations, or may be so unfamiliar with gay men that they think they don't know how to evaluate them. Costs for public adoption can range from practically nothing, particularly when the placement is for a "special needs" child, to about $2,500 for various legal fees, health exams, and home studies.[14] As I will discuss further in chapter 2, potential parents who are not heterosexual married couples typically are devalued as adoptive placements, most likely to be offered "hard-to-place" children who are older, nonwhite, male, and/or categorized as having special needs. In a system that ranks prospective parents according to a calculus of relative desirability, gay men tend to move to last place when children are allocated.

Private Adoption

One way to circumvent the challenges of public adoption—and to avoid having to choose a special needs child or one of a different race—is to undertake a "private" or "independent" adoption. Prospective parents who can afford the fees and other expenses involved can use the services of private agencies or other middlemen, usually placing an advertisement in a suitable venue—either in print or over the Internet.[15] The facilitators who broker these adoptions specialize in matching pregnant women who plan to relinquish their babies to adoptive parents, generally chosen by the pregnant women from among various applicants. Biological mothers may back out of agreements at any point, so these processes are notoriously risky.

The course of private adoptions varies considerably, but they most often are "open" adoptions, at least at the outset, with both the birth mother and the adoptive parent(s) intending some level of future interaction. Adoptive parents may not only pay fees to the various intermediaries, local agencies that must conduct home visits, and attorneys, but often pay medical expenses for the pregnant woman and subsidize her rent, maternity clothes, medical costs, and other expenses she incurs during the pregnancy. In many instances the adoptive parents are invited to be present at medical appointments (especially for ultrasounds) during the pregnancy and at the birth, with varying levels of active involvement being negotiated in each of these contexts.

International Adoption

Another pathway gay couples, like others who wish to adopt, may take is international adoption. While some American agencies that facilitate international adoptions may be willing to work with gay and lesbian adoptive parents, this information must be concealed from authorities in the countries from which U.S. couples acquire children. As well, many countries will not consider single men—the category typically used to label gay men, even when they are part of a couple—as adoptive parents. In some instances, when "single" men are considered, they are offered older children, or only boys—the theory being, it seems, that a man seeking a female child on his own might be likely to have an unwholesome (hetero)sexual agenda. Although China is currently the country from which the largest number of U.S. couples adopt, the Chinese government has restricted access for "single" men for some time and recently established new guidelines that prohibit a range of other persons not deemed as optimal from adopting Chinese orphans.[16] At the time that I conducted my research, virtually all of the children that gay men I interviewed adopted from overseas came from Guatemala, which permitted both couples and singles to adopt with no age restrictions.[17]

Surrogacy

Yet another way to bypass the uncertainties of various types of adoption can be found through surrogacy. The use of a surrogate to form a family, however, imposes its own material and emotional challenges on potential fathers. As I will discuss more fully in chapter 2, unless fathers can make personal arrangements with specific women—as in cases where a joint parenting arrangement is intended—locating a surrogate and (probably) an ovum donor and navigating around geographical and medical obstacles requires not only a willingness to invest large amounts of money but the determination necessary to endure the lengthy process that may unfold.

*   *   *

All of the methods by which gay men can hope to become fathers involve significant investments of time and often money in processes that can be bureaucratically dense, emotionally demanding, and sometimes frustrating and disappointing. In chapter 2, I will address factors that enter into men's calculations among the options available to them. As they seek to become parents, men are confronted with a cascade of financial, emotional, and moral dilemmas. None of the options are ethically neutral and all may produce problematic results—money spent without a child at the

end of the process, adoption of a child compromised physically or mentally, and the frequent need to disguise gay identities, to render one's way
of life shameful and invisible in service of an elusive end. Men may not
have all the information they need to make optimal decisions, and in any
case probably cannot fully gauge how parenthood will affect their lives
and their relationships with others. That they forge ahead, even as they
are mired in uncertainty, speaks to the sense of urgency that fuels their
quest for fatherhood.

Talking to Gay Fathers

My concerns with gay fathers center on the meanings that attach to their
struggles to become fathers and the subsequent challenges they face as they
navigate between seemingly contradictory identities. I listen with particular attention to the men's stories of how they move across spaces defined
as "gay" and those understood as relating to "family," and hence conventionally "not gay." Some of these men yearn to join the wider society, to
have people around them acknowledge them as ordinary parents and citizens. They may also be keenly aware of the challenge their existence poses
to the "family values" espoused by conservative opponents of gay rights.
In some cases, being ordinary may stand as the more compelling objective; in others, staking out pioneering terrain as gay fathers looms larger.
But these emphases are unlikely to be sharply dichotomous. The fathers
I spoke to accomplished a delicate balancing act between the impulses so
inadequately characterized as "accommodation" and "resistance" to heteronormative standards. Their positions shift in the moment, sometimes
beyond their ability to account for them. I hope to do justice to the themes
around which they organize their stories in the chapters that follow.

    The stories I tell here represent only a few of the many ways in which
gay men achieve fatherhood and experience its complications. As might
be expected, gay fathers' lives vary along many different dimensions. I
noted earlier in this chapter that different routes to achieving fatherhood
all have their own social, economic, and cultural attributes. Maintaining a
relationship with children born in an earlier heterosexual marriage presents a very different set of challenges from traversing the bureaucratic
obstacles necessary to complete a public adoption. Adopting privately,
seeking a child in a foreign country, or working with a surrogate to produce
a child that is biologically related to its father are each different not only

in their formal attributes but in terms of how potential fathers imagine
their results. Each of these methods involves different investments of time
and money, requires different kinds of interactions with public agencies,
and implies different sorts of personal negotiations as gay men find themselves required to justify their desire for fatherhood and to substantiate
their credentials. Gay men make particular choices about how to seek out
fatherhood depending upon their financial wherewithal, how they imagine
the moral foundations of fatherhood, and what characteristics they imagine to be essential in "their" children.

Setting the Scene

These accounts are based on research I conducted with gay fathers between 1999 and 2003 primarily in the Chicago area, but also in the San
Francisco Bay Area, in and around Los Angeles, and in Iowa City, Iowa.
After early interviews I hoped to undertake a relatively traditional community study of gay fathers centered in the suburban village of Oak Park,
Illinois, known for its large and active gay and lesbian population. But my
work with a number of gay fathers there made it clear that no narrowly defined, geographically bounded community of gay fathers had a strong local
presence. I also learned that although many gay fathers were acquainted
and socialized with others like themselves, they generally were proud of
being part of more broadly defined, i.e., not just gay, networks. To the
extent that some of the men participated in gay fathers' organizations and
support groups, those entities drew participants from many different parts
of the metropolitan area.

Early on, I focused my research primarily on "intentional" gay fathers,
i.e., men who had sought out fatherhood as gay men, but as I met with
many such men, I found that they interacted with formerly married gay
fathers, and that many gay men who had become fathers through heterosexual marriages also saw themselves as "gay dads," particularly those
who had joint or fulltime custody of their children.

I interviewed ninety-five gay fathers (or, in a few cases, prospective fathers) across the spectrum—men who had children in heterosexual marriages and as gay men, and in the latter category, men who had become
fathers through various kinds of adoption—public, private domestic, international—as well as men who had used surrogacy or crafted co-parenting
agreements with women. Of the ninety-five fathers or partners of fathers,

seventy-seven were Caucasian, fourteen black, and five Latino. I located men who had become fathers alone and in couples, and tried to achieve racial and socioeconomic variation among those I interviewed. In addition, I interviewed two women who were co-parenting with a single gay man, and the adult foster daughter of a gay couple.

I interviewed forty-two couples, usually meeting with both partners, but in some cases with only one. Among the couples, fourteen had completed a public domestic adoption, seven an international adoption, and six a private domestic adoption.[18] One couple had their first child through a domestic private adoption and a second through an international adoption. Also included among the couples were seven where one of the men was formerly married. One man considered himself a gay father, but was still married to the mother of his children. Six couples had one or more children through surrogacy, and one couple had established a shared-parenting arrangement with a lesbian couple.

Sixteen men were single at the time of the interview. Of the single men, eight had become fathers in earlier heterosexual marriages, one planned to create a shared-parenting arrangement with a lesbian friend and another had a child that he co-parented with a lesbian couple, one of whom was the biological mother (I also interviewed the lesbian couple). Five had become parents through domestic adoption, one through international adoption, and one became a father (of triplets) through surrogacy.

Unlike some other works that have commented on the political implications of particular actions for the future welfare of lesbians and gay men in the U.S., this book will not present an argument for or against any of the phenomena I discuss. That is, I do not claim to know whether fatherhood represents a goal that should be sought by gay men, or whether entering into parenthood promotes resistance to conventional gendered values or deepens acceptance of these same values. Rather, my work is ethnographic and seeks to frame gay fatherhood in the meanings it holds for the men who are engaged in it.

In the chapters that follow, I focus most intensely on the stories of intentional gay fathers, not because they inhabit a separate world from other gay fathers, as I have mentioned, but because the careful planning and self-examination they must undertake most fully evoke the complexity of gay fathers' lives. Processes that may be vaguely recalled for formerly married fathers, e.g., why they wanted to be fathers, are sharply etched in the stories of intentional fathers. While both kinds of fathers must come to terms with intersections and possible conflicts between being gay and being fathers, intentional fathers often take on these challenges more directly, as they must reorganize their performance of gayness to make parenthood possible.

This book depends on narrative sources for most of its substance: I focus on what men *say* about their experiences as gay fathers and about how they make sense of these experiences in the particular context of conversation with me—an anthropologist with a specific set of personal attributes. That is, my understanding of culture for the purposes of this project depends on a reading of discursive strategies—I am concerned with what they choose to tell me, what themes seem to preoccupy them, the specific terminology they use to describe themselves and their families, and other elements of their narratives. My concern is what they *say* and what that indicates about what they imagine and value, rather than what they *do* as a matter of daily practice. This emphasis is unavoidable in research in which the people under study are neither spatially defined nor in regular interaction with one another. Since I studied a population that was defined by shared characteristics but was temporally and spatially dispersed, it was not possible for me to undertake direct observations of behavior on a long-term basis. While some of what the men tell me seems distinctively connected to specific circumstances associated with being gay (e.g., adoption restrictions in some jurisdictions), other accounts reflect a complex intersection of "gay" perspectives and those typical of members of the wider society. In line with anthropological convention, all names I have used are pseudonyms; I also altered some details to enhance the narrators' anonymity.

My research draws on understandings of "community" that benefit from the insights of multi-sited ethnographic methods (Marcus 1998). Many earlier studies of gay and lesbian populations have focused on the "community" as a unit of study (Beemyn 1997; Kennedy and Davis 1993; Krieger 1983; Murray 1979; Newton 1993), but I contend that research that seeks to examine practices that cross boundaries between communities or that illuminates the more complex meanings of community that emerge through multilayered social life must extend beyond geographical definitions.

The questions that animate this book reflect anthropology's increasing interest in studies of identity that have emphasized the contested, unstable, and actively negotiated properties of nation, race, and politics as well as gender and sexuality—questions that take on heightened importance when shifting boundaries make it difficult to claim a geographically defined site as the locus for research. Anthropologists have been concerned to situate various sources of identity in relation to one another and to document the kinds of negotiations that characterize their intersections and collisions. They have also sought to specify the processes through which different aspects of identity are formed and maintained, and to examine how these are played out in different interpersonal and cultural arenas. Much of this work has focused on racial, ethnic, and national identities, and on the changing, often strategic nature, of particular configurations of identity and the evolving meaning of ethnic (or other identity-based) categories (Brodkin 1998; Leonard 1992; Takezawa 1995), issues that become particularly central as one heeds instances in which boundaries are breached and traversed.

In other words, my inquiry follows from the understandings that I outlined above of both family and masculinity as neither stable nor fixed. Gay fathers' stories reveal that neither gay identity nor the constitution of gay community is rigid or immutable. Gay men who are also fathers often find themselves shaping identities and social worlds that do not conform to the expectations of most scholarship of gay life. Whether their understandings of their situations constitute resistance to conventional gender paradigms or whether they recapitulate such forms is by no means readily ascertained; neither are the men's beliefs about what fatherhood means necessarily configured in relation to specific imaginings of gay—or other—community (Anderson 1983).

In line with the narrative emphasis of my research, I focus the chapters that follow on themes I identified as particularly central to the stories gay fathers told me in the course of the research. These men offered strikingly patterned accounts of their desire to be fathers, the steps they had to take to achieve this goal, and their subsequent experience as parents. They framed their stories in terms of larger concerns: what material circumstances shaped their pathway to fatherhood; what they identified as the "natural" sources of their parental desires; how to either adopt or rebel against values and norms they associated with families; connections they articulated between parenthood and morality; and the contentious intersections they had to navigate between paternal and gay identities.

While I don't characterize the men themselves in terms of "types" derived from the narrative analysis, I do seek to call attention to the culturally consistent themes that arise in the stories they told me. Stories often draw on more than one of these themes or particular narrative strands fit into a number of different thematic phrasings, pointing to the complex negotiations gay fathers engage in as they make sense of their situations, moving from one stage to another. The stories are also artifacts produced in interviews with me—a middle-aged lesbian researcher with longstanding interests in gay and lesbian family life. But I am also not a parent and not a man. That is, while most gay men I met with seemed to consider me a sympathetic figure, and someone whose work is grounded in a good understanding of gay life, I do not share many features of their identities, including race and ethnicity (except in the case of the Jewish families). I say all this not to discredit the stories I collected or my own skills as an ethnographer—I believe that most narrators were motivated to share their experiences with me as honestly as they could—but to remind the readers that all such findings are the product of specific, individually mediated circumstances and are not, for that reason, replicable in the usual scientific meaning of that term.[19]

My concern with "stories" is one that has been central to all of my ethnographic work. As I explain in *Lesbian Mothers* (1993), I see my mission as one that avoids the problems of explaining events that I (usually) have not witnessed, and instead focuses on the constructions narrators put on them, *in conversation with me*. That such narratives are characterized by patterns that reveal the imprint of culture has been attested to in the work of many of my predecessors. In her now classic study of the abortion debate in Fargo, North Dakota, Faye Ginsburg (1989) explains how shared "procreation stories" reveal distinctive similarities between the narratives of pro-choice and anti-abortion activists; although their actions and political beliefs are strikingly at odds, both groups of women draw on shared ideas about nurturance and caretaking in forming their views.

Studies of illness, pain, and suffering have provided a particularly vivid ground for the analysis of narratives and storytelling. Medical anthropologist Arthur Kleinman (1989), for example, shows how patients organize their descriptions of various symptoms and medical disorders into orderly patterns that imbue those experiences with meanings that have broad cultural applicability. As Linda Garro and Cheryl Mattingly observe, stories are useful "in helping the anthropologist address life as an unfolding affair, an engagement of actors who very often find themselves in interpretive and practical struggles" (Garro and Mattingly 2000, 17). Narratives, they point out, offer useful sites for teasing out the relationship between the individual and the culture, and thus, for representing the culture without doing violence to the particularity of individual experience. Other work by medical anthropologists has shown how the need to represent one's life produces identities that are processual creations rather than fixed entities (cf. Frank 1997; Kaufman 1986). Gay Becker suggests that in the United States, where "verbal self-expression is highly valued," narrative becomes the most accessible means of understanding our experience. This is a profoundly cultural experience, as cultural processes enable "people to take in and reformulate the external world" (1997, 194).

Viewed another way, narratives constitute key elements of what political scientist Mary Katzenstein has dubbed "discursive politics." She uses this term to describe the nature of the work women activists do when they come together, rewriting through talk, text, and symbolic acts their own understanding of themselves and their relationship to the world (Katzenstein 1995). Sociologist Verta Taylor (1996) argues that such maneuvers can foster the formation of new maternal identities for women suffering from postpartum depression, and thus have substantial political import for those participating in the discourse. I would suggest that fathers' self-presentation through the accounts offered to me may constitute a similar process, as the men move toward language that will situate their seemingly anomalous situation—being gay fathers—in a recognizable cultural logic.

Renato Rosaldo reminds us that "narratives often reveal more about what can make life worth living than about how it is routinely lived" (Rosaldo 1986, 98). It is with this in mind that I build my project around the stories of gay fathers. Their perceptions of how particular events unfold are in this sense more crucial to our understanding of their circumstances in a particular cultural setting and historical moment than a descriptive account of "what happened." To be sure, the real-life exigencies of becoming and being a gay father are the raw material of their stories, but these themes could be fashioned in various ways, and, indeed, different fathers do construct different kinds of stories from similar foundations.

Because intentional fathers have to carefully consider not only whether they want to be fathers but how to go about achieving this goal, they are confronted with a range of choices at every stage of the process. Should they adopt through the public system of foster care, most likely ending up with a nonwhite or mixed-race child who is no longer an infant? Should they seek out a domestic private adoption, which might entail a protracted struggle with an ambivalent birth mother, but in which such variables as race and age might be more reliably specified? Or should they attempt an international adoption, which might yield an older child or one who is medically compromised, and which would require an extensive involvement with an even more congested bureaucracy than that which oversees domestic adoptions? How do preferences about race figure into their deliberations? Does the desire for biological paternity loom over their deliberations and ultimately lead them into the dizzying—and very expensive—world of surrogacy and assisted reproductive technologies, a world that makes a science-fiction territory of egg donors, in vitro fertilization, ultrasonography, and endocrinology as familiar as one's home town? Deciding on a pathway to fatherhood means making choices that depend on access to economic resources, but it also involves making moral judgments about how one wants fatherhood to resonate with other values that animate men's lives. It may also entail framing particular pathways as "choices" even when they have largely been determined by economic and other constraints.

All of the actions taken by fathers, whether they perceive them to have been produced by affirmative choices, or whether they accept whatever possibilities come their way, can be traced back to fantasies the men have about what it means to have a family. I have sought in this analysis to understand what it is about fatherhood that inspires gay men to pursue it, even in the face of a multitude of obstacles. What underlies the yearning for family and children that permeates the stories these men told me? How do gay men dream their families?

CHAPTER TWO

Consuming Fatherhood

My trip to Liam McGee and Matthew O'Donnell's home takes me to the west side of Twin Peaks, an area of San Francisco with spacious Spanish-style homes surrounded by lawns and shrubbery. The fog has rolled in, obscuring the view of the ocean and the sunset. This is assuredly not the gay ghetto; it's a neighborhood of children and families, reputed to be more conservative than other areas of the city. Liam and Matthew both grew up in large, extended Catholic families in California. They've known each other since their first year in college, though their relationship started years later. In 2000, when we meet, they are both forty-five years old, successful professionals, and parents of a twelve-year-old daughter, Jessica, who attends a local parochial school.

Liam and Matthew privately adopted Jessica at birth, after working with a lawyer whose specialty is arranging open adoptions. Liam explains their process: "Step one was to decide to have a child, and then step two was how. . . . Now's the time, we're settled, we've been together, we have a house. Now is the time to raise this question. We talked about it. . . . But all the time thinking, 'How the hell are we going to find a baby?'"

I ask why having a house was such an important part of their decision making. Matthew explains, "Well, I think for us, we thought that was as close to a wedding as we would have. For other gay couples we know roughly our age, [it] was like, well, once we bought the house it was real that we were together as a couple. And I guess we just kind of figured, you know, we're certainly as stable as a lot of people we know. For me it was stability. But also financial stability to bring a child up as well. But it just also symbolized we're in this together."

So the two men began to explore adoption in the mid-1980s, long before gay fatherhood had acquired a public face. Matthew continues, "We were seeing a therapist as a couple during this time. He was very neutral. But later he said the two of you were just crazy. Where were you going to get a baby? Just remember, we're talking 1986, 1987."

They didn't know any other gay men who had children, and the few lesbians they'd met who were parents had all been able to use donor insemination to become pregnant. Liam began calling around to all the adoption agencies in the Bay Area and was decisively turned away wherever he made inquiries. One agency was astonished that they imagined they could have a child placed with them. "There are too many deserving couples waiting for a child," they were told.

Both men were convinced that it was important to adopt an infant, to avoid "fixing the horrors" of a child whose development might have been compromised by a traumatic beginning in life. They finally located an attorney who specialized in brokering open adoptions. She had never worked with a gay couple before, but she was willing to take them on as clients. As she explained her procedures, Liam had a revelation.

> All of a sudden [the conversation] took a shift that I wasn't understanding in terms of that this is a business, and we're going to market you. You're going to have to write letters. She showed us examples. We need to have a picture that will really catch someone's eye. We will be the only picture in the binder of two men. We won't be in front of a Mercedes-Benz with a home in Atherton [a wealthy San Francisco suburb]. We just were going to stand out no matter what! . . . So we wrote up a letter . . . our one-page "Dear Birth Mother." And we put our picture on it. We thought we'd give it a year. That was perfect for us. She said you're going to find an older woman, maybe someone who's been around the block, maybe a gay woman, who will be comfortable having two men with her baby. So we gave her the letter.

Liam and Matthew were convinced that the entire process was very unlikely to yield results. Why would an expectant mother choose two gay men to raise her baby when she could have her pick of heterosexual couples with more material resources and certainly more respectability? But less than two weeks after their letter went out, the attorney called them to say that a woman had liked their letter and wanted to meet them. Rather than the kind of mother the attorney had told them to expect, Isabella was seventeen years old, mixed Filipino and white, and firmly convinced that they would be the best parents for her baby. Rather than having to persuade her, the two men had to resolve their own anxieties about whether they were, in fact, ready to take this step.

LIAM: We then went through our doubts. Are we ready? I wasn't sure. And on the radio, there were two stories right in a row. There was the story of a woman in the East Bay who dressed her son up like a pig and put him on the front lawn with a sign, "I am a thief." A five-year-old child. The same newscast had a story about a woman who, on an airplane, a national flight, stuffed a newborn child into the garbage in the airplane bathroom. And I looked at him, and I said, "We'll *never* do that. Never."

MATTHEW: I think we were doubting our abilities, and then when we heard that, it's like, what are we doubting?

But they also needed to reassure themselves that Isabella was neither HIV-positive nor someone who had been abusing drugs or alcohol. These misgivings were quickly addressed. They also paid to provide her with separate legal advice, counseling, and medical care, in an effort to reassure themselves that she had every opportunity to consider her options and to make the decision to relinquish the baby freely and fully informed of her rights. Isabella told them that she chose them from the many other couples whose "Dear Birth Mother" letters she had read because they were Roman Catholic and would raise their child in the church and because they were both part of large, extended families. She also indicated that she was reassured that no matter what else happened, placing her child with a gay couple would assure that she would forever be her child's only mother.

Only about two weeks after their initial meeting with Isabella, Liam and Matthew attended the birth of their daughter at San Francisco General Hospital. Their further fears, that Isabella might change her mind after the delivery, were also unfounded, so two days after her birth, Jessica "came home" with them. Jessica knows who her biological mother is—she has photos and letters from her. But Isabella has long since moved back to her previous home in another state, and visits are now quite rare.

Liam and Matthew began their efforts to become parents years before gay fathers were in the public eye, at a time when the idea of gay men adopting a child was simply implausible. "Why would two men want an infant?" they were asked repeatedly as they approached adoption agencies and searched for information about how to negotiate the obstacles that were put in their path. They found that they had to market themselves to all the intermediaries they met, to tell their story in a way that would capture the attention of a pregnant woman trying to find a good placement for her baby. On one level, their being gay was less important to Isabella than their Catholicism and their large families. She clearly imagined a future for her child that would draw on particular values and images that she associated with good family life. But she also didn't want to be "replaced" as her child's mother; her only continuing bond with her daughter is the knowledge that she remains the only mother Jessica will ever have, revealing a deeply held assumption that fathers and mothers are inherently dissimilar.

Liam and Matthew's attorney hadn't anticipated that expectant mothers might find a gay couple particularly attractive as parents for their babies, but in fact such placements, and others that also seem improbable, are not rare. In some instances, a couple's gayness simply is superseded by other characteristics compelling to birth mothers: birth mothers' reading of what sorts of families and values the couple has, of their affection for one another. Some pregnant women indicate that the fact that a couple is not conventional speaks to their commitment and sincerity; their love must be more authentic since they receive so little public acknowledgment. Others actively embrace the opportunity to do something to redress the injustices that gay people face in the world, in some instances because of a personal connection to a lesbian or gay man. And, as Liam and Matthew note, some birth mothers are thrilled to find a situation that leaves them as the permanent mothers of their children, even when they have little ongoing contact with them.

Liam and Matthew had only limited options available to them when they decided that they wanted to be parents. It was the 1980s, during the crisis years of the AIDS epidemic (especially in San Francisco), and few men in the gay community were confident enough in the future to imagine parenthood. The technologies that would make surrogacy feasible were in their infancy, and certainly wouldn't have been available to gay men. Domestic adoption agencies shunned them. Even with these limitations, however, the two men had preferences and priorities for the kind of child they wanted to adopt. Most centrally, they wanted a newborn; race and sex were not issues, or at least were beyond the options they thought they could realistically control. They were not wealthy, but had sufficient

resources to spend money on an attorney and on the expenses of the birth
mother. It was with this set of desires and obstacles that they ended up
completing a private adoption; while they "chose" to take this path, their
choices were made in a climate of constraint. Most of all, they managed to
become parents while everyone around them told them they were wishing
for the impossible.

Investing in Fatherhood

As we can see in Liam and Matthew's account, consumption enters the
story of gay fatherhood in two ways. On the one hand, there is the matter of
desire and need. Having children enables people, gay men among them, to
achieve the insignia of adulthood and stability. Liam and Matthew are conscious that some of these markers, notably marriage, are not available to
them, so they adapt to the situation first by buying a house, and second by
deciding to become parents. This is the kind of consumption that has to do
with performing identities, akin to the way that Americans use particular
acquisitions to represent who they are and what they have accomplished.

But Liam and Matthew also find themselves in another sort of consumption scenario, that associated with the raw economics of the marketplace—what they have to do to get what they want. In their case, they
must devise a strategy that compensates for what they perceive to be their
precarious status as consumers. They search for a sympathetic interme-
diary who can help connect them to a birth mother; they write a "Dear
Birth Mother" letter intended to present themselves in the best possible
light; and they choose to pay for an array of support services for the birth
mother to assure that the transaction will go smoothly and that the birth
mother's interests will be served.

We will see in this chapter how gay men engage with consumption in
both senses as they move toward realizing their dream of being fathers.
Gay men are under no obligation to be fathers and must actively seek out
this status, so one element of the story has to do with *why* they want to
be fathers—what fatherhood will produce for them that is not otherwise
accessible. We will also examine their interactions with the marketplace,
the calculations the men make as they try to balance their devalued status
as potential parents against the resources they bring to the venture. The
resources are themselves diverse—material, of course, since achieving fatherhood may require considerable investments of money, but also social

and ethical. Each pathway produces particular obstacles—bureaucratic snarls, hostile officials, children's health problems, and the like—and anticipating these is part of the negotiation that each father must complete. The object sought, a child, may thus be valued along various scales. For some, getting a newborn who matches their race is of primary importance; for others, accomplishing an act that stands as an ethical response to an unjust world is most desired.

"You Need to Realize That I'm a Grown Man"

Becoming a parent can solidify a person's claims to being settled, adult, and responsible, which has a special resonance for gay men who are often seen to be immature and irresponsible, or at least not completely mature.[1] This was particularly clear in the story told by Enrique Morales, a Latino man who lives in San Francisco and who adopted three half-siblings through the foster care system. I visited with Enrique in the small Victorian row house he owns that hugs a steep hillside on San Francisco's Bernal Heights, on a somewhat shabby block that overlooks the hills to the south. Enrique is employed as a social worker for the city of San Francisco, specializing in child welfare, and his decision to become a parent is tightly interwoven with his professional activities and his knowledge of the ins and outs of the foster care system. A former Catholic seminarian, Enrique moved to San Francisco from Southern California to attend graduate school in social work. For as long as he can remember, his dream was to settle down by age forty and to have children. His first child actually came into his life earlier than that, when he was thirty-two, but at the time we met, he was forty and was living with his three adopted children and a male cousin in the little house, which he had purchased some six years earlier. Enrique felt that being a parent has allowed him to confront his parents' assumptions that his life hadn't fallen into place or that he wasn't quite grown up. Soon after adopting his first child he reminded his parents that he had a family, one just as legitimate as those of his married siblings, but he's struggled with the perception that they continue to see him as not quite grown up.

At the time of the interview he had just turned forty and told me that he had arrived at the "best time" in life. He bought a house in a less expensive part of town than where he used to live, got a cheaper car, and invited his gay cousin to move in with him and help him work on the house. He enjoys what he calls "the stability" of his current situation.

I guess everything is in a way settled. Not in a negative way. Not settled where I don't think things are going to change for me. But I feel like all my work has paid off, the things that I want out of life have come to fruition. I've worked hard at my education and my career and relationships with my family—my family is my children. And even though the children are all very young still and very difficult—one particular child with very special needs—it's challenging, but it feels good. It feels really good right now.

Enrique's desire to become a father cannot be separated from the frustrations he experienced with his family. Despite the fact that he had achieved many of the markers of adulthood, particularly in his career, he felt that his parents continued to see him as not really grown up. As a gay man he was stuck, as meeting their requirements would conventionally only come through heterosexual marriage. But adopting children and establishing a household, however unconventional its form, enabled him to demonstrate that his life was stable and mature, to present evidence to his parents that was unassailable.

Why Children?

So what is it about children that is so compelling—for people in general and, in the current context, for gay men? What makes it worthwhile to enter into the legal and medical labyrinth of becoming a parent when procreation cannot be achieved heterosexually? Forming a family is an emotional and sometimes biological, medical, or legal process, but it also reveals desires by potential parents, whether they are gay or not, to perform "family" in a convincing manner. As we see in Enrique's account, creating a family signals adulthood, responsibility, and community stature; it entitles parents to make social and material claims, to achieve a kind of cultural recognition not otherwise available (Calhoun 2000; Cott 2000). It is, on many levels, a key scene in a script that most people in society hope to enact, though the narrative form it follows shows considerable variation. From this perspective, children are an acquisition without which full claims to family status are void. Particular kinds of children further these objectives more easily than others, and questions of differential value attach to many different family narratives.[2]

The question that has driven much scholarship on fertility and family size in the West is a seemingly simple one: Why do people want children, when they are expensive, require an intensive labor investment, and rarely produce an economically measurable benefit? A version of this question was central to early second-wave feminist theory, as some feminists argued that both pregnancy and motherhood exposed women to a host of social and cultural disadvantages, and were essentially at the root of women's devalued social status (Firestone 1970; O'Brien 1981; Rich 1976).[3]

Not surprisingly, the sociological and demographic literatures are congested with competing theories of family formation, many of which are rooted in debates over fertility rates and what sorts of forces radically alter the normative sizes of desired and/or achieved families. Some, most notably those advanced by the sociological economist Gary Becker, have argued that both the wish for children and the size of completed families must be framed as analogous to consumer desire. Assuming that the family in the West has "perfect control over both the number and spacing of its births" (Becker 1960, 210) because of the availability of birth control, Becker claimed that the desire for children was no different from any other economic motive, so that couples who have higher incomes will seek better-quality children (i.e., by providing more education, health care, and other advantages), while those with lower incomes may have more children but invest less in their "quality." Because children cost more than they produce, they are analogous to consumer durables, though "since children cannot be bought and sold they are a less 'liquid' asset than ordinary durables" (Becker 1960, 227).

In 1968, demographer Judith Blake posed a challenge to Becker and other scholars who had approached the question of family size with the same conceptual tools developed for analyzing the desire for and acquisition of consumer durables like cars and refrigerators. Her now-classic article "Are Babies Consumer Durables?" disputed notions that rich parents would want more children in the same way as other "goods" by highlighting non-economic forces that influence parents' desires for children. Blake's answer, which has been echoed in the work of scholars who followed her, is that the importance of children exists in terms of "the goals to which children are intrinsically related" (Blake 1968, 22). She goes on, "One can become a 'parent,' 'have a family,' be a 'mother' or 'father' only by acquiring children. That one should desire these statuses is the final result of complex institutional control, but *given this desire*, children and only children can satisfy it" (Blake 1968, 23; emphasis in original).

But since few of those seeking to become parents actively engage with these analyses, it is more pertinent here to consider the ways in which the

addition of children to a family may permit particular kinds of cultural performances. In this light, the acquisition of children may be said to resemble
the pursuit of consumer goods that signal class status, moral value, or other
desirable traits associated with parenthood. As Blake asked, is there any
way to claim status as a family, to access the attributes of full citizenship
without having children? "Family" is a term widely understood to refer to
the family of orientation, at least for adults; those persons who are childless
are described in many different contexts as lacking families. The serious-
ness of this omission sometimes surfaces in nervous jokes about people who
have seemingly substituted pets for children: the nurturance directed at
companion animals is equated with parenthood, but always taken as com-
pensatory and, as such, a bit pathetic (Grier 2006). Having a family allows
us to claim adulthood and full citizenship; it also facilitates the acquisition
of a "home" as opposed to a mere "house" (Douglas 1998; Garber 2000).[4]

Gay Men in the Baby Market

Gay men who seek fatherhood, who like other potential adoptive parents
are predominantly white, must compete with heterosexual married couples for the small number of highly valued white infants available through
the public and private adoption systems.[5] They thus find themselves more
liable to be matched with a child considered less desirable across a range
of racial, gender, age, and health-related categories. Gay men of color, like
other families of color, in contrast, are more apt to parent nonbiological
children through informal, often familial, arrangements. Such "adoptions"
often do not appear in public records and are thus difficult to enumerate.
White heterosexual couples have greater success in adopting younger children, children who appear not to have a physical or mental deficit, and
girls.[6] They are more willing to consider children who are racially different
from themselves if the children are Latino, Asian, or mixed race, i.e., not
black, apparently perceiving all colors other than black as somehow occupying an intermediate position only slightly removed from white (Pertman
2000). Barbara Katz Rothman reports hearing Asian and Latin American
children "called 'a discreet shade of off-white,' not white perhaps, but most
assuredly not black" (2005, 49). In other words, just as white infants are
more highly valued as potential adoptees, white heterosexual couples are
the conventional standard of appropriate placement, and are more likely
to obtain the kind of child they prefer than gay men or other "singles."[7]

Gay men differ, of course, from most heterosexual married couples in that they enter the adoption system without having first struggled with infertility, and thus regard the possibility of adopting as an exciting opportunity rather than the only option left after failing to produce a biological child (Savage 1999). They are also keenly aware that as gay men they are usually more tolerated than actively sought as potential parents. Nonetheless, in the face of large caseloads in the foster care system, some adoption workers do recruit gay men, lesbians, and single people as potential parents, as they come to understand that any capable adult can help remove children from the cycle of foster placements (Mallon 2006).

Potential parents who find that the system is unlikely to yield a child that meets their racial, health, or age requirements have a number of options. They may choose to remain in the public system and adopt a child categorized as "hard to place," which, as I outlined in chapter 1, typically means one who is no longer an infant, not white, and/or classified as suffering from a mental or physical disability. These children tend to be categorized as having "special needs," an ambiguous category that can include everything from relatively minor physical or mental problems to significant developmental or psychiatric impairment. The term is so ambiguous, in fact, that agencies tend to use it to refer to *any* factors that make a child difficult to place, including children who are black and biracial, in sibling groups, and who have experienced more than one foster placement, even when they are healthy (Pertman 2000). But while the attribution of "special needs" may tarnish a child's desirability, adopting such children can bring a host of state benefits and other financial entitlements that make adoption more affordable for parents of modest means.[8]

For some gay men (as well as many other potential adopters), adoption from the foster care system is the only path available since they lack the resources to seek more costly options through private agencies, international adoption, or assisted reproduction. In these cases, a counternarrative to the usual evaluative schema may emerge, as a child who might have been rejected by some families comes to have special value because he cries out for rescue, allowing his parent(s) to achieve a level of moral stature that attaches to successful completion of difficult projects; some gay men (and others) who could invest more money in the quest for a child are thus morally compelled by the social value of public adoption. For them, the racial and gender attributes (nonwhiteness, maleness) that lower the market value of these children are precisely the qualities that make them appealing; potential parents who take this position affirmatively choose to adopt a "hard-to-place" child.[9] By adopting a child otherwise devalued, these men (and others) can achieve their dream of being parents while also enacting what they experience as an affirmation of the value of every human being and, as some explain, striking a blow against injustice. To be sure, gay men are not the only potential parents who maximize altruism or battle racism in choosing a child, but gay men may be under particular pressure to do so, as the other options even occasionally available to conventional families are less likely to come their way.

But not all gay men approach fatherhood as a route to community service or as a way to right the wrongs of an unjust social system. Instead, like many prospective parents, these men particularly hope for children who (at least superficially) resemble them, children whose ethnic, medical, and/or genetic backgrounds are at least partly open to examination, and in most cases, children who are not black. Hispanic, mixed-race, and Asian children can meet these requirements; as we shall see, their incorporation into a white family is imagined as less difficult, the problems of racism that a mixed-race family might encounter understood as less intractable. Such adoptive parents are unlikely to couch their racial preferences as based in active dislike of black children or people; the explanations offered draw on the logic of popular sociology or psychology. "It's not fair to the child to subject him to these racial pressures," or "the black-white racial divide is just too enormous for us to manage," phrases that recall Heather Dalmage's (2000) description of "tripping over the color line." These preferences speak as well to how families are conventionally imagined, that is, "as if" naturally formed (Modell 1994), with the assumption that the more likely a particular family configuration might occur in "nature," the less likely it is to be subjected to hostile scrutiny by outsiders.[10]

The classic artifact produced in these transactions is the "Dear Birth Mother" letter, in which the individual or couple describe themselves, speak of why they wish to become parents, and provide other information intended to impress birth mothers (Handel 2002; Silber and Speedlin 1991). Often these documents resemble advertisements more than conventional letters, striving to demonstrate the wholesomeness of the prospective adoptive family, typically by providing photographs of them involved in stereotypically "family-oriented" activities—outdoor sports, playing with pets, or decorating Christmas trees, often in the company of relatives. They also may signal the economic solidity of the family by including pictures of their home, referring to their occupations, and making prominent mention of vacation travel that would not be accessible to persons of lesser means. But as we saw in the story of Liam and Matthew that opened this chapter, how birth mothers actually select the persons who will adopt their children is hardly a straightforward process, as the actual "winners" of the implicit competitions may not always be the most affluent or conventional. That significant numbers of these women knowingly select single parents or gay couples makes clear that complicated calculations govern their thinking (Lowe, Wittmeier, and Wittmeier 2006; Melina and Roszia 1993).

Private adoption, however, can be a risky proposition. Prospective parents can become involved in a circuitous process that does not necessarily produce results even after large financial investments.[11] Birth mothers may change their minds at any time during the pregnancy or immediately thereafter. And some adoptive parents find that birth mothers may become troublesome and demanding in the months preceding the birth and even long after relinquishing the child. The birth mothers and the adoptive families tend to come from very different economic circumstances, so the temptation for low-income and working-class women to form bonds and try to intensify feelings of obligation with the relatively affluent people who adopt their child can be substantial. From the adoptive parents' perspective, continuing ties to the birth mother through "open adoption" may signal their commitment to head off the identity dilemmas they assume their children, like other adopted children, may eventually face (Pertman 2000).

International adoption allows gay and nongay parents to circumvent the uncertainties of working with a known biological mother; while requiring some compromise on matters of race and age, it sidesteps the more stigmatized adoption of an African American child.[12] Anthropologist Christine Ward Gailey interviewed parents who adopted from other countries, and while they rarely invoked race directly in speaking of their decision, it lurked as a "submerged motive" in their accounts. "One woman said international adoption was a way of '*making sure you get a blue-ribbon baby.* . . . *Well, you know, smart, blond, blue-eyed.* . . . *Well, I mean looking like us as much as possible*'" (Gailey 1999, 68; emphasis in original).[13]

Consuming without Consuming

As we have seen, there are intrinsic rewards that come with being a parent that are difficult to produce in any other way. Performing adulthood and full citizenship in the absence of a "family" is not convincing; by attending solely to oneself, one risks appearing to be selfish and socially disengaged. Achieving parenthood is a process that requires explicit consumption strategies, but considering the stereotypes that cast gay men as egocentric and self-indulgent, it is particularly essential that they diminish and deny the material features of these transactions.

Sociologist Viviana Zelizer details the changing valuation placed on children over Western history, as children moved from being "useful," when they provided agricultural or other labor in support of the family, to "useless," as they have come to require substantial outlays for education, food, and other investment unlikely to yield direct or measurable benefits. Drawing on Philippe Ariès's classic argument (1965) about how the meaning of children developed historically, she relates these changes to the conversion of instrumental evaluation of children to a new emphasis on emotion. As middle-class women became increasingly isolated in domestic units in the nineteenth century, children were sentimentalized and conceived of as "precious" (Zelizer 1985). That is, materially "useless" children became emotionally "useful," a cultural shift so hegemonic in its reach that most people cannot imagine that it could have ever been otherwise.

This shift to conceiving of children as emotionally valuable cannot be accomplished without a firm rejection of any suggestion that they have instrumental importance. Maternal (and parental, by extension) love is supposed to exist apart from material considerations, to be unsullied by selfish desire, urges for financial benefits, or other marks of impure motivation. Any situation in which parents are thought to seek profit from their children is understood to reveal a uniquely evil form of corruption (Hancock 2004).[14] Similarly, any suggestion that children are consumer acquisitions contaminates parents' moral claims.

"Like a Neon Sign That I Couldn't Forget"

Andrew Spain, a resident of Chicago, adopted a gravely disabled boy he located through a national registry. He describes the entire decision-making process as somehow mystical, and claims to have been taken unawares by an ad he saw in the *Reader,* a local community newspaper. The advertisement was for an agency that sought foster placements for special needs children and specifically urged unmarried people to consider foster parenthood. Andrew experienced the ad as being "like a neon sign that I couldn't forget." He was particularly motivated to follow up on it both because he wasn't in a relationship at the time and because he felt that the "traditional values" he grew up with would make him a good parent. In other words, he believed that a set of circumstances simply came together that made becoming a parent the inevitable direction for his life.

Even with the siren call of the advertisement driving his desire, Andrew began to think about his preferences, weighing various desires against the realities of his situation. He quickly decided that he didn't want to just foster, but to adopt a child. First he thought that it would be best to adopt a child that was as young as possible. "To be there from day one. To be there as early on as possible" was important, he explained. But other competing conditions had to be taken into account. He didn't have the financial wherewithal to adopt an infant, realizing that as a single gay man, he would be less likely to get his first choice than would a two-parent heterosexual family. This realization helped him solidify a commitment to adopting a "special-needs" child, as he reasoned that such a child would be the most likely match for a man in his position.

So Andrew began to scan the volumes that detail the condition of special-needs children available for adoption around the country, essentially searching for a child whom he could identify as "his child." He finally located a gravely disabled child, describing to me the experience of looking at the picture and realizing immediately that this was "his child." As we will see later, narratives of this sort also speak evocatively to themes of nature and suggest the intervention of mysterious forces that link the fates of a particular child with a particular parent (or, in another domain, the bonds between adults who fall in love). They also highlight how powerful visual images can be in generating compelling emotions that are coded as part of nature.[15]

But Andrew was also very pragmatic as he devised a route to achieving parenthood. Considering the material and social constraints he faced as a gay man, he determined what sort of child he could realistically acquire and then elaborated his final plan so as to enhance the moral significance of his choice. By approaching adoption as he did, he obtained a child he could call his own and also a righteous position of personal sacrifice. Both of these, in turn, make his fatherhood even more compelling as an ethical stance. His choice of a profoundly disabled child, one that in fact had already been returned to the agency by other adoptive parents, potentially shielded him from accusations of consumerism; that is, he drew on a widely held belief that only profoundly antimaterial forces could cause a person to choose a child who lacked all the characteristics usually desired in an adoptive placement.

Achieving his goal required careful strategizing. Andrew found himself increasingly frustrated with the bureaucratic roadblocks that slowed the process and thus began to bypass regular procedures, walking boldly into adoption agency offices and, without gaining official permission, consulting books with information about children waiting for adoption. He could only assume that personnel at these agencies took him for a fellow social worker, and thus never questioned his presence. With the information he gained, he contacted social workers around the country directly and found himself accelerating an otherwise glacial process.

He was also carefully conscious about how he presented himself, adopting what he considered "clothes that specifically would look like the all-American father would wear. I remember buying an Izod v-neck sweater that had a little alligator and looking the part. . . . I was playing the part." Although he had resolved that he would not deny being gay if asked directly, he decided not to volunteer this information. "One, because it [made] no difference to the way I was going to parent my child and my abilities to parent. And two, I didn't want to screw up the possibility of my getting a child." Fortunately, none of the social workers and other adoption gatekeepers he dealt with ever asked him about his sexual orientation.

As we shall see in chapter 3, Andrew embeds his choice in a discourse of nature that makes every aspect of the process seem to exist beyond calculation and choice, even as he proudly describes the carefully considered path he took to achieving fatherhood. This narrative also connects with several themes that I will discuss in greater detail in later chapters. First, it is clear that Andrew ranks fatherhood as an appropriate alternative to having a partner, and given the choices he makes in locating a child, fatherhood emerges as the expression of a kind of love superior to that he would have with a lover. Second, Andrew's story, like others we will discuss, reveals an intense desire to do something morally significant by becoming a father. He wisely adjusts his parental goals to both economic limitations and the obstacles he knows he will encounter as a gay man. But the realization of his larger objective, to be a father, is achieved through a kind of "shopping" venture in a catalogue, which is followed by the choice to adopt a particular child. This man never "settled"; he pursued this child actively, even bending some rules to get to meet him sooner than the procedures would have allowed. He perceives the adoption as an achievement that was premised on his savvy manipulation of the adoption system at various stages. But at the same time, he understands his parenthood as having been preordained, not consciously sought at the beginning. The intersection of agency and destiny enables Andrew to make overlapping claims to both adulthood and citizenship, which demand purpose and agency, and to goodness and abnegation, which are rooted in forces that resist explanation.

The Revenge of Consumption

But disengaging the desire for children from the notion that the children themselves generate economic benefits doesn't remove consumption from the analysis of reproduction. As anthropologist Janelle Taylor reminds us, many of the cultural mechanisms mothers invoke allow them to mitigate, at least partially, the vexing connection between money and children, affirming that motherhood is a site wholly removed from the domain of the material. "Motherhood is supposed to be a special kind of human relationship, uniquely important because uniquely free of the kind of calculating instrumentality associated with the consumption of objects. It stands for 'love,' in sharp contrast to 'money'—a simple but persistent opposition that structures American middle-class cultural values concerning family, parenthood, and child-rearing" (Taylor 2004, 3).[16]

Other scholars note that the acquisition of children cannot be separated from those global and economic forces that determine access to both reproductive technologies and various kinds of adoption. Some of these analysts point out that it is no accident that particular developing countries have emerged as "exporters" of children to the more affluent West (Bhabha 2006; Briggs 2006) as part of an economic strategy that takes advantage of the forces of supply and demand, and some scholars have noted the relationship between trends in international adoption and the history of military operations during U.S. history (Gailey 2000). Adoption patterns appear, as we have seen, also to reflect categorizations of Asian and Latin American children as more acceptable, i.e., less colored, than blacks (Gailey 2000). Still, interracial and international adoption demand management of racial difference within the precincts of the family. Is a Chinese girl adopted into a Jewish family Chinese or Jewish?[17] Should the Anglo parents of a baby adopted from Guatemala learn to speak Spanish?

Can the white parents of a black child ever do justice to the complicated demands of African hair?[18]

Some emerging discourses of the meaning of parenthood and the value of children focus not on the instrumental utility of children, but on their new position as consumer acquisitions in themselves or as instantiated through consumption practices (Bourdieu 1984; McCracken 1988).[19] At the same time, however, parental narratives operate to disengage the process from motives that might be seen as corrupt or materialistic. By emphasizing "nature" and "love" in their most idealized forms, the authenticity of parental virtue remains intact. Nonetheless, in the U.S. all steps in reproductive processes are deeply entwined with consumption practices, from the transformation of ultrasound pictures into family photos to the decoration of the baby's room and the plethora of objects alleged to be essential to an infant's development.[20] Just as adults use consumption of objects they use themselves to perform identity or to express affiliations and loyalties, so consumption associated with their children can invoke particular meanings for families.

Welcoming Diversity

I settled into Josh Goldberg and Brent Martin's suburban living room one cold January evening, nibbling on pizza the two men had ordered in for the interview. The room was filled with children's playthings; their son Samuel, about seven months old, had been put to bed before I arrived. Their two Siamese cats settled on the back of the sofa, adding to a feeling of domestic serenity. Josh is in his early forties and has established a solid career as a litigator in a major Chicago law firm. Brent is about ten years younger, and has temporarily left his work in clinical psychology to be a fulltime, stay-at-home dad. Josh comes from Chicago and is Jewish; Brent grew up in the Deep South in a fundamentalist Christian milieu. He now considers himself Jewish, though he has not converted. The two men had a Jewish commitment ceremony about three years earlier, which sparked their discussions of becoming parents. Josh was the official "father" for the adoption process, but they have already filed the necessary paperwork to complete a second-parent adoption that would make Brent a legal "second" parent.

The two men investigated a number of adoption options, quickly deciding on international adoption. They had considerable anxiety about domestic adoptions, largely based on horror stories they had heard about birth parents changing their minds, particularly if they learned that their child would be adopted by a gay couple. When I asked them what made international adoption seem like a better choice, Brent explained, "It sounds horrible, but in large part not having to deal with a very nearby birth family who might go ballistic or fundamentalist on us." Josh continued, "Just the fear of vulnerability that people always have that someone could later change their mind as they see what a wonderful child you're raising and somehow the system wouldn't necessarily abide by you even though you have rights. That was part of it. . . . I'm a litigator, so I always think of the worst-case scenario. But that was only one of the many reasons." Josh elaborated on these.

> I'm someone who very strongly welcomes diversity. . . . We began our conversation talking about how the American ideal is not fully realized for us—I believe very strongly in the power of the country as a place where energy from all over the world has come for years to make this a stronger place. And I thought there are so many children, I mean there are so many children in the United States. But within the United States there's a certain threshold of care you're supposed to be getting, so it was just a way of bringing some of those benefits to a child who might not otherwise get them, and also bringing another culture into our lives, too, which I thought would be neat.
>
> ELLEN: Did either of you have previous experience in Latin America?
> JOSH: I had been to Costa Rica. And we didn't go in thinking about Latin America. At the beginning of the process—I mean a lot of it is sort of food-driven. We love Ethiopian food, so that would have been a fine country, except for they don't let gay people—they don't let men adopt. We know gay couples that have adopted from Ethiopia, but they're female. We love Indian food; [but] India is another country that would prefer to let its children starve.

Josh and Brent approached a local adoption agency not far from where they live, attending an informational evening on international adoption. They had numerous links to this agency as one of Josh's law partners had been adopted himself through its auspices and another had gone there to adopt a child as a single mother. Once they began working with a social worker there, they explored adoption from a number of Southeast Asian countries, and learned that they would face a thicket of bureaucratic obstacles if they pursued adoption from Vietnam or Cambodia, two other countries that seemed attractive to them, perhaps because of their cuisines.

Finally, their social worker at the agency asked whether they would consider Guatemala. Josh explains,

> One of the reasons I wouldn't have considered Guatemala, from what I knew of it, it's one of the more homophobic and macho countries in the hemisphere. And that scared me a lot. But then as we started to investigate, there were so many good things about adopting through Guatemala that that was what we targeted.
>
> ELLEN: What were some of the good things?
>
> BRENT: You get the children early—that was the big one. That it was one of the few countries where you could get the children early. Almost certainly under a year, and possibly under six months. And he was not quite five months when we brought him home.
>
> ELLEN: What was important to you about getting a child early?
>
> BRENT: I'm a nurture-over-nature kind of person, so my sense is the sooner you get the blank slate, the sooner you get to give the child everything you want to give them. He was marvelously cared for, but nutrition, socialization, everything is going to be better with two parents on one child versus one [caretaker] for three children in a large institutional setting. That being said, the Guatemalans do care about their children, and the people involved in the adoption process care about the children, and make sure they get to good places. It just seemed like a good system.

Josh added,

> There are several other things that were attractive. One is, candidly, there's a very low incidence of alcohol and drug abuse in Guatemala, and so the chance of fetal alcohol syndrome was much reduced, and that's something that if you can avoid, we prefer to avoid. And also, Chicago is a place with a fairly large Guatemalan community, and proximity-wise it's much easier than going to Vietnam. So if you want to integrate Samuel's heritage into our lives and give him exposure, it's an easier place to do that than other places.

Although neither Josh nor Brent speaks Spanish, Josh indicates that he doesn't see this as an insurmountable challenge. "We can both order food off menus in many languages. At some point, I think we'd like to learn Spanish." They have also arranged to attend meetings of a Chicago-area organization of parents who have adopted from Guatemala, which they see as a potential support. Josh continues, "We love all kinds of music. We have ten-thousand-some CDs. Through music, through literature, through the food we cook, through the places we go eat, to the places we travel, we'll do the best we can."

While they have talked about adopting a second child, Josh and Brent are leaning toward just having Samuel. Josh explains, "Samuel's so perfect and the equilibrium seems so right that the odds of hitting that kind of success another time just seem remote. He's just really easy. And if you have a child who's violent, let's say, or difficult, it could be difficult for Samuel, it could be difficult for our cats, it could be difficult for a lot of how we live."

The difference in physical appearance between Samuel and his fathers has created some awkward moments in public settings. About a month before our interview, Samuel had to be taken to the hospital to have an infection treated. Josh describes a conversation with a technician.

> First of all he said, "That's not your baby, is it?" And I said, "Yes, I'm his fa-ther." "Well, he's adopted, isn't he?" "Well, yes he is." "So you don't have any kids of your own." . . . Brent was holding him and I was asking questions like do they know what organism it is, is it in the blood stream? And she said, "What, are you a microbiologist or something?" I said, "No, but I just want to be as informed as possible." And she goes, "Are you the child's uncle?" And I said, "No, I'm his father. He has two." And her tone changed.

Josh and Brent's story weaves together a number of consumption-related themes that move expectant parents into international adoption. First, there is a matter of "quality." Children from overseas are unlikely to be encumbered by ambivalent birth parents, and once they are removed to the U.S., the possibility of having to negotiate with blood relatives appears to be negligible. Along the same lines, children from countries like Gua-temala are perceived not to be subject to the problems that are thought to be common among American children, particularly the impact of drug or alcohol abuse. Despite the fact that the children live in institutional settings while awaiting permanent placement, a circumstance the fathers regard as less than optimal, these are environments that, nonetheless, are well run by nurturing and skilled caretakers.

But adopting a child from another country raises a number of cultural challenges for American parents. Despite Brent's firm belief in "nurture over nature," the two men still feel a mandate to bring something they gloss as Guatemalan cultural content into their home. They imagine this as requiring them to learn (at least some) Spanish, explore Guatemalan cuisine, and play music from Samuel's native country, activities that will insure that the child is not robbed of key dimensions of his heritage. That this and other foreign cultures are imagined primarily as culinary and musical sites speaks to the way foreignness is consumed in many U.S. milieus.

Overseas adoption also presents Brent and Josh with particular challenges as they perform fatherhood in various public settings. Although some of the difficulties they experienced at the hospital where their son was being treated had to do with their status as gay fathers, they had to struggle even harder to make themselves visible as Samuel's parents because they aren't seen to resemble him. It appears that hospital employees felt entitled to interrogate the two men about their status and to tell them directly that adopted children are not "kids of your own." We will see that resemblance is a key concern for many fathers, leading some of them to try to find a biological route to parenthood.

As we have seen in Josh and Brent's story, many potential adopters see international adoption as a "safer" alternative than private, open adoption, since the birth mother is located in a distant country and is unlikely to change her mind during the pregnancy or seek an ongoing relationship with the family. On the other hand, international adoptions rarely allow access to newborn infants, as bureaucratic processes in most countries delay release of a child for months. Often, the children are considerably older, and developmental delays are not uncommon among them. While international adoptions do not require a letter to the birth mother, who is not a visible participant in the process, they often necessitate similar sorts of documents intended for those who manage private agencies in the U.S. and organizations in various countries who oversee the process. They also demand enormous amounts of paperwork, including government background checks, fingerprinting, home visits, translation of documents into the relevant foreign languages, and one or more trips, of varying length, to the country from which a child will be adopted.[21]

The Cost of Fatherhood

Brent and Josh's account shows that desire alone cannot bring children into the lives of gay men. They must venture into an adoption or assisted reproduction market in which children are differentially valued and in essence "priced." Cost is related primarily to the qualities of the child sought and secondarily to the methods used to accomplish parenthood. That is, gay men who desire fatherhood cannot escape encounters with the market, as both supply and demand contribute to the conditions under which they can form a family. In these and other ways, a troubling connection between parenting and consumption overshadows gay men's discussions of parenting.

Gay men, of course, are not alone in experiencing the family-formation process as deeply immersed in market forces, part of the wider phenomenon Ginsburg and Rapp (1995) have called "stratified reproduction."[22] The demographics of adoption in the U.S. inscribe the differentials of race, age, health, and nationality across every aspect of the process (Pertman 2000). As we have seen, healthy, white infants are not available in the U.S. in sufficient numbers to meet demand, particularly in the public foster care system, but nonwhite, older, and/or disabled children are abundant.[23] In western European countries, virtually all adoptions must be international because children native to those countries are almost never available (Altstein and Simon 1991; Andersson 2000; Howell 1999; O'Halloran 2006; Rothman 2005; Selman 2000). But in the U.S. the economics of unwed or low-income motherhood and irregular access to contraceptive and abortion services, coupled with the intense stigma now attached to abortion, mean that large numbers of children end up in foster care or become available for adoption through private agencies.

Both feminist historian Rickie Solinger (2001) and legal scholar Dorothy Roberts (2002) have called attention to the ways that foster care and other institutionalized placements for children of color speak to "class privilege" embedded in the system. As sociologist Barbara Katz Rothman puts it, "Adoption most often means moving a child up from its point of origin to a family higher in the social and economic hierarchy. Poorer women and families are put in the position of relinquishing children; wealthier women and families take those children in, take them on" (2005, 68).[24]

In a recent analysis, Debora Spar (2006) examines both assisted reproduction and adoption (among other family-building technologies) through the lens of business, illuminating how both depend on market forces at least as they are practiced in the United States. In the current climate, the value of children is sharply differentiated depending upon age, race, and the sorts of problems the children available might have. Infant adoptions are primarily private, with birth parents essentially selecting the adoptive parents, reversing the marketing process that obtains in the public sector. At the same time, low-cost foster system adoptions account for only about 10 percent of the number of children eligible for adoption.[25]

In like fashion, Spar shows how the development of technologies that permit egg donation and the use of gestational surrogates not genetically related to the fetus they are carrying sparked the growth of the surrogacy industry. These technologies effectively separate egg donors and surrogates into two distinct populations. Egg donors are required to be young, and to have attributes aspiring parents seek in their offspring—good looks, educational accomplishments, and the like. But these donors are unlikely to want to carry pregnancies for others. Surrogates, in contrast, need not have the characteristics sought in a child; they only have to be healthy enough to complete a pregnancy, willing to meet the requirements of surrogacy (e.g., no smoking or drinking, no sexual activity during the insemination period, agreement with going through diagnostic procedures and having an abortion if the results are not favorable), and willing to regard the fee paid them—usually about $20,000—as attractive recompense for bearing a child for someone else.[26]

While surrogate arrangements have been sharply restricted in many countries,[27] the legislative response in the U.S. has been ambivalent and uneven, resting on an ideology that understands the family as part of a private domain that should be immune to public interference. Sociologist Susan Markens accounts for this situation by pointing to the characteristically American celebration of individual rights, along with our "laissez-faire approach to the marketplace and our protective stance toward families" (Markens 2007, 23).[28]

Anthropologist Diane Tober (2001) points out that altruism is a key element of the evaluation of donor semen, with its marketability increasing to the extent that donors express altruistic motives that balance the more materialistic (and perhaps egoistic) rewards that lead them into "reproductive work." That is, altruism, which seems to remove the act of donating sperm from the nexus of commercial relations, is actually a key element affecting the market value of the sperm. Not unlike ova, sperm is regarded as "the prototype for the child that will be produced" (138), revealing the influence of what Tober calls "grass roots eugenics."[29]

Going for the Gold

In a process reminiscent of the "Dear Birth Mother" letter, individual men or couples who wish to obtain surrogate services must go through a variety of processes to locate surrogates and/or egg donors and negotiate the medical procedures needed to achieve pregnancy. One couple interviewed by journalist Liza Mundy explained that "they put together what they called a 'marketing profile': a computer-produced mini-newsletter with articles about their interests and personalities, spiced up with photographs that they hoped would make them look like good potential fathers" (Mundy 2007:134).

Unless the couple has a friend or relative who wishes to serve as a surrogate and/or ovum donor, they will need to work with an agency that specializes in facilitating all the necessary arrangements. The agency conducts some sort of evaluation of the potential fathers, though standards for acceptance vary widely, and matches them with potential surrogates and with ovum donors who are similarly subject to varying screening procedures.[30] Each phase of these negotiations requires financial outlays that may be quite large, particularly since the agencies and the surrogates may each be located in a different part of the country. Both surrogates and potential parents select one another, typically through written profiles and often, as well, through some sort of personal interview, and this connection may be solidified with ongoing e-mail and telephone communication. Fathers-to-be typically seek a woman who is personally likeable and whose personal health practices—diet, smoking, alcohol use—are acceptable. Like the sperm purchasers Tober described, they are also concerned with the donor's motives for serving as a surrogate. A similar, though usually less personal, process may be undertaken to identify ovum donors, when required.[31]

Surrogates may be either "traditional," that is, artificially inseminated with the sperm of the father-to-be, or "gestational," meaning that they are impregnated with embryos resulting from the in vitro fertilization (IVF) of donor eggs with father-to-be's sperm (Ragoné 1994). In recent years, as I discussed above, fewer women have chosen to be traditional surrogates, presumably because of their wish to avoid a genetic connection with the fetus they are carrying, a condition they feel will better enable them to relinquish the infant. The assumption that comes into play here is that maternal bonds proceed "naturally" from genetic relatedness and that carrying a fetus not biologically related to the surrogate will allow her to feel like a disinterested vessel rather than a mother-to-be (Ragoné 1998).[32] For either kind of surrogate, most agencies select women who have already had one or more children and claim to have achieved their own maternal ambitions.

While artificial insemination (AI) is relatively low cost, about $500 per attempt, expenses associated with IVF, necessary when attempting gestational surrogacy, can be very high.[33] Considering the fact that multiple IVF and embryo-transfer attempts might be necessary before achieving a viable pregnancy, each of which may involve significant travel for egg donor, surrogate mother, or father(s)-to-be, as well as the high fees paid to the medical personnel, the process of completing a single surrogate pregnancy may exceed costs of $100,000, even costing as much as $150,000. If men who have worked with a surrogate decide to have a subsequent child with the same woman, they will save some money on the selection process, but will incur all the medical costs again and will also be required to pay the surrogate a higher fee. Since fertility specialists typically implant four or more embryos in hopes that one will successfully "take," it is not uncommon for IVF pregnancies to produce more than one baby. Such pregnancies are, of course, more risky for the surrogate (who will be paid more if she is carrying more than one fetus), and are likely to result in a premature birth, long periods of neonatal intensive care, and possible disabilities as the children develop.[34] As is typically the case in private adoptions, the prospective father(s), who are generally far more affluent than the surrogate, arrange for her medical care, and may also subsidize maternity clothes, rent, and other expenses she incurs while pregnant, in addition to traveling to participate in prenatal medical visits and the delivery.

Perhaps unexpectedly, Liza Mundy reports that some surrogates affirmatively choose to work with gay male couples (or singles) instead of heterosexual married people. One explained that infertile (heterosexual) couples are desperate after long periods of failing to conceive and that this sometimes leads to acrimony between the surrogate and the intended mother. Gay men, in contrast, are perceived to have selected surrogacy as their first choice and thus to be happy with the arrangement and more appreciative of the surrogate's efforts on their behalf (Mundy 2007, 135).

Many of the potential parents who choose to bypass the public adoption system have financial resources at hand that will permit traversing the worlds of private domestic adoption, international adoption, or assisted reproduction. But even when they are not so affluent that such expenditures may be contemplated without anxiety, they may be able to reallocate resources in pursuit of fatherhood, as one might save up for an expensive purchase or finance an acquisition over time.[35] As with many choices that have economic components, a decision about a pathway to parenthood is framed not only by actual financial resources, but by cultural preferences of various kinds. Does an intended parent feel comfortable with a long waiting period for a child? Is a family with an only child, the possible outcome when expenses and bureaucratic expenditures are weighty, com-

patible with a parent's understanding of how a "healthy" family is configured? Is the preference for an infant a more powerful engine of choice
that the possibility of an international adoption, which is less costly than
surrogacy? How do particular kinds of adoption choices become normative in some communities? Since the purchase of genetic materials and
the gestational services of a surrogate are commercial transactions, how
do fathers who choose surrogacy understand the ethical components of
their decision?

"It Just Fell into Place"

One afternoon I met with Alan Zuckerman and Art Keller at their large
Chicago apartment. Located on an upper floor of an elegant art deco
building, with a stunning view of Lake Michigan, Alan and Art spoke passionately about the many reasons they chose to become parents. I had
met the two men through the local gay synagogue; they are both Jewish,
now that Art has converted, and this identity is central to how they see the
meaning of their having children. Alan told me,

> I don't think I could experience all the joys and some of the pains of life—and I
> mean in a positive way—without having kids. I think that watching a first step,
> teaching somebody certain things that I think are important, and helping to,
> to a certain extent, make the world a better place through a child, and making
> me a better person through a child, I think I would be partially, selfishly miss-
> ing out on life if I didn't have children and even grandchildren. I want to see
> grandchildren!

The two men decided on surrogacy after investigating various kinds
of adoptions and participating in a group for gay and lesbian prospective
parents.

> We had decided to raise the kids Jewish. . . . And pretty much what you can ex-
> pect in the state [system] is adopting an African American or biracial child. And
> we had thought that it would just be too much for the kid—it was more focused
> on the kid than on us. And there is a high population of those kids that are born
> with drug dependency, and so you really have no idea about them. . . . And then
> we talked to people who had done foreign adoptions. We didn't go through
> any formal process, but we talked to people, and it just seemed liked they were

buying a baby. And we couldn't do it as a gay couple—someone would have to pretend to be my wife and all that. It was just way too complicated and I just couldn't do that—it just didn't feel right. . . . I was thinking that what if we tried to adopt from Latin America or somewhere where at least the child would feel [comfortable], well because I'm definitely ethnic looking.

Alan and Art are careful to situate their decision making about race in terms of how they can be responsible parents. On the one hand, they worried that having a nonwhite baby in a Jewish family would cause difficulties for the baby; on the other, they present themselves as distressed by the moral ambiguity of international adoption, which they felt was steeped in an ethos of consumption. That the decision to eliminate both public and international adoption was located in their imaginings of what their family would look like emerges in Alan's comment about the importance of having a physical resemblance between parent and child, or between siblings. Family is defined by phenotypic parameters, and there is only so much flexibility possible before a family no longer "looks like" a family.[36]

Having ruled out domestic and international adoption, the couple then settled on surrogacy, which they planned to undertake twice. Art explained that having the opportunity to have a biological connection to the child was a major attraction of this method. When I asked how much all this would cost (in excess of $100,000 per child) and whether that would be a strain on the couple's finances, Art crisply responded, "Let's just say we can afford it." It is worth noting that their earlier qualms about international adoption as the moral equivalent of purchasing a child do not surface in their discussion of surrogacy.

ALAN: It's just like, well, if we can do this, wouldn't it be great to have someone who is actually related to you?
ELLEN: What would be good about that?
ALAN: Well, you just feel like you have part of yourself. You see part of yourself in the child, it's kind of like carrying on a family tradition. . . . I think that part of it is selfishness. You want something of you to see in your child. I think it is selfishness, part of it is selfishness. And I'm guilty of that.

As these comments show, for Alan, biology, as represented by perceived physical resemblance, makes consumption disappear as a component of the transaction. The actions taken to have a child through surrogacy are rooted in *nature* in that they maximize genetic connections and allow the parents to "see something" of themselves in their child. In line with their rhetorical rejection of their reproductive arrangements as commercial, the two men emphasize that the surrogate who is working with them is someone who is really focused on helping gay men have a family, that she is not in it for the money. As a gestational surrogate, her ethnicity is irrelevant for their purposes since she has no genetic relationship to their baby. In a later interview, after the birth of their son, I learned that the surrogate's altruism was further demonstrated by her insistence on providing breast milk even six months after the delivery. She sent the milk by Federal Express and refused to be compensated for the cost. While she is not technically "related" to their baby, her stated desire to help Alan and Art have a family and her commitment to many acts of generosity that fall far beyond the normal expectations of a surrogate erase some of the commercial attributes of the transaction.[37]

More complex issues arose when the men began the process of selecting an egg donor. In their early thinking, a Jewish egg donor would have been ideal, as Alan explains,

> And for me it was more the connection, I wanted them to feel the connection to Judaism. And maybe that's because I grew up in such a Jewish home. That they would feel, whether it's my biological offspring or Art's, I wanted them to look at that picture, right there, and see my great-grandmother and say, for one, that could be their great-great-grandmother, or for them to look at it and say, "Oh my gosh, she's from Russia," and that could be someone, so that there's more of a connection to both of us.

But the reality is that there are very few Jewish egg donors, so they decided to settle for someone whose coloring would likely produce a child that would be "between" the two men. Alan is dark and Art is very fair, and their eventual plan was to have two children with each of them being the biological father of one, using the same egg donor for both. Their strategy, then, involved finding an egg donor who was "between" them in complexion, thus, in their eyes, maximizing the chances that the children will resemble each other and easily see themselves as siblings.

> There were some women in there, it was unbelievable—they looked like models, with IQs like you wouldn't believe. And we were looking at them, and we said, "That just isn't us." We wouldn't date them!! [Laughing.] And it wasn't even so much that, it was just that they didn't seem like nice people and we were

getting that sense, and we don't want that. And the funny thing was, it all just kind of fell into place. It was one of those things where you know that someone is watching out for us. It just fell into place.

Working with an agency that facilitates matches between potential gay and lesbian parents and donors, they engaged in a lengthy selection process, relying for the most part on photographs and general information about the donors: physical attributes, education, and reason given for donating being particularly central.[38] Both men claimed to be skilled at predicting a person's personality from a photograph. This was the method they used to select a donor who would have the personal qualities they required for the genetic "mother" of their children. In this case, of course, genes did matter, but supply and demand also entered into their calculations. Since Jewish donors were extremely scarce, the two men accepted the alternative—that their baby would have to be formally converted to Judaism.[39] Instead, they focused on selecting a donor who exhibited qualities associated with being a "good person." Their understanding was that the sort of child they would have had a great deal to do with personal qualities of the egg donor. Alan explained,

> Most of it was getting a very good sense of, well, is she going to be someone who we would perceive to be warm, genuine, and just a good person. We wanted somebody who was intelligent, but not too intelligent. . . . And we didn't want a kid with an IQ of 160. We didn't want that. We wanted someone who was above average, who seemed very well rounded. Like even though my brother-in-law is very intelligent and very well rounded . . . his brothers were, like, off-the-charts smart, but they're so off the wall that I was just worried that, well, that was where it would be nice to have someone who was above-average intelligence but genius level to me was, well, I was worried. Because we could actually go to certain Web sites and we could pick a kid, or pick a donor, who went to an Ivy League school and whose SAT scores were perfect. We didn't want that. We didn't want that.

A number of consumption-related strategies emerged as these men moved toward fatherhood. They had the opportunity to get the "best possible" egg donor, but modified that objective because of their ambivalence—or perhaps anxiety—about donors who might surpass them intellectually or otherwise, and who therefore (they feared) might disrupt their future family. They had everything mapped out, from the eggs to the sperm to the surrogate to the goal of having a Jewish family, and all of this was facilitated by their substantial incomes ("just say we can afford it"). As affluent consumers, it's not unlikely that they are accustomed to being able to purchase what they really want, rather than having to compromise and choose the second-best, bargain item. This previous consumption experience reveals itself in their strategies for achieving parenthood.

This narrative also reveals a cluster of ideas about what it means to have a family, how a family should be defined, and how genetic information can be interpreted in creating a family. Appearance, or rather resemblance, plays a central role in this story, though as gay men who have no choice but to use donor eggs, Alan and Art are willing to settle for a lesser degree of resemblance than are some heterosexual couples (Becker, Butler, and Nachtigall 2005). Both Jewishness and being legible as a family are understood as interpretations based on how individuals look—interpretations that are made both within and outside the family. Race is a key variable here, but within the larger category of "white," complexion and hair color are vital indicators of kinship. Similarly, Jewishness is affirmed by resemblance to artifacts like family photographs; being able to recognize oneself in the images that circulate in families is the foundation of belonging in that unit, according to Alan and Art. To feel that one belongs in a family is a self-attribution, but that assessment requires facilitation through perceptions from the outside. If family members are "read" as related, then the reality of their kinship connection is confirmed.

"Personality," by which Alan and Art mean being "warm, genuine . . . a good person . . . [and] well-rounded," also registers as genetically mediated, but in practice something one can assess through physical appearance. The authenticity of the family unit that results from pairings with donated eggs is certified by the choice of a donor who could have conceivably dated one of the two men. If the donors were too perfect, too smart, or too beautiful, Alan and Art suspected them of not being "genuine" and, worse, of not being someone who could have actually come into their lives. The seemingly farfetched question of whether the egg donor is the sort of woman either of them might have dated situates their decisions in the domain of nature, even as they pay large sums of money for the genetic material, in vitro fertilization, gestation by a surrogate, and all the other costs that attach to the larger project of becoming a family. When they explain that "It was one of those things where you know that someone is watching out for us," they locate their reproductive process in the domain of nature; even after enormous expenditures and complex decision making, their success at achieving fatherhood appears in retrospect to have happened almost of its own accord.

Putting Consumption in Context

We have seen that the processes of acquiring a child when conventionally "natural" methods of procreation are inaccessible entail a particularly focused engagement with a world of commerce and consumption.[40] Prospective parents must "shop" for a child—or for genetic material and service providers—and must weigh monetary costs and other investments against their images of what they expect from a child and from parenthood (Spar 2006; Triseliotis 1999). As Rothman observes, consumer behavior in selecting a child (or genetic material) involves gathering information and making careful decisions, much as one might approach another major acquisition, what she characterizes as "good consumer behavior" (Rothman 2005, 62). Parenthood is a cultural construction that brings certain benefits, but it cannot be attained in just any manner. American parents must meet stringent moral requirements that dictate separation between material advantage and parenthood so that parental motivations can be experienced (and viewed by others) as purely affective. To do this, they must transform the commercial, monetary, and consumption-related dimensions of becoming a parent into appropriate categories: love, nature, and notions of preordination.

For all who desire to have children but cannot procreate conventionally—either because of infertility or sexuality—a number of decisions need to be made, each of which calls for clarification of some feature of the familial dream. What sorts of financial resources do they bring to the process? How does phenotypic resemblance figure in their imagined families? How daunting is racial difference, and how, indeed, do the aspiring parents recognize and measure differences? How important are the age and sex of the future child(ren) perceived to be? Resolving these quandaries depends both on how potential parents imagine a future family and on moving toward these goals within the constraints imposed by the system of supply and demand that governs adoption and assisted reproduction.

Gay men move through the same processes as straight people who seek parenthood, but they do so with the knowledge that their parental desires are less valued by the wider society. They enter the market for children, then, as disadvantaged consumers; just as children are evaluated according to race, gender, age, and health, potential parents who are single rank below married couples, and gay men (or lesbians) appraised below them. In other words, gay men enter the world of reproduction at a disadvantage, and can only succeed in achieving parenthood if they negotiate wisely. As we shall see, gay fathers make explicit assessments of their ability to traverse various obstacles, often finding that maximizing virtue by seeking to adopt a devalued child or that spending money on mechanisms outside the public foster care system can enhance their odds of achieving their dream. Whether they spend a lot of money in the process of becoming fathers or not, they cannot readily escape the consumption stories that surround reproduction; their choices are inevitably "about" consumption even when they minimize specific instances of it. In the accounts they provide, gay men who pursued and achieved fatherhood in different arenas reflect on their decisions and reveal ways in which they traversed complex worlds of consumption in the process.

The stories told by gay fathers who formed families under a range of circumstances indicate that consumption is a vital piece of the process by which families are formed and evaluated. However, consumption doesn't occur in a vacuum. References to the work of consumption are embedded in larger narratives that elaborate themes of family and nature, morality and belonging. In the context of acquiring children, consumption is not a simple process of "buying" children, genetic material, or the services of persons who can channel genetic material into the essential elements of family. Rather, consumption plays out in a complex locus of meanings in which family, love, and goodness are articulated against the background of what being gay means in America. One doesn't just "become" a father in this location. One becomes a father within a web of meanings in which gayness, family, love, sacrifice, belonging, and other attributes compete with each other for starring roles. As is the case for putatively mainstream families, gay fathers and their families accurately anticipate the need to perform their kinship status in a context in which none of the elements of performance occurs in a neutral environment.

One also becomes a father in the context of particular material constraints or opportunities. Prospective gay fathers, like others seeking access to parenthood through adoption and/or new reproductive technologies, must evaluate their options and chart a course that is affordable and socially feasible. But these more concrete exigencies don't operate in a vacuum: each man must also take account of the ethical boundaries he has established for himself or that prevail in his community, and must calculate not only material factors but the cultural costs and benefits of particular pathways to parenthood. Being gay sometimes figures into these reckonings explicitly as men explain why they have a more limited range of children available to them than other prospective parents, as Andrew did, or that they face specific challenges in trying to demonstrate that they are real adults, capable of overcoming images of self-indulgent gay men, as Enrique explained. Liam and Matthew start their process in an environment that denies the possibility of gay adoption, directing them toward private domestic adoption, which they perceive might be more flexible because it is more visibly commercial. Josh and Brent eliminate pathways that discriminate against gay men and acknowledge that they have no choice but to deal with the problem of "resemblance." At the same time, they perceive their son's ethnicity to resonate with their love of "diversity," plotting a strategy of engagement with it through a series of consumption options.

In other cases, being gay is more obliquely referenced. Alan and Art, for example, use their gayness as the starting point for investigating various reproductive options. Because, as gay men, their choices in the various adoption markets are unacceptable, and because they have the financial wherewithal to consider more costly routes, they decide to become parents with a surrogate. Since a gay-friendly agency can facilitate matches with a surrogate and an egg donor (for a substantial fee), they are shielded from having to struggle against antigay sentiments as they move through the selection process.

Of particular importance as I review these stories is the disconnect between consumption required for family formation and the kind of kind of toxic acquisitiveness that has been attributed to gay male populations. As economist Lee Badgett has persuasively argued (2001), gay populations in general do not have more disposable income than heterosexuals, nor do gay men necessarily "reek of the commodity," as anthropologist Jeff Maskovsky has explained (2002). To frame gay men's struggle to become fathers in the context of consumption is not to say that these men have the ability or inclination to consume more than others. Instead, I intend to demonstrate that adoption and assisted reproduction, and perhaps the allegedly more "natural" procreative practices used by nongay parents (which rarely receive much scrutiny), all have consumption dimensions that bring them into line with other market-mediated processes that have become prominent in recent years. All of these processes seem to enable the expression of *choice* and thus convince actors that they have been free agents in forming their social lives. That these constructions can conceal the action of those constraints that also shape the actions taken may not be easily discerned.

The most compelling instance of how consumption gives meaning to procreative practices is found in the performance of family. As a number of the cases presented in this chapter indicate, much of what fathers (or other parents) must achieve in the process of claiming their legitimacy is a convincing performance of belonging. Most essential to this performance is physical resemblance, the emergence of phenotypic attributes that can be read as emerging from a single strand of kinship, imagined, as David Schneider famously explained, as "blood" (1968). Whether such appearances are authentic or not is hardly the issue; the question of authenticity is an interpretive exercise negotiated by parents, children, and various audiences under a variety of contingencies. We will see in later chapters how perceptions of who is likely to belong to whom, and who is not, can be manipulated in various contexts and made to do the work of testifying to family authenticity.

CHAPTER THREE

"Something Inside Me"

Gay Fathers and Nature

Forty-four-year-old Frank Miller and his partner of twenty-one years, Carl Bowman, own a hair salon in a small Midwestern city. About seven years before I met with them, they adopted six-year-old twin girls who had been removed from parental custody as infants because of sexual and drug abuse. Both men grew up on farms with parents who "worked hard" and, as they explain, taught them what they know about being part of a family. Frank describes his parents' values, particularly the importance they placed on honesty, as central to his own approach to raising children. Becoming parents, he told me, was a natural part of the larger story of his relationship with Carl. The two men had built up a successful business, had owned a number of homes, and saw themselves as established community members. "We were happy; we had everything we wanted—except children. And we both loved kids." Frank explained the decision to explore adoption even as they worried that as gay men there would be numerous obstacles and limitations. And his commitment to honesty—another value that he associated with the way his parents raised him—meant that he couldn't embark on adoption without being open about being gay. Because they were gay, he and Carl decided to only inquire about adopting girls, in hopes that their motivations would be seen as more acceptable by the agencies they would have to deal with.

One indication of the naturalness which gay men assume to account for their aspirations to be parents can be seen in their tendency to describe the transition into parenthood as part of a self-evident sort of development. In many of these narratives, an account of family history or tradition represents the force of nature in that it is assumed to be deeply rooted and unchangeable. It is also embedded in definitions of family that depend on the presence of children for legitimacy.

Echoing the comments of Frank and Carl, Mark Friedman, who lives in Marin County with his partner, Rick, and their baby, Abraham, told a story anchored in his family history. Mark grew up in Los Angeles in a three-generation Jewish family. Now a social worker, he laughingly told me, "I grew up thinking that I was going to have a child, that I was going to be a rabbi, that I was going to be a botanist. . . . And that I of course was going to get married to a girl from Beverly Hills or the Valley." He continued, explaining that living in an environment that included "having people around of every generation constantly in the house" and that his active involvement in Jewish and Zionist youth activities further convinced him that he would be a good parent. But when he came out at eighteen, he at first believed that this would be the end of his dream of being a parent. He and his first lover, Ted, had actively discussed having children, but put those hopes aside when Ted was diagnosed with HIV. Mark cared for Ted until his death, just after their tenth anniversary. But when he met and fell in love with Rick, the new relationship "inspired in me the dream that I could have children . . . so our second date was to an adoption workshop." After a lengthy process, they successfully completed a private adoption that allowed them to be present at Abraham's birth. Although taking a new baby home from the hospital terrified both men—they kept frantic vigils while he was sleeping lest he perish from crib death—Mark says, "Something inside me knew that it would be inherent, the ability to do it."

Nature plays a varied role in Mark's story. He grounds his desire to be a parent in an inheritance passed down to him by the multigenerational family in which he was raised. Mark sees children as integral to the continuity of the family; by becoming a parent, he acts out a biological legacy much as he might reveal a physical trait typical of the family. The selfless caretaking that is called for when one has an infant is similarly something he didn't have to learn; there was "something inside" him that could be counted upon to provide him with abilities one needs to parent. This unnamable interior quality is part of him in the same way that his DNA is. He doesn't question its authenticity; it is simply there, along with other physical and temperamental traits.

It's Only Natural

What could be more natural than having children, or wanting to have children? Whether we find an explanation in science or religion, most Americans regard reproduction as something that cannot be questioned: it simply *is* one of the fundamental impulses that drives human life. While the specific features of marriage and kinship differ depending particularly on class and ethnicity, childrearing methods and behavioral norms may also vary dramatically, Americans readily understand the desire to reproduce to be something normal, natural, and instinctual. In particular, gender theory and popular wisdom both tend to assume that motherhood has a particularly intense genesis in women, who, indeed, are virtually defined by their reproductive and maternal preoccupations.

But does a desire to parent present itself with the same kind of urgency for men? As we have seen, gender theorists have tended to explain fatherhood quite differently from motherhood, focusing on aspects of fatherhood that are assumed to be less fundamentally embedded in their essential personhood than are the factors that produce motherhood. Though none of these views suggests that fatherhood is unimportant to men, they tend to situate the impetus to father in the public domain and in men's relations with one another. Fatherhood thus enables men to achieve the status of *social men* and to craft themselves as "whatever women are not" (Gutmann 1996). In other words, maleness is just there, but to be a man, one must perform one's masculinity in a legible fashion.

But even when motherhood and fatherhood overlap behaviorally, a trend that has increased (or been better documented) in recent years, the *perception* of the two conditions continues to emphasize "natural" distinctions between them. So, for example, even though men perform many of the tasks associated with motherhood (e.g., changing diapers) and women carry out work presumably assigned to men (e.g., economic support of the family), popular perception continues to sharply dichotomize motherhood and fatherhood so that parents undertaking roles that diverge from their conventional assignments still do not change their identities. Insofar as motherhood and fatherhood are tied to definitions of femininity and masculinity, cultural cognitions demand that they be distinguished, regardless of the degree to which their performance is actually blurred (LaRossa 1997).

Examinations of fatherhood and masculinity have offered consistent evidence that fatherhood does, indeed, have a core emotional dimension and may entail intimate and domestic-caretaking obligations. At the same time, however, the prevalence of dichotomous gender paradigms reinforces stereotypes, allowing women and men to continue to imagine motherhood and fatherhood, femininity and masculinity, as virtual polar opposites. And even in the absence of empirical evidence for the solidity of these distinctions, most of us understand them to be natural. Nature, then, is a conceptual scheme rather than a designation for any particular set of causalities.

So What Is Nature, Anyway?

It's not easy to pin down what we mean by "nature." Nature, it would seem, is just *there*, filling in gaps where culture does not have a defined presence. Like material reality, it defies interrogation. But anthropologists *have* scrutinized nature, treating it as a culturally constructed category that plays varied roles across the ethnographic spectrum, and those efforts inform my approach here. The concept of nature, Marilyn Strathern argues, may be particularly strained as reproduction and technology intersect, seemingly removing procreation as being simply a "natural fact of life . . . in a world where couples can seek assistance to beget offspring without intercourse" (1992, 43). That is, the biological foundation of kinship becomes less "real" under conditions in which it is manipulated by commerce and calculation. That we have come to define kinship in terms of blood or DNA as something "real" demonstrates the hold that Western culture has over intellectual domains including anthropology. Such definitions fit comfortably into contemporary theories of evolution in that they connect human existence to larger patterns of nature; these are what we unreflectively name "the facts of life."

Nature has a particular set of referents in the West, and has become a markedly embattled concept as technological advances have been interpreted to threaten its survival. We see such uses of the idea of nature in discussions of the world around us. The built environment is usually understood to intrude on some pre-existing natural order, but such intrusion can be mitigated by the use of less harmful—more "natural"—materials and practices. In this context, nature is conflated with the "earth," imagined as female. Exploitation of resources and disfigurement of her splendors are coded as masculine enterprises that entail rapacious greed. But nature is also an explicitly imagined and constructed domain, as when a particular landscape is designated as a "natural." When applied to food, nature reads as uncorrupted or pure and hence safer, an association drawn from widespread suspicion of agribusiness practices and fears of pollution of food and water supplies. An associated idea, that foods can be evaluated in terms of their nutritional components, is also connected to images of nature; natural foods, in this construction, are readily assumed to be healthier than those subject to processing or other artificial interventions—even when they are manifestly the products of domestication and agriculture. In a particular version of this story, "raw" is imagined as intrinsically better than "cooked," which entails interference with the natural state of particular foodstuffs.[1]

Because nature is typically taken to be a domain lacking in premeditation, one that resists conscious manipulation, it also connotes authenticity. If something is natural, we assume that no one planned it, that it is uncorrupted by the desire for gain or by the need to accommodate orthodoxy. It is, in a sense, the default mode—what would be there if no one interfered with the environment. The power of nature is often understood to manifest itself in mysterious ways and through displays of what seems to be preordination. "It was meant to be," people may say as they absolve themselves of planning any particular outcome, or "Everything happens for a reason." Things that are meant to be, intended in this cosmic way, can't be questioned; they are felt to be true and to defy analysis (Lancaster 2003).

In the current climate of fascination with all things genetic, nature is also commonly conflated with biology, and hence with deterministic understandings of the impact of DNA or other biological mechanisms on our lives. Scholars from many different fields, as well as popular writers, have joined this debate, either enthusiastically endorsing the notion that almost everything in our lives can be traced to the actions of our genes or condemning the tendency of such thinking to foster an unreflective faith in a biologically driven destiny (Keller 2002; Lewontin 1993; Nelkin and Lindee 1996). In particular, a number of authors have taken issue with the political conservatism and downright racial determinism they see as authorized by DNA discourse, as notoriously epitomized in *The Bell Curve* (Herrnstein and Murray 1994), which proposed that deficits in intelligence among African Americans could be traced to hereditary factors.

At the same time, however, biology and nature have come to be overlapping if not equivalent concepts in much popular discourse, with particular salience in discussions of reproduction. These assumptions seep into our understandings of families as units defined not only by certain generational and structural ties, but instantiated in physical resemblance.

This level of connection is also commonly represented as "blood," understood, according to David Schneider (1968), as the most stable element of American kinship. He pointed, in particular, to what he argued was the implicit assumption governing American kinship: "that Blood Is Thicker Than Water" (1984, 165). "This assumption is but a particular instance of the more general characteristic of European culture toward what might be called 'biologistic' ways of constituting and conceiving human character, human nature, and human behavior. Man's humanity tends to be formulated in terms of his place in nature, with a few caveats about his free will, intentionality, conscience, and his (self-defined) extraordinary intelligence distinguishing him from other natural organisms" (175).

That blood connections are imagined to be the foundation for the most sturdy and solid relationships is revealed even in the language of "chosen" family, famously presented by Kath Weston (1991). Among the lesbians and gay men she studied, close relationships are "like" biological kinship; the only metaphor that worked adequately to express the level of reliability and loyalty of their friendships was that of biological family. Weston's account also makes clear how fragile and "chosen" blood relationships can, in fact, be, as families may ostracize a gay child or otherwise refuse to acknowledge a bond.

As I will discuss below, motherhood has been centrally implicated with nature in popular discourse as well as in theoretical analyses of gender. It is, on the one hand, something that biology reserves for women, who singularly possess ovaries and wombs that permit them to undertake the most time-consuming and visible part of reproduction. It is, at the same time, conventionally related to a bundle of social practices that define and limit women's status. Just as kinship and family organization are immensely varied, so are the attributes that make children worth having. In agrarian societies their labor is integral to the family's economic success; in many kinds of cultures children constitute a kind of insurance for one's old age, as they are called upon to care for the needs of their elderly parents (Ariès 1965; Frykman and Löfgren 1987; Zelizer 1985). Children have ritual obligations across the ethnographic spectrum and their existence assures the continuity of the kinship line, however that might be configured. The centrality of children to the continuity of the family or lineage is variously imagined as consisting in particular substances. In the West, blood serves as a durable metaphor that evokes kinship as ground in actual physical matter. But the way the materiality of kinship is figured differs across cultural lines. For example, Carol Delaney (1991) has noted the salience of "the seed" as an analogous expression in Turkish society; in early modern Europe, the notion of the homunculus served a similar purpose (Pinto-Correia 1998).

In the industrialized West, in recent years, the ascendancy of genetics has provided new imagery for kinship ties, offering an amplification of the meanings attached to blood. DNA, chromosomes, genomes, and the mechanisms by which biological characteristics are passed from generation to generation are not only the stuff of science but of the popular imagination, offering new foundations for believing in the reality of the blood ties in kinship (Finkler 2000; Schneider 1968; C. Thompson 2005; Wiegman 2003). Among other reflections of the growing centrality of genetic imagery in Western cultures is the growth of explanations for various attributes in biology. Not only racial heritage and diseases but personality characteristics, gender, and sexuality are increasingly accounted for with reference to their biological and genetic foundations. Nature and nurture are locked in ever more bitter competition, and at the present moment nature seems to be gaining ground as the most central explanatory model for, well, everything (Duster 1990; Nelkin and Lindee 1996; Reardon 2004). The burgeoning field of science studies has taken on many of these issues, directing careful attention at how medical and scientific language and images shape collective understandings of gender, race, identity, and character—and, indeed, the way these connect to something that reduces to "nature" (see, for example, Downey and Dumit 1997; Dumit 2003; Franklin and Roberts 2006; Lock 2001; Martin 1995; Rose 2007).

Sylvia Yanagisako and Carol Delaney expand on some of these ideas in the introduction to their important collection, *Naturalizing Power*. "Evolutionary theory or ideas have so permeated human consciousness in the West that it has seemed 'natural' to compare human society and behavior to that of animals. . . . Especially are sex and reproduction held to be quintessentially natural activities; indeed they are considered our 'animal' behavior" (1995, 6). In the West, we readily assume that human sex and reproduction are organized more or less as are such processes among nonhumans; we draw lines between animals and ourselves in other arenas. Nature has acquired particular salience not only in the discourses associated with motherhood, but in narratives of adoption, the use of assisted reproductive technologies, and the satisfactions parenthood can bring (Modell 1994; Ragoné 1994; C. Thompson 2005).[2]

In recent years, nature has assumed a new ideological position as a counterweight not only to culture, but to more broadly construed expressions of artificiality. In these usages, the nature-culture or nature-artifice binary assumes a particular moral valence, with whatever is understood to be natural coded as beneficial along a number of axes: purity, safety, health, hygiene, ethics, decency, and so on. For example, nature has been particularly sharply invoked in relation to fertility, pregnancy, childbirth, and lactation, that is, all the physical dimensions of motherhood. Some objections voiced by feminists to assisted procreation rest on concerns that such interventions are unnatural and hence morally suspect and possibly economically exploitative (Spallone and Steinberg 1992; Stanworth 1990). Other feminists have elaborated the association between motherhood and virtue, framing these in terms of women's presumed affinity for caretaking (Bobel 2002; Eller 1993; Elshtain 1981; Griffin 1980; Merchant 1980). These approaches celebrate motherhood as embedded in "nature" and repudiate perceived incursions from mainstream culture into the purity of that domain.[3] The valorization of the "natural" may extend to invoking animal models as the prototypes of purity in regard to motherhood; in these constructions, motherhood is understood as an embodied domain. Interference with its performance—whether that involves conceptive technologies, obstetrical interventions, bottle feeding, or even hired childcare—denies women access to their authentic (maternal) selves (Blum 1999; Hausman 2003; Klassen 2001; Nelson 1991).

Despite some consistencies in the way the concept of nature is deployed in various maternal and gender discourses, the set of ideas nature evokes also proves to be remarkably flexible. For example, while some women see the use of procreative technologies as interference with nature, others understand it in precisely the opposite sense, as a method for restoring their natural fertility to what nature intended it to be (Franklin 1997; Sandelowski 1993). And, as I have shown elsewhere, lesbian mothers have proved to be enthusiastic users of nature imagery as they explain their desires to become mothers and their claims to cultural legitimacy as such (Lewin 1993).

Disentangling parenthood from consumption shapes the way parents and potential parents think and speak about their reproductive activities. Emphasis on the "natural" attributes of all sorts of reproduction, including the use of assisted procreative technologies and adoption, serves as one obvious example. Users of these reproductive methods tend to understand their experience as "natural" no matter how extensive the interventions undertaken. Thus, couples who have achieved parenthood through complex procreative interventions, such as IVF, describe the resultant pregnancy and birth as "natural" (Sandelowski 1993). This discursive strategy distances the procreative process from the commercial attributes embedded in assisted reproduction, allowing couples to resist thinking of their ability to become parents as fundamentally linked to their capacity to absorb the costs of reproductive technologies.

Similarly, adoptive parents routinely characterize their first meeting with their child as an event with mystical attributes, in essence reuniting them with the child they were "meant" to have. The arrival of the adopted child is consistently called "coming home," as adoptive parents insist that connections with their new child overcome apparent biological distances, as well as geographical barriers (Modell 1994). While private and international adoptions parallel reproductive technologies in being available primarily to potential parents with the economic wherewithal to purchase them, even low-cost public adoption depends on choosing the "right" child from catalogues and other materials that describe the children awaiting placement.[4] Such discourses allow adoptive parents to avoid direct engagement with images of consumption. Anthropologist Judith Modell reports, for example, that adoptive parents tend to use metaphors of birth and nature to describe the process that brought them their child and to resolve the challenges presented by a process that is not rooted in blood and thus arguably not natural: "The first challenge [for adoptive parents] involved transforming a *deliberated* (by them) and a *designated* (by someone else) parenthood into a 'destined' parenthood. A bond that was as sure as birth was a bond as unpremeditated as nature. Adoptive parents talked about knowing 'instinctively' the child was theirs. They also talked about falling in love with the child. . . . The second challenge involved 'naturalizing' their parenthood, which adoptive parents did by identifying with their own parents; the parent-child relationship was an inherited one" (Modell 1994, 200–201; emphasis in original).

In other words, accounts of adoption parallel the language used to describe birth. Love for a newborn child is understood to be instinctive, particularly for mothers, even as some experts speak of "bonding" as a mediated process (Arney 1980; Eyer 1992). Becoming a parent entails reproduction on several levels, including the reiteration of connections with the previous generation.

Similar rhetorical strategies to those that emerge in domestic adoptions can be found in the narratives of parents who adopt internationally. Despite the enormous geographical and cultural distances that are traversed in these adoptions, the bureaucratic complexities that must be managed, and the inability of the prospective parents to "meet" their child except through photographs during much of the time the adoption is in process, parents almost universally describe a feeling of pre-ordained connection with the child they will adopt and the arrival of the child as a "homecoming" (Yngvesson 2005). In her research on international adoption in Norway, anthropologist Signe Howell quotes an adoptive mother of a Korean girl as follows: "We felt that our daughter was born at [Oslo International Airport] on the day that she arrived home" (Howell 2001, 203). In another article, Howell (1999) compares each step of the international adoption process to a stage of biological family formation: pre-pregnancy, pregnancy, birth and family life, with parents convinced that they and their adopted child "are meant for each other," and that their child could not possibly have been adopted by anyone else. The "birth" occurs when the child arrives "home."[5] The intense feelings of love and loyalty that prospective parents feel once they have been matched with a child can be put to the test if something goes wrong with the adoption or they find that the child is compromised in some way not revealed (or known) by the agency. Such losses are experienced much as the death of an already existing child might be felt. The commitment is there, even in the absence of physical connection.[6]

Gay fathers' accounts of themselves commonly draw on one or another of the meanings attached to nature. Recourse to nature in personal narratives does not obstruct the use of other images in those same narratives; indeed, the stories fathers tell are often saturated with overlapping themes. Still, metaphors of and appeals to nature appear prominently in all kinds of reproductive discourse. No matter how economically or socially driven the need to create a family may be, Western accounts of procreation are firmly anchored in images of natural impulses, often conveyed to individuals through mysterious forces and unpremeditated behaviors. As we saw in chapter 2, images of nature seem to be especially compelling strategies parents use as they attempt to blunt the salience of utilitarian and commercial elements of achieving parenthood. The authenticity of parental love depends on its purity and disengagement from material concerns and explicit calculation. But as we have seen, nature is typically a more prominent marker of motherhood than of fatherhood, so invoking it may be particularly problematic for gay men who wish to be fathers.

As we have seen, popular understandings of fatherhood in the West draw on matters of status and gender performance far more than they do on notions of either biological or emotional necessity. Ideas about motherhood, in contrast, cluster around definitions of nature to such an extent that it is sometimes difficult to distinguish one from the other. But for gay fathers who told me their stories, nature often plays a starring role. But these men are not equating themselves with mothers. When I asked them whether they think of themselves as mothers, most were perplexed. "How can I be a mother? I'm a man and I'm not confused about that." They might acknowledge that they do the kinds of things mothers do—fixing meals, tending to skinned knees, participating in the PTA—but those activities don't define their gender identities. At the same time, however, they are willing to avail themselves of the imagery of nature and blood to understand the impulses that led them to pursue parenthood and to give form to the feelings connected with being fathers. They deploy discourses that draw on nature in a number of ways, not always explicitly invoking the term "nature" as they construct their claims.

"That Extra Bond"

Jeffrey and Tony Pearl live in San Francisco. They are jointly parenting a son, Isaac, with a lesbian couple, Nancy and Patty. Isaac is the biological child of Tony and Nancy, and in an effort to craft themselves as a coherent family, all four adults decided to adopt a shared surname, Pearl. They reside in two flats in the same jointly owned building, and Isaac moves back and forth between his female and male parents according to a regular schedule.

Jeff explained that he'd always wanted to be a parent, but coming out as gay led him to assume that dream was unrealistic.

> Actually, [having children is] one of those things that I had kind of put out of my mind when I came out of the closet, and back then there weren't gay and lesbian people having kids very much. And so to me it was just kind of one of the choices I had made with coming out, you know, well this just means that I won't be able to have kids. And I think that over time, I did become aware of people having kids, but it didn't seem like very much of a reality for me. You know, then I met Tony and he was already involved in [trying to have a child] and it was kind of a reawakening for me of interest in this area. . . . [It] did tell me when I met Tony that he is someone who is serious about life so he might be a good life partner. So it was a clue that this might be someone who is marriage material.

Even though Jeff and Tony knew gay couples who had children together, they hesitated before trying to adopt because of their firm belief that children should have both a mother and a father. Tony explains, as he describes his earlier efforts to become a father with a female co-parent: "I just felt like all kids should have a mother and a father, and in the context of gay culture, that's really kind of radical or reactionary, I'm not sure which. But I didn't, I couldn't imagine it without, maybe because I'm close to my mother. Or, I don't know: I just wanted my child to have a true biological mother involved."

Jeff and Tony joined a support group for prospective gay and lesbian parents, and briefly considered adoption when it seemed difficult to find a woman (or lesbian couple) interested in co-parenting. They eventually met Nancy and Patty through another member of the group who thought they would be well matched. Like Tony, Nancy had made an earlier effort to have a child, and was very familiar with the medical issues, particularly age, that they would have to take into account. Jeff described the process:

> There's kind of a courtship that happens when you first get together. You know, we met them, we got together and we had to kind of talk about values and what their vision was for raising a child with another couple, and all that. So it took a while before we made the decision to have a child. But . . . we knew that it wasn't something that we could take too much time [deciding], so there was a trade-off between examining the situation forever and then moving forward.

Tony sees the decision to have a child biologically as "natural," a key element of what makes people want to have children in the first place. "It's like a drive. I assume that most people who want to have kids want their own biological kids." Jeff adds, "But there is kind of, sort of a curiosity that is tied back to my own biological family of, well, wanting to have that sort of bond, that extra bond that one has with their biological child. I don't think that is necessary for the kid to be happy, but I do think it is a nice thing."

Jeff and Tony's social life is embedded in gay worlds that are supportive of family life, although they are still recovering from the defection of some of their gay friends after Isaac's birth. At the same time, both men remark that they can now relate to other men at their jobs through their shared experience as fathers, and Jeff notes, "I think I feel like more of an adult in some ways. You know, some of it is getting older, but I think it happens more rapidly when you have a kid and you adjust your life to taking care of a kid." Jeff has a leadership role in a predominantly gay and lesbian synagogue, where they were married some years earlier, and they have made friends through the synagogue and the parenting group that helped them find Nancy and Patty.

Both Tony and Jeff's families have struggled with the fact of their sons' being gay. Tony's Italian Catholic family has been particularly troubled, but despite their original ambivalence about the family arrangement their son had chosen, they have gradually become more comfortable as they have gotten to know Isaac and slowly come to acknowledge him as their grandson. Jeff's family is Jewish, and while they had been somewhat more accepting over the years, the arrival of a grandson, even one with whom they have no genetic connection, has made them far more comfortable with his being gay. Jeff explains, "I think they're just very happy, in an odd sort of way, my life is a little more conventional than they expected it to be. So they can sort of relate to having kids and having a household with kids in it, and I think it's nice for them. We can relate to each other a little bit more as adults now that I have a kid."

For Jeff and Tony, parenthood has allowed for a softening of the distance between an image of the life they want to have—as parents in a family with a mother and a father—and the realities of being gay men. While being gay never posed a conflict with the demands of high-pressured careers, parenthood has made both men reevaluate their commitment to work, as they have come increasingly to see their responsibility to their family as being at odds with professional dedication expected for men in their fields. Although they care for Isaac on a half-time basis, they have still found that being parents has changed their relationship to other areas of their lives, demanding time and energy that get in the way of other obligations. Jeff works for a computer start-up company and feels that other employees see him as "less dedicated" to the job, while Tony, an engineer, says "I'm not really that interested in moving up anymore," and thus has tried to move into a less demanding position at his company.

At the same time, their new family status, unconventional though it may seem from the outside, makes them intelligible to their parents in a way that they never were when they were "just" a gay couple. They have formed a family based on blood, linking them to past generations, and are doing it in a way that even the most ardent defenders of conventional families might find at least marginally acceptable. Their adherence to a model of family based on the existence of a mother and a father and expressed in a coherent unit that is readily identifiable as a family, i.e., a unit with a shared surname, speaks to a commitment to recreate a kind of nature that they always desired but never considered attainable.

No Reasons, No Decisions

For some fathers, the very naturalness of their situation is encapsulated in an inability to pinpoint a decision or a moment of conscious desire leading up to their becoming fathers. For Matt Parker there was no specific motivation to become a father; he claims, in fact, that this wasn't something he wanted to do. I spent an evening with Matt in his comfortable home on Chicago's far North Side. His two small dogs napped on the sofa and his three boys ran through the room periodically, with Matt reminding them that he'd told them to stay in the basement family room where a movie was playing on the VCR.

Matt is white, and works alongside his parents and siblings in a family business. His former partner is black. When his partner's sister found herself unable to care for her new baby and asked her brother to do so, Matt at first protested that he really didn't want to take care of the infant. Yet, he describes a process during which he simply fell in love with the baby. When I ask what made him fall in love, he can't quite explain his feelings:

> I don't know. I couldn't tell you. I looked at him and he had these big eyes, and curly hair, and it's always been easy to be around each other. I can't explain it. I don't know. We're right for each other. We are a lot alike personality-wise. Our birthdays are a couple of days apart. . . . We're both pretty quiet, low threshold for anger and stuff. Both of us are vegetarians. And mostly for the same reason, he doesn't like hurting an animal. He's very gentle. At school, the teachers always tell me he's the sweetest kid in my class, he's never a problem. I don't know why I connected with him. Who knows? I always say that there's a purpose, so there must have been some reason he came home that day.

His partner eventually adopted Marcus, and shortly afterward he went to court and was granted a second-parent adoption. He then took on most of the primary obligations of parenting. When he and his partner broke up a couple of years later, it seemed appropriate for him to become the custodial parent, and while his ex-partner visits with the boy and gives the family some financial support, there was never any question about who was the primary parent. He found the experience of parenting Marcus so rewarding that once he was on his own he decided to adopt first Malcolm and then Karim through the foster care system. At the time that I met him, the boys were 4, 9, and 10. The boys he had adopted through the foster care system were well past infancy when they were placed with him, and he was firm about having wanted to adopt older children. "In the whole scheme of things, for me personally, I'd rather have a child of Malcolm or Karim's age and stabilize their life than a baby. A baby always has a chance. There are people that want babies. Why should I be greedy? I had my baby. They're still my babies. Sometimes with babies, people want them because they think the child's not theirs, and for me, it doesn't matter. They're children."

At first glance, Matt seemed to be extraordinarily lacking in introspection about a decision—or series of decisions—that are quite atypical for gay men, particularly when they are single. But that very inability to name a specific motivation for his becoming the single father of three, a white man raising three black sons, speaks to its naturalness. He seems to be saying that one can't really speak about something that simply comes from one's core. It's just there, his story tells us, and requires neither explanation nor analysis. His social life largely revolves around events suitable for children. Many involve his large family—his parents, siblings, and their children—so that there is a year-round schedule of holidays they all participate in.

> Because there are so many of us we usually have a monthly birthday thing. Then the November and December people get lumped with Thanksgiving and Christmas. We always have Thanksgiving together, Christmas together. It's often at my one sister's house. We do sort of a potluck thing and assign different items for people to bring. Christmas we usually go to church and go to my parents' house for breakfast and then open presents in the afternoon. We look forward to holidays with my family.

He also spends time with other parents and families he's met through his kids' school or around the neighborhood. He describes these connections:

> We just got through soccer season, so that was a big part of our socializing, with soccer people. The two older boys, their teams. People from their schools. A lot of people from their schools were playing, so they were at the soccer meet. I have some really close friends. There was a woman who wandered into my office one day who had children. I knew her because her kids went to [the same school as the boys], but we never connected. We both had a child the same age. He goes to school with her daughter. And now I'm friends with her husband. And now we socialize. We see them on vacations. One of the boys on Malcolm's team has

a family that goes to Mexico, and so those kinds of people are better for us. And then Karim's got friends, so I socialize with their parents outside of soccer. Another mother, Rose, is single and she'll bring [her son] over and they play.

In like fashion, when I asked him about his social life and his prospects for finding a partner, he shrugged, "I'm 48. I don't feel like I need to anymore." He thinks it unlikely that he will settle down in a steady relationship. "It doesn't much interest me," he tells me. "With kids the traditional reaction I get is, 'Oh, this is wonderful.' They'd kind of dig being a parent. And that will usually last a day or two and then it's like, 'Can't you get a sitter for that kid?'" Occasionally, he goes out to dinner with gay friends who aren't parents, what he calls his "friends who are single," and he maintains a telephone relationship with one old friend. But when the possibility of going to a show comes up, he opts for something the boys would also enjoy. His account suggests that he views this as a natural progression, with age as the central determinant of what is appropriate for him. Sex is for the young, he seems to say; he has better things to do now.

"I Knew This Was *My* Child"

All of these uses of nature coalesce in a kind of mystical discourse that poses parenthood as an ineffable force with origins in something mysterious and spiritually deep; paternal love enables men to perform acts of goodness that would otherwise not have been possible for them, especially given the image of gay men as self-indulgent and pleasure-oriented. This notion of fatherhood is couched in terms of a spiritually intense connection to a particular child that is somehow foreordained. The individual isn't responsible for making it happen; it's beyond ordinary control or decision making. We will see later that this kind of discourse also informs a notion of parenthood or fatherhood as a moral force, an arena in which goodness triumphs. Things that can't be explained through rational discourse can only be attributable to some force beyond human intention, and since such forces are not experienced as premeditated or self-serving, they must originate in nature.

We met Andrew Spain in chapter 2. Now in his early fifties, Andrew adopted a three-year-old boy some twenty years before my interview with him. As he reflects on his decision to adopt and the experiences he had raising his son, Jared, he expresses an implicit sense that everything simply fell into place for him once became a father. He has great difficulty pinpointing the factors that prompted him to start the lengthy process of seeking to adopt, explaining that as a gay man he had never seriously entertained the idea of being a parent nor had he even considered it desirable. As he tells the story, he was browsing through an alternative weekly paper in Chicago when he saw an advertisement urging single men and women to consider fostering special needs children. He explains, "I was not in a relationship then. And I began to think about it. I literally joked myself into, 'Well, you don't have any major plans for the next twenty years.'"

In his account, the quest to become a father seems to have been generated almost by sheer chance. But once he embarked on the process, which he describes as so time-consuming it was like having a part-time job, he decided that he should be an adoptive father rather than a foster parent. Part of his conviction to take this path stemmed from the fact that as a single foster parent he could count on having a teenager placed with him. He saw this as "inappropriate" for two very different reasons. First, he says that he wanted a child who could plausibly be his own; since he was then in his early thirties, he felt that this ruled out a teenager. Beyond this, he raised a larger ethical issue: "I did not feel it was fair for a ten-year-old child, a boy probably, who'd been beat up by the foster care system, to all of a sudden now be living with a gay man. I just did not think it was fair to the child. It would be yet another adjustment. I thought it would be hard for the average heterosexual boy to deal with."

Andrew framed his notions in terms of what would be a recognizable family and also in terms of attending to larger social issues, issues that went beyond his own need to be a parent. He also assumed that whatever child might be placed with him would most likely be heterosexual, apparently accepting popular discourse that frames heterosexuality as more "natural" than homosexuality. While he doesn't reflect on how this might affect his understanding of his own identity as a gay man, the fact that not being in a relationship, i.e., not actively gay, opened up the possibility of parenthood does suggest that the natural urge to be a parent trumps his sexual interest in men, also presumably natural. In other words, the underpinnings parenthood possess in nature produce a ranking of natural urges, one that marks sexual desire as less worthy. I will return to this theme later, but it implies a judgment that personal fulfillment is morally flawed in a way that the altruism parenthood embodies is not.

As he continued through the foster parent licensing procedure that is the first step toward adoption, he made a critical discovery about himself.

ANDREW: [The interview process] really opened up a lot of things for me about why I was doing this. I proceeded through several interviews. . . . I said to myself, "Wait a minute, you'd be a damn good parent." I really started thinking about some of my traditional values, the way I was brought up.

ELLEN: Can you describe what a traditional value is?

ANDREW: The importance of the family. The importance of the closeness of the family. The commitment to each other in that family. And even part of the mother who is a fulltime mother and a fulltime parent, who dedicated herself to being a parent, that was her job.

It seems that actually being a fulltime parent wasn't really the point here: it was his *realization* that he held these values and that they are the appropriate foundation for the formation of a family. As Andrew moved through the arduous adoption bureaucracy, he was energized by the notion that his ability to be a father was somehow intrinsic to who he was, a commitment he arrived at without conscious purpose.

Besides having been drawn to adopt by an ineffable force that somehow emerged out of a chance encounter with a newspaper advertisement, his eventual selection of a child couldn't be easily explained.

Well, I opened the book up one day to [another state] and there was a little boy . . . with a horrible prognosis who'd had a stroke when he was six months old. The book had him as two [years old]. They said he had grand mal seizures, petit mal seizures, cerebral palsy, had had a stroke, had severe brain damage, didn't speak, probably never would, but the only things he said were "no" and "what's that?" I was excited because stroke rehab was what I had done before [professionally]. And I was so intrigued by this little kid. And I did not know that much about early childhood, but I looked at the picture and I thought that's pretty profound for a kid to say "no" and "what's that?" Something does not jibe here. On the one hand, saying he's so severely disabled with this horrible prognosis, but the only thing he chooses to say is "no" and "what's that?" To me there was a seed there.

Andrew went on to describe his determination to adopt this child, who he instantly recognized as "my baby." His description of the sequence of events that then took place is as detailed and fresh as though it had happened yesterday rather than twenty years earlier. Jared "looked pretty pathetic. He looked like the runt of the litter." Andrew went on to tell me that Jared had been placed several times for adoption but that he "failed" these placements and each time was returned to the agency. Recalling this moves him to tears: "I'm sorry. Knowing later what those adoption placements were like, that's what's bringing this up. . . . One, he was placed and he had a stroke, and they returned him. The second place he was in, he was abused, and they found out and took him back to the original foster parents."

The agency he dealt with in Chicago began the process of trying to arrange a meeting, but the wheels moved with excruciating slowness. Anxious to speed up the process in order to rescue Jared from the situation he was in, Andrew skirted official channels, contacted the out-of-state agency on his own, and concocted a story about a business trip to the state where Jared was living so that he could plausibly visit almost immediately. Once he met the boy he became even more persuaded that they had a special bond. Even as he describes the care the child received from various state agencies and treatment facilities as "excellent," he also emphasizes the inability of all of the therapists and medical personnel to accurately assess his condition or to recognize the child's potential. In particular, the doctors told him that Jared would never be able to make eye contact with another person, learn to speak, or achieve meaningful social interaction. They also predicted that within a few years, he would simply stop developing and never make further progress. Andrew simply didn't accept these appraisals, arguing that because of the power of the diagnoses used to treat Jared, the boy had been socialized into a sick role that then became the only way he knew how to behave, particularly if he wanted to get attention.

He recalls their initial encounters with a series of dramatic discoveries—that the child was overmedicated and thus propelled into a drug-induced lethargy, that some of his diagnoses were probably induced by medication, and that his capacities for sociability were far better than doctors had assumed. Even without medical training, Andrew simply felt he knew better than the professionals, probably because this was "his baby." Once he succeeded in adopting Jared, he quickly decided that the child needed to be taken off the heavy medical regimen he had been on almost since birth. He stopped the routine of taking Jared to multiple medical appointments, trying to limit the occasions that would foster a patient identity. Indeed, the fact that Jared responded well to coming off these medications suggested to Andrew that many of the diagnoses in the child's record were just plain wrong; for example, he never had any seizures even after stopping the phenobarbital regimen that he had been on almost since birth. He also succeeded in motivating Jared to give up some of the infantile behaviors that had been his only way of getting attention—grunting and having tantrums. His response to both was to ignore them, forcing Jared to speak and to behave more reasonably. The ability to implement both of these approaches didn't come from any professional knowledge, but rather was simply instinctive. When I asked Andrew how he decided how to treat Jared he answered, "I don't know. I guess I just felt that there was so much trapped inside of him which needed to come out." As he explained it, Andrew was the only person who recognized these capacities in Jared. He was meant to be his father.

Gay Fathers Appropriating Nature

Gay fathers' use of discourses of nature tends to be more subtle and nuanced than it is for women and mothers. They rarely use the word "nature" and are unlikely to claim biological justification for the pathways they followed to fatherhood and for their parenting practices once they have achieved it. But they do mobilize ideas that draw on assumptions about nature in their accounts of their experiences.

As we have seen, ideas about nature underlie accounts that ground the desire to be a father in deep histories, often embedded in family. Frank and Carl, the two men in a small Midwestern city, traced their desire to be parents to the values they recall from growing up on farms. The image of the Midwestern farm offers what is arguably the quintessential image of wholesomeness and tradition (Duquaine-Watson 2005), and by explaining themselves with reference to these values, Frank and Carl located themselves in a long and honorable history. They also positioned their desire to parent as undeniably worthwhile, as it was based on connections quite separate from their lives as gay men.

Mark Friedman used a similar strategy. In recalling his boyhood in a large Jewish family, he emphasizes how typical he was—except for being gay—"I grew up thinking that I was going to have a child. . . . And that I of course was going to get married to a girl from Beverly Hills or the Valley." The urge to become a father never went away, even after he came out, grounded as it was in his Jewish upbringing and his continuing involvement in Jewish community activities, and his relationship with his current partner, Rick, was solidified when he also expressed interest in adoption. This foundation proved to have prepared him for parenthood, as he was convinced that there is "something inside" him that would enable him to take on the care of a child.

Jeff and Tony Pearl also recall fatherhood as something they always wanted, and thus not something that can be traced to a specific external motivation. Their connection to nature is instituted as well in their decision to seek a child through a co-parenting arrangement with a lesbian couple. By having a biological baby together, and living in an arrangement in which their child has both mothers and fathers with a single surname, they not only replicate "natural" processes of reproduction, but a particular structural arrangement associated with normative family organization. They further assume that this biological connection is something that links their family arrangement to a sort of universal desire, and see their adherence to the priorities of family life as enhancing their connection to coworkers and family members. In other words, being fathers breaks down divisions between themselves and the nongay world. The implication is, of course, that there is something artificial about homosexuality, but that is not a point that they make in any explicit way. Having a baby, even through the intervention of assisted reproduction, seems fated, a perception that effectively erases the considerable planning and manipulation that the four adult members of the Pearl family had to employ in order to achieve parenthood. While their use of these technologies seems to indicate a triumph over nature, they interpret their experience as a kind of submission to natural impulses that simply had to be fulfilled.

Other fathers also locate their decisions in forces outside their control, a way of invoking nature implicitly. Matt Parker describes becoming a father as something serendipitous. His connections with his sons are mysterious, beyond calculation or planning, and he sees things as simply having worked out because they make sense. As it does for some other men, being a father has provided him an alternative to a gay social life. He is now embedded in a network of family and friends who also have children in a way that is appropriate for the adult he now is. While he doesn't speak explicitly of trying to leave gay life behind, there is little doubt that it is no longer as alluring as it was when he was "single."

Finally, as we see in Andrew Spain's account of the process surrounding his adoption of Jared, his understanding of how he succeeded against the formidable obstacles of the adoption bureaucracy is grounded in his view of nature. While not conscious of having desired fatherhood earlier in life, once the idea formed—inspired by the advertisement in the *Reader* that appeared as a mystical beacon ("like a neon sign that I could not forget")—the inner resources to pursue the goal emerged from somewhere inside him. Similarly, his conviction that Jared was "his baby" and later his instinctive understanding of how to care for him both flow from some inner knowledge that he can't account for logically. None of these processes can be explained with reference to ordinary ideas about how to live as a gay man; nor do they help any of these men achieve financial or social success. But their authenticity, drawing as they do on internal, natural truths, can't be denied.

Nature, in all of these accounts, stands in opposition to the logical, the material, and the advantageous. The forces that led these men to fatherhood are not the same as those that shaped their careers or helped them to find fulfilling adult relationships. In other words, nature is conceived of as a force for good, a system that moves people toward doing the right thing, even if they sustain material losses in the process. Their accounts also suggest that parenthood is a natural condition even for gay men; the notion that it is not within the repertoire of gay men's lives reveals a disconnection from the natural order. Gay men can be as embedded in this natural order as anyone else, these stories seem to say.

These narratives bear a marked resemblance to maternal discourses of nature that have been documented elsewhere. Most notably, they resist assertions that the desire to be a father can be attributed to some external cause. These men just "know" what they should do, drawing their convictions from family history in some cases, from mystical processes in others, or from the irresistible pull of falling in love. That is, the need to be a father may be in one's genes, in one's history, in nature, or God-given, but it cannot be regarded, in these narratives, as artificial or, by implication, self-serving. Even the legalistic mechanics of adoption or the multiple medical interventions that make assisted reproduction work are "natural" in this discourse, as they bring the individual to a condition they view as mandated by nature.

These narratives of nature also erase any implications of artificiality that might attach to adoption or to reproductive engineering of the sort the Pearl family pursued. Embedding the formation of their families in nature enables these men to restore biology to their reproductive stories, perhaps a different approach to attaining full civil rights, but still legible as that sort of enterprise. Even if biological processes in the literal sense are absent from these procreative events—as is the case with adoption and the use of conceptive technologies—the men's accounts situate biology in intention, legacy, and the inability to find rational explanations for the events they have experienced.

Our Own Families

R andall Johnson and Trent Williams live in a comfortable townhouse on Chicago's North Side, and I joined them in their spacious family room for our interview. Their three-year-old son, Raymond, was playing on the carpet while we chatted. It had only been about six months since he had come to live with them, and they were beginning to make plans for their first Christmas with their son. Randall and Trent are both black; they work in technical fields and clearly do well: the room was tastefully furnished with soft leather sofas, and both men and their son were wearing stylish sportswear.

The two men have been a couple for over three years, and about two years ago had a "covenant ceremony" to solemnize their union. It was held at their church, a large black congregation known for having a pastor open to gay rights—"respecting of my lifestyle," as Randall puts it—but not a predominantly gay church. They describe themselves as religious; Trent sings in the choir and both trace their involvement in the church to childhood. They agree that they both always wanted to have children, and despite being gay neither man had thought this would be impossible. More fundamentally, the two men see parenthood as a necessary component of their relationship, something that makes it complete not just in terms of their connections with the outside world and their families, but with respect to the ongoing quality and fullness of the relationship.

ELLEN: What's so important about having a child?

RANDALL: I think it was having a fulfilling life. To kind of round out my life. The one thing always missing to me, especially on the holidays, was not having my own family. I always felt that to go to my mother's house, my sister would bring her husband and her children, there was always Uncle Randall there. I had a great time with my nieces and nephews. But I never felt that I had my own family unit to bring into the fold. And I always thought that once Mom dies or moves on, am I going to be the lonely uncle, you know, poaching on everyone else's family? I wanted to have my own family unit of my *own*, to grow with, to nurture. I wanted that desperately, to have my own family. To have my family over to my house. To not always be the single uncle, or the fourth wheel, going to another family member's home. Really, having my own family.

ELLEN: So having a partner didn't do that.

RANDALL: Having a partner did it, but it was still, it still seemed that there was something more that we could offer. Trent said we have so much love to offer, more than just a little. We even talked about doing a Big Brother thing. We have so much more love to offer. So having a partner did that, we were a family, but not, I don't think, a fulfilled family.

As the two men plan for the coming holiday, they talk about how having a family entitles them to begin to define their own traditions—what sort of decorations to have on the tree, what customs to follow about open-ing presents on Christmas Eve. Their discussion of the possibilities sets off a good-natured debate. Randall's family always opened one gift each on Christmas Eve, but that wasn't the routine at Trent's house and he's not sure whether he wants to have that become a standard part of their family's holiday celebration.

Randall and Trent's story points to a complicated process through which parenthood offered them something they both desired—recognition as an authentic family unit—and an enhanced ability to fulfill their obligations to God and the wider community. Their goal, then, was not only to have a family, but to have what they call "a fulfilled family," one that performs for the benefit of a larger collectivity, one that is kin-defined. Randall and Trent's account depends on construction of a particular kind of family to achieve both consumption and moral objectives. As black men, they have obligations that they believe exceed those facing other men; thus, their op-tions for achieving parenthood are limited by the social facts of the foster care system. In becoming parents, they do something for themselves and something for their families, but they contribute to the wider community by providing a home for at least one black child who would otherwise be lost in the system.

Holidays are particularly central repositories of family memories and traditions, and it wasn't surprising that many of the fathers became quite animated when they began to contemplate the importance of children in annual celebrations. Children transform couples into families, and make them equal players in the larger universe of kin with whom holidays are typically observed. Before they had children, some men found holidays painful reminders that they were only tangentially part of their larger families. Having children both makes their homes suitable locations for holiday events and allows fathers to have equal status with their straight siblings.

Discovering Gay Kinship

Every anthropologist has a deep reverence for the topic of kinship, even as our belief in its disciplinary centrality has been shaken by the critiques of the past few decades. David Schneider (1968) famously confronted us with the ways in which the discipline's construction of kinship reflects its prevailing uses in our own culture, and since his reading of American kinship began to influence the field, once unquestioned ideas about the interplay of biology and culture have come under scrutiny. As Schneider led us to understand, American kinship is a system for ordering our relationships into those based on "blood" and "law," but those concepts are best understood as symbolic rather than concrete. Rather than drawing on biological universals, kinship generates ideas about biology and uses these to make social life legible and predictable. Since the life sciences have achieved a level of authority about the organization of nature in Western cultures, biology easily provides a model for explaining kinship.

> There are certain cultural notions which are put, phrased, expressed, symbolized by cultural notions *depicting* biological facts, or what purport to be biological facts. Sexual intercourse and the attendant elements which are said to be biological facts *insofar as they concern kinship* as a cultural system, are of this order. Kinship is *not* a theory about biology; but biology serves to formulate a theory about kinship. . . . So much of kinship and family in American culture is defined as being nature itself, required by nature, or directly determined by na-

ture that it is quite difficult, often impossible, in fact, for Americans to see this as a set of cultural constructs and not the biological facts themselves. (Schneider 1968, 115–16; emphasis in original)

Gay and lesbian existence has long been assumed to float somewhere outside the domain of nature and kinship. Prevailing views on this topic are familiar: gays cannot reproduce "naturally," and thus their numbers can only increase through some form of "recruitment"—in apocalyptic scenarios put forward by homophobes this translates into seducing and abusing children. Even when not imagined to prey on defenseless children, gays and lesbians are not only understood to lack families of procreation, but are assumed to be almost universally alienated from the families in which they originated. Indeed, popular discourse on coming out almost always centers on the terrors of revealing homosexuality to one's family, especially parents. The outcome of such exposure is usually expected to involve some type of exclusion, varying in intensity and duration, but nonetheless consisting in an attenuated connection to one's blood relations. Indeed, the coming out story as bildungsroman routinely hinges on the dramas that unfold from such perilous revelations (Weston 1991; Zimmerman 1984).

Across the spectrum of race, religion, and nation, the news that a child is gay or lesbian is expected to bring down the curtain on full membership in one's kin group. Stories abound, for example, of Orthodox Jewish parents observing the traditional mourning period (shiva) for a gay child much as they might for a child who has converted to Christianity, married a non-Jew, or, of course, died, though less drastic forms of exclusion are probably more commonly reported. As for procreation, as noted, gays and lesbians are conventionally imagined outside its boundaries. Of course, the occasional presumably heterosexual mother or father might come out as gay or lesbian, creating the contradictory status of lesbian mother or gay father, but these "lapses" in family development have been understood to be rare. Even in such cases, full disclosure doesn't necessarily occur, particularly as such parents may have to worry about its impact on visitation and custody, a concern that (among other pressures) can mask the existence of gay parents.

Nor have such stereotypes been confined to the general public and the popular media. Notions that "family" and "gay" are contradictory and irreconcilable categories are widespread in gay and lesbian discourse, even amounting to de facto antonyms in some instances. In her ethnohistory of

Cherry Grove, Fire Island, a predominantly gay beach resort town outside New York City, anthropologist Esther Newton reports that "gay" and
"family" are used conversationally as mutually exclusive, with "family"
even serving as a synonym for "heterosexual" in some contexts (Newton
1993). In the more recent history of the community, she shows, the arrival
of lesbians alarmed old-time residents not only because of their effect on
the gender balance but because numbers of them brought children along.
Along the same lines, gay father Jesse Green vividly describes the general
consternation that occurred when he and his partner arrived at a posh
Hamptons party with their baby, Erez, in tow.

> I saw how Erez's appearance had sent shock waves pulsing from canapé to cock-
> tail. Among the younger men, it seemed that the presence of a giggling baby
> jangled the erotic energy they were attempting to cultivate. Some turned their
> backs to block out the interference; others looked over with sour expressions
> that suggested we were about as welcome as a chaperone at a prom. When we
> laid Erez down on the grass to change him, one gleaming gym-bunny actually
> squinched up his nose. Older men, on the other hand, looked balefully at the
> boy as he held our hands, perhaps envious of an opportunity that had largely
> been denied them. One sixtyish gent, fussily patting Erez's head for a moment,
> laughed off his embarrassment by saying, "In my day we could have been ar-
> rested!" I was not sure whether he thought it was such a good idea for gay men
> to be around children even now. (1999, 158)

Such dichotomous thinking also pervades much of the academic research on gay men and lesbians, as I indicated earlier. Most notably, community studies undertaken by anthropologists, sociologists, and historians
tend to proceed as though their boundaries are crisply drawn around gay
people. In ethnographic studies like *The Mirror Dance* (Krieger 1983), for
example, a Midwestern lesbian community is presented as a closed system
in which interactions with nonlesbians are virtually invisible. The women
seem to have no blood relatives, children, co-workers, or neighbors whose
reach extends beyond the echoing networks portrayed in the text. When
relatives or others are mentioned, they seem rather like intruders regarded
with suspicion from the vantage point of the inner circle (or the author).

The reasons for such myopia are not hard to discern. In an effort to
counteract the influence of deviance models, scholars have labored to provide alternative views of those whose lives were once casually relegated to

the margins. Documenting the internal logic of gay and lesbian communities helps to remedy the problem, as does research that puts so-called marginal people at the center and shows that the lives of gays and lesbians are more than just reactive, but rich and rewarding in their own terms. But this body of work and the popular assumptions that help to constitute it both fail to acknowledge the continuing power both of the concept of "family" and of the actual connections it may describe.

Kath Weston's now famous study, *Families We Choose* (1991), established the foundation for a generation of kinship-related research that has come since. And, as I noted earlier, the grassroots movements for access to the insignia of family membership have changed the conceptual terrain for a large population of gay people. Weston's work, in particular, made several things about kinship clear. On one level, she detailed the ways that gay men and lesbians create social networks for themselves out of the raw materials of friendship, at least partly in response to the uncertainties of relationships with blood kin. On another, she showed that the language her narrators used to explain these relationships—"families we choose"—was deeply embedded in ideas about family that resisted replacement. Calling these friends "family" clarified their importance and their possession of the qualities of diffuse, enduring solidarity conventionally ascribed to blood ties only. In contrast, many of the blood relations of gay men and lesbians she described resembled (conventional images of) friendships in that they were unreliable and conditional on meeting family standards, i.e., being straight.

And, as we shall see again in chapter 6, the idea that gayness and parenthood cannot coexist generates a dilemma of incommensurability (Povinelli 2001) for those who find themselves (or wish to find themselves) in this strangely contradictory condition. How some of these parents devise identities that make sense to them will be discussed in that chapter. Here, I would like to focus instead on more straightforward understandings of "family" and how these are revealed in gay fathers' stories of becoming and being parents. We shall see that a number of discursive strategies accompany the use of the language of family among the men whose narratives I present. These strategies do not only derive from their being gay men, but are drawn in very specific ways from how they understand their race, ethnicity, and/or religious values. Inscriptions of family are heavily influenced by how men are situated in larger worlds that intersect with the boundaries of sexual identity.

"It Just Feels Right"

One thing having children can do for parents—whether gay or straight—is to open up connections with difficult relatives, facilitating lines of communication that had earlier seemed sealed shut, or inspiring both sides to devise ways to make the connection manageable. In earlier research with lesbian mothers, I found a pattern of often unexpected reconciliations between families and daughters who had long been estranged from them because of their sexual orientations once those daughters produced treasured grandchildren (Lewin 1993). In like fashion, gay fathers I interviewed reported that relatives who had resisted meeting their partners, or who had expressed explicitly homophobic sentiments, in many cases were won over by the arrival of children and seemed to let go of their reservations.

Josh Goldberg and Brent Martin, whom we met in chapter 2, live in a suburb north of Chicago with their son, Samuel, whom they adopted in Guatemala. Josh is a corporate attorney in his early forties and Brent, about ten years younger, is a clinical psychologist, though he is a taking a break from his profession to be a fulltime father to their son, not yet a year old. Their decision for him to stay home was based partly on the fact that Josh has a considerably higher income but also on Brent's firm belief that there was no point in adopting a child only to "have someone else raise" him. He plans to return to his career in a couple of years, explaining that opportunities for practicing his profession will not change dramatically during the two years he plans to stay home with Sam.

Having a parent at home makes them quite a lot like many of their neighbors, and Brent finds himself hobnobbing with stay-at-home mothers when he takes Sam to baby gym and other activities. Brent says, "I'm just very acutely aware that I'm doing what mothers typically do when I go to particularly the supermarket, because people look at me with a mixture of awe and fear when they see me competently managing a fidgety child while doing the family shopping." But when I ask him if he sees himself as a mother, he is clear that he does not. Josh adds, "I think a mother is a female parent, just like a father is a male parent. And Brent's equipment doesn't make him female."

Both men have family members who have found it difficult to come to terms with having gay sons. Brent's parents live in a small town in the South and are fundamentalist Christians ("they truly believe we're damned") with little exposure to other gay people or to big city life. They were skeptical when they learned about the adoption plan, displaying little interest in Sam when the men first returned from Guatemala. But things changed dramatically when Josh and Brent took Sam to their home at Christmas. Josh explains: "That came around with a vengeance when we went to visit over Christmas and [Brent's mother] got to meet him." Brent continued, "They just adore him. . . . They're not demonstrative, emotionally expressive people, [but] they just light up when they see Sam."

Josh's father has also had a change of heart now that he has a grandson. Josh says,

> My father was one of the most homophobic people in the world and was always obsessive about gay people. One of the factors that made it hard for me to come out was that this had been such a drumbeat of his for as long as I can remember, for reasons one can only speculate. And he's also a sexist person, a racist person. . . . And he wasn't particularly interested in Sam in the abstract. . . . [But] he stops by every couple of weeks to see Sam and recognizes Sam as his grandson. And that's more than I expected. Whereas my mother is very much like I expected. She's very involved, calls every day about him. Shows pictures to all her friends. And constantly dispenses advice about how we should be doing things differently. And that's what grandmothers do.

Parenthood has also changed the way both men think about and position themselves in the world, making them much more emphatically adult, in their view, than they could have been before they had children. Brent speaks thoughtfully about the profound effects fatherhood has had on him as a person.

> The thing that sort of freaked me out was contemplating being "dad" to someone, being what my dad was to me, being that big person role model to another person, in the abstract, is very daunting. In reality, although we haven't gotten to the real role model part of things yet, it just feels right. It feels like who I am. . . . I think that ultimately makes me more of an adult in a strange sort of way, making that transition. Without any chauvinism against people without children, [it] really does feel . . . [that] being a parent, you have to be disciplined all of the time that you're parenting and that's just a different kind of challenge. And I guess, in that regard, I have changed.

Josh and Brent have no doubt that their decision to start a family positions them in the larger struggle over gay and lesbian citizenship and civil rights. While they are fortunate in that Josh's firm offers comprehensive domestic-partner benefits ("I wouldn't be there if it didn't"), they both resent being categorized differently from other (married) couples. They were united in a Jewish commitment ceremony some years ago, and considered themselves "husbands." Josh says, "I bristle at 'domestic partner.' Brent is my husband. I like the notion of partnership because, between us, that implies a certain equality and reciprocity. . . . [But] I anger at sort of having an alternative universe created where we can't use the same terms." Nonetheless, Brent suspects that their seemingly benign suburban existence sends a particularly powerful political message to the antigay world: "In my mind politically we frighten Pat Robertson far more than a bath house or anything more sexually transgressive does, because we are being completely ourselves and we are doing it in suburbia along with all of the other parents. And we're going to be at the PTA meetings. And we're going to be demanding that we be treated like everybody else and that Sam be treated like everybody else."

Josh and Brent's narrative of fatherhood highlights a number of key issues, some of which speak to multiple meanings of family generated by having children. On one level, having a child opens up connections with their families, even with specific relatives who were particularly hostile to homosexuality, in a way that no other sort of outreach can accomplish. On another level, it catapults them into adulthood, highlighting their responsibilities and the need to serve as "role models" in a way that no other activity, to their way of thinking, does. But even as both of these changes propel them more firmly into a kind of family life that they can share with people in the mainstream, it also is confrontational and potentially subversive, posing a particularly potent threat to the forces of homophobia. It is noteworthy that they characterize their suburban domestic existence as authentic to who they really are, presumably more so than when they were a childless gay couple. Having a family, in their account, has a particularly motivated quality: it is what ought to be and what it truly means to have a marriage.

"I Always Imagined Myself as a Family Man"

When I first met Peter Levine and Ben Kaplan in their Chicago townhouse, they were the parents of a young son, Ari, and were expecting a second baby in a few months. The townhouse is in the Lakeview neighborhood, just a block from Lake Michigan, in an area colloquially known as Boys Town because of the visible concentration of gay men among its residents and the many local businesses catering to them. Peter, 40, is a real estate agent and Ben, 38, works in a manufacturing concern located in the suburbs. Both come from large, close, Midwestern Jewish families. They've been a couple for some sixteen years and had a commitment ceremony— "under the chuppah [the Jewish wedding canopy]," as they explain. Early in their relationship the question of having children didn't really come up; they didn't know other gay people with kids and were struggling with what were then more immediate issues like whether to come out to their families. At that time, Ben explains, coming out meant admitting one couldn't have children, a reality that made telling one's family more difficult than just discussing being gay.

> I knew I always imagined myself as a family man. I grew up in a family where it was ingrained that there was nothing better than having children. A family is the way to go. . . . That was one of the main reasons why I struggled [with being gay] as long as I did. Because I loved kids, I always assumed that I was going to have kids. And when I came out to my folks, that was probably a huge blow to them, that I wasn't going to be a parent. It was one of the hardest things that my folks had to deal with when I came out to them.

Peter went through a similar struggle. He understood that he was gay from an early age, but resisted coming to terms with his sexuality as a way to hold out hope for a family. "Who ever heard of a gay parent? I mean, early on, I couldn't think of any role model." For years, Peter and Ben let their families think they were just roommates, with each man joining the other's family for holiday dinners and other occasions. Peter explains, "The funniest line at our wedding was one that my mother made in her toast. She said that during all the time that Ben came to our house for Passover and whatever that she always thought that he would make a good mate for my sister. And then she paused and looked at the room and said, 'Little did I know that one day he'd be marrying my son!' "

It was Ben's sister who raised the issue of children. She offered to donate her eggs so that they could get pregnant with a surrogate. At the time, they couldn't afford to take her up on her offer, but once the possibility had been suggested they never seriously considered any other way to have a baby. In the meanwhile, however, they were having an active social life—doing things they enjoyed without the encumbrance of children and not giving much thought to anything being missing. The spark for their final decision, however, came from the arrival of a very immediate role model. Their neighbors, Chris O'Neil and John Stone, had twin girls with a surrogate. Peter explains, "So it wasn't really until *they* had their children—they used to live right there, across the courtyard. You open our door and they were ten feet away. Right there. We used to wave. And they were the trailblazers. They found the agency. They figured it out. And before you knew it, they had the twin girls. And it was wonderful. And we saw them every day. And we sort of followed in their footsteps."

As Peter and Ben explained, seeing two gay men close at hand raising a family made a huge difference to them. They not only had a model of how two gay fathers could manage their lives, but living in such close proximity they were able to absorb some of the pleasures of parenting. Also, as they moved into their late thirties, they began to think more about how they wanted to move into full adulthood. It occurred to them that they didn't want to wait too long to start having children, feeling that it would be important to still be young enough when children are young to be able to keep up with them. Also, as Ben's sister got older, they realized that her ability to donate eggs would decline. At the same time, the gay life of parties and cultural events and restaurants started to look shallow and immature. Ben says,

> We wanted to be active and you see these older gay men participating in the party scene and you wonder. Some of this is sort of pathetic, and you wonder how long are we going to want to be in that part of the gay scene and not sort of finding reward and value and pleasure exploring different aspects of gay life. And we just saw this as something we could find a great deal of pleasure in. I think we saw a tension—both of us think it's pathetic when we see a middle-aged man trying to act like he's twenty years old.

Peter adds, "I feel like we [were] coming at this at the end of the cycle, being very involved in a lot of different things, and we [were] ready for a new challenge. Life is passing us by, and if we're going to do it, then do it now."

The two men continued to think over their options, while still participating in the round of gay-centered social and cultural activities that they had been involved in over the years. But in the summer of 1998, they had an epiphany.

BEN: I think the crystallizing moment was at the airport in Amsterdam. We had gone to the Gay Games. We had, like, fourteen days and fourteen nights of just nonstop, all-out party. And we were just exhausted, and we both had gotten really sick from no sleep and too much everything, and we were at the airport. And across from us were two guys, and an adorable little baby who they adopted.

PETER: Adorable little baby. And [Ben] was the one who expressed that like the bolt of lightning struck. Honey, look at that. And they had obviously not been into the scene of the Gay Games and the party and on and on. They were warming a bottle and changing a diaper.

BEN: The two guys were pretty cute, too. They were adorable, these two guys.

PETER: It was like the juxtaposition of what we'd done over the two weeks. It struck him first. And he was just like, look at that. The clouds cleared, and a ray of light came down.

The men in the airport provided another accessible image of gay men with a baby. The tenderness of the scene was compelling and the fact that the fathers were "pretty cute" made the situation look even more desirable. Part of the power of the scene came from its occurring on the heels of the frivolity of the Gay Games. When Ben describes himself and Peter as being "sick" from "too much everything," he encapsulates a number of thoughts about having a meaningful life. Can one go on forever doing the same thing? Or is there a time—adulthood—when even a gay man has to settle down and figure out what life is really about?

Making the decision to have children was only the beginning of the process. Besides harvesting eggs from Ben's sister, a difficult endeavor since she was by then in her late thirties, Peter and Ben had to locate a surrogate and manage the complicated set of medical and legal arrangements that are connected to surrogate births. Working with an agency in Los Angeles that specializes in surrogacy for gay men and lesbians, they found a surrogate, a lesbian whose only criterion for choosing a couple was that they be in a long-term relationship. Finalizing the arrangements, doing the ovum transfers and inseminations and all the other medical procedures involved numerous trips to California. But the pregnancy, with Peter's sperm, worked out, and at the time of our first interview the same surrogate was pregnant with their second child. This time, the egg donor was Peter's sister and Ben provided the sperm.[1] Each of these pregnancies cost over $100,000 to bring to completion, including fees and other allowances to the surrogate, the costs of egg retrieval, embryo storage, multiple insemination attempts, fees to the agency, a medical policy for the surrogate, and the many trips to California associated with every step of the process.[2]

A few months later, Peter and Ben's second son was born and I attended the bris, the Jewish circumcision ritual, held at Peter's brother's spacious home in Chicago. The crowd attending consisted mainly of relatives from both sides of the family but a substantial number of the two men's friends were also there, gay men and some lesbians, Jewish and non-Jewish. Both a rabbi and a cantor participated. An abundant buffet lunch was spread out on the dining room table, and people circulated and chatted both before and after the ceremony. Since the birth of their first son, Peter's mother had died, so the two men devised a male version of her name to be given to the second boy, adhering to the Ashkenazi Jewish custom of naming children for deceased family members. Ben and Peter had no difficulty integrating themselves into their extended families. Over the years since I interviewed them, Peter and Ben regularly e-mail photographs of their sons, so I have been able to follow their progress as they have grown, seeing them playing in the snow, frolicking at the beach, and playing musical instruments at family gatherings. If this photographic record has a theme, it is the easy integration of their family with the wider constellation of both extended kin groups, with clusters of cousins and aunts and uncles all involved together in the business of being a family.

Passing Down Tradition

Tyrone Landon and Thomas Palmer live in a spacious flat in Chicago's Hyde Park neighborhood with their eleven-year-old son, Damian. Damian's adoption by Tyrone became final a few months ago and Thomas has started legal proceedings to complete a second-parent adoption. Two of Tyrone's cousins, also gay men, currently live with the family, and they often assume responsibility for activities involving Damian. Thomas is a lawyer and works in a judicial position for a government agency; Tyrone, who has a business degree, is currently enrolled in divinity school. He keeps up a complicated schedule of various community-related jobs and activities, ranging from teaching, to consulting, to social service. Both men grew up in African American families that struggled to help them achieve academically, and both are close to their large extended families. As they talk about their parenting practices and their hopes for Damian, they each invoke their respective families, situating themselves relatively seamlessly in deep histories passed down through kin.

Ritual is a serious part of both men's lives, through their involvement in church and through special events, like the holy union ceremony they held some five years earlier. They eagerly show me the album from that occasion and tell me that they have begun to plan a ceremony to renew those vows. Their home also has become the focus of Christmas and Thanksgiving celebrations; they take considerable pride in being the "focal point" for holidays among their families. Tyrone tells me what the qualities of a good home should be.

> It should be warm and inviting. I had a wonderful experience growing up, extended family, church family. It felt very warm and right. I've always cherished that and wanted to pass it on. I want to create that here. Christmas with a tree and the fire going, and the dogs, you know, running back and forth. That's family, that's home. That's what I like. It's so traditional anyway.
>
> ELLEN: When you say traditional, what do you mean?
>
> TYRONE: Like a picket fence and those types of things.

This image doesn't necessarily require living in the suburbs, nor does it describe their Hyde Park apartment building. For Tyrone and Thomas, the metaphor of the "picket fence" is less about a physical reality than about an image of warmth and inclusiveness. The involvement of biological kin and a circle of close friends, all black gay men, who have become like uncles to Damian, all contribute to the realization of this ideal. Their actions as parents—particularly, as they explain, their emphasis on how important it is for Damian to get a good education—recapitulate the stories of their own upbringings, sons of working-class black families that struggled to be sure their sons would achieve. But "family" is also invoked through the ongoing actions of Damian's "uncles," who spoil him with trips to Toys "R" Us and take him on excursions to various places in the Chicago area. In other words, family in Tyrone and Thomas's framework is constituted both from history and ongoing action. Tyrone and Thomas also host an evening event about once a week they call "family night": "We play board games and stuff. Everybody's home. The five of us and maybe one or two other people will come by. We cook a big dinner. We sit and talk. Play games."

Interestingly, the detachment that many white gay fathers report on the part of their friends who don't have children doesn't seem to be typical of

Tyrone and Thomas's circle of black gay friends. Though none of the other men they know are fathers, the adoption seemed to have sparked excitement among their friends and some have begun to investigate adoption for themselves. In any case, the notion that a larger group of people can and should be incorporated into their family is central to their account. Tyrone tells me, "It's not unlike things I experienced as a child culturally. . . . The opportunities are there to take advantage of." He was an only child, but explains that he had lots of cousins and never felt alone. Since Damian is the first grandchild on either side of their families, both grandmothers are indulgent and involved in his upbringing. While this sometimes means explicit advice to the two men, more commonly Tyrone and Thomas draw on their memories of childhood to devise solutions to parenting problems. If Damian fails to make his bed before leaving for school, for instance, his eight-dollar weekly allowance is cut by a dollar. Tyrone explains that the boy needs to learn that there are consequences to his actions; he sees conveying this message as one of the central obligations he faces as a father. These are lessons that he makes clear have come from his and Thomas's boyhood, lessons that both of their mothers took pains to deliver. Their own mothers are very much the model they rely on as they figure out how to be parents to Damian.

On the other hand, the two men also see their home as fundamentally different from the ones in which they were raised. This is a "male household," Tyrone tells me, which means to him that when they adopt again, which they hope to do before long, they should only consider a boy. He's hard pressed to define a "male household," and my attempts to unravel its meanings give way to silly jokes about chastity belts and girls' hygiene, but as he goes on, he also stresses that African American boys are more in need of adoption than girls, and that they have an ethical obligation to consider that. While responsibility to their community, then, offers at least a partial explanation (or a comfortable rationalization) for the adoption decisions they have made, Tyrone believes that being gay men properly situates them in a male household. Thomas is less committed to this view, making the case for adopting a girl, but Tyrone cuts the argument short with his judgment that a girl would need her own bedroom, an amenity their flat will simply not provide. On that practical note, the discussion ends.

Though Tyrone and Thomas move in a mostly gay, black, and male world socially, their sense of self and their understanding of the meaning of family are firmly grounded in their experiences growing up in African American families. The idea of family defines their immediate social world, populated with a number of gay black men who constitute their family on a daily basis, what Kath Weston has characterized as "chosen family" (1991), but it also links them to the past and to larger conceptualizations of African American life. That history is about using firm discipline and clear notions of who's in charge to train children to do their best on every level—in school, at home, and in church. Their obligation is to use their memories to pass this basic ethic on to their children. Even as their immediate social world is composed of mostly gay people, they staked a claim to the wider black community in a broader way when they adopted Damian.

For Tyrone and Thomas, as for many other men whose stories I heard, understandings of tradition are virtually indistinguishable from ideas about what family is. Families are where traditions are first experienced and taught, and one does honor to one's family by passing on the content of this learning. But family is also imagined as an absolute necessity if these traditions are to be fully realized in the next generation, and families, by definition, include children. Tyrone and Thomas cannot establish a fully functioning family without being parents and they cannot, therefore, carry on traditions or help to generate new traditions otherwise. That they understand their obligations in this regard as flowing directly from their African American heritage doesn't negate the fact that virtually every ethnic group constructs the function of family much the same way. What distinguishes their obligations as black men to carry on tradition and extend family into the future is the urgency of the crisis facing black children in the foster care system, particularly when they are boys. In other words, their affinity for tradition and family constitutes more than sentiment or nostalgia: it is about the very survival of many of their young people, about the weight of the knowledge that some children will have no future unless responsible community members take action. Thus, family comes to have a broader meaning for Tyrone and Thomas: it encompasses both the personal, domestic experience that takes place on "family nights" and their obligation to take action on behalf of the larger black community. Adopting an older black boy is one such action, and the fact that it also allows them to honor the traditions of their individual families is a further benefit.

As in many American families, the affection showered on Damian by the "uncles" often takes the form of gifts and trips to stores like Toys "R" Us (Seiter 1995). Being able to engage in extravagant consumption very likely has special resonance for black families newly arrived in the middle class, not long removed from a time when such purchases were routinely out of reach (Chin 2001). But Thomas and Tyrone also stress the importance of a kind of family togetherness that is not specifically focused on consumption when they explain the "family nights" that have become routine at their house. Attending church together every Sunday is also a marker of family cohesion as are routine chores and making sure that homework gets done. These are rituals that connote obedience and recognition of parental authority and are key markers of orderly family life. Tyrone and Thomas's account of their family puts routine and order at the center of its structure; adherence to what they see as traditional forms of parental authority, performed through the repetition of specific activities, anchors their family in a larger history to which they feel responsibility as black men. Being gay only inflects the style through which these obligations are enacted; the obligations themselves are neither negotiable nor subject to revision.

"A Sense of Connection"

We met Enrique Morales in chapter 2, when he explained how his family of adopted children allowed him to prove to his parents that he was as fully adult as their other children. Enrique first considered parenthood when he was in graduate school in social work. A letter from the Department of Human Services was included in the orientation packet given to each student that talked about the department's policy of recruiting adoptive parents. In particular, it made clear that all sorts of people were welcome to apply, including gays and single individuals. For the first time, it occurred to Enrique that his longstanding dream really could become a reality.

About eight years prior to our meeting, Enrique had adopted Carmen, then six months old. Although he had originally imagined adopting two children, things were going so well that he began to reconsider.

> After my daughter, I was toying with the idea of adopting a second. Then I decided, no, life is good. My daughter was three or four at the time, and things were moving where she was a little more independent, she could go to a friend's overnight. I could actually start dating again and getting out. And I was enjoying that. So I thought, no. But at the time I was also aware that there was another child out there. I knew that my son was out there. And there was always the possibility. . . . And two months later, I get a call. And so that was it, and then

a year ago, about a year and a half ago, I was at work and came across information that [the Department of Human Services] were going to have another child [from the same biological mother] that was in foster care. First I said I really couldn't do it. . . . I just thought I couldn't handle it all. But the more I thought about it, since they're siblings, I couldn't see myself living knowing that there was a child out there that felt like mine already. You know. I have this bond with their biological mother somehow.

All three children, Carmen, Antonio, and Miguel, have the same biological mother but different biological fathers. Although Enrique has never met the mother, he knows her name and a great deal of her story. Besides the three half-siblings he has adopted, he is aware of five other children she had earlier; all are being raised either by her relatives or are in foster care. The mother is a drug-addicted prostitute often sighted hanging out at a particularly notorious corner in San Francisco's Mission District. Carmen came to him in good physical condition, but Antonio suffers from attention deficit disorder, and Miguel is living with the consequences of having been born with methadone and cocaine in his system.

Enrique feels strongly that he had no alternative but to adopt both Antonio and Miguel, that both of them were destined to be his children because of the bond he has with their biological mother. Once he was aware of the other children's existence, he literally felt he had no choice in the matter, a commitment shared by his daughter, nine years old at the time of the interview.[3]

There's a bond to her [the biological mother]—I'm raising her children. And my daughter had such a strong response to my other son that I thought I owed it to them. Whatever sacrifices. . . . I knew her [my daughter] enough to know that in hindsight as an adult she would have chosen to do that. To have her other brother. So we sat down and we talked and I told her. And it's been like a dream. She loves having two brothers. She loves helping out. She's quite the little mother now.

Although he says that he was open to adopting a child of any race or ethnicity, he hoped to be able to adopt a Latino child so that they would share an ethnic background. His children's mother was part-Latina, and at least two of their fathers were also Latino, so this worked out with his kids. "My preference was a Latino child. To me it's important to have your children have a sense of connection to you. Not just through the adoption and the parenting. But also to have that physical connection, too. It's important. And I've seen it in the kids. They like having that connection as well."

Enrique's family, then, is uniquely defined by blood even though it was created by adoption. His gay cousin, Rafael, has lived with them since Carmen's adoption, and his presence helps to make parenting manageable; he can babysit for the kids when needed and he has worked with Enrique in reconstructing the house, which was only affordable because it was extremely dilapidated when he purchased it. Enrique understands his family as being destined to have taken its particular shape because of the biological bond among his children. While he chose to adopt them, he also sees himself as having made that choice in response to a kinship imperative that was irresistible.

There are many ways we can interpret Enrique's comments. He emphasizes a desire for a naturalized family and situates himself as morally responsible and virtuous, a theme that echoes the language used by mothers when they describe their bonds to their children (Lewin 1993). But Enrique's narrative also resonates with questions of consumption. Becoming a father allows a person (in this case, a single gay man) to achieve a particularly valued condition: stability and full adulthood. This goal was achieved through *choice*; that is, no one expected Enrique as a gay man to take this path to moral engagement, but he also sees it as compelled, in some way, by an imperative grounded in nature to raise the three half-siblings as a family. He had to make choices that were practical given the financial limitations he faced and so never considered any option other than public agency adoption. Taking this path made clear to him, as well, that he would need to seek economies in other areas of his life, leading him to move to a less expensive part of town, to settle for a cheaper car, and to invite his cousin to move in with him and his children. Enrique's choice of Latino children also underscores the element of nature he feels he has achieved in the formation of his family: because all members of the family are "Latino" he understands them to be kin in a way not possible without that designation.[4]

Like many other fathers, including Josh and Brent, Enrique's decision to become a parent brought him closer to his parents and other family members. He is the only one of their children who went to college, moved away from home, and is gay, and he had only revealed that last bit of difference to his parents a couple of years before he began the adoption process. Once he decided to adopt, he wrote them a long letter, detailing not only his adoption plans, but his commitment to have his family live in a particular way—as an "out family, a gay-identified family." While he would raise his children to be Catholic, his commitment was to a far more open type of Catholicism than what was familiar to them. "I wanted them to know because I didn't want to feel like when I had children and we went down there that my children would have to watch what they say. I didn't want them to hear things that would discount their family or their lives."

Enrique has been enormously gratified by the outcome of the process. His parents have, in his words, "embraced" his family, flying up to the Bay Area almost immediately after he brought Carmen home because they couldn't bear to wait until his planned visit to them to see their new grand-daughter. "My mom came up and she spent a week. It was a good thing. I think it's helped them because from that point on, they felt reconnected to me. Because before I was their son who went off. I was the only one that went to college in my family. I was an independent thinker. I went off to seminary. I went off to college, graduate school. I'm gay, I was living in another part of the state. So this was a way for us to reconnect." The grand-children made a level of communication, intimacy, and openness possible that had not previously existed for Enrique and his parents. It is clear from his account that he felt far more motivated to work things out with them than he might have had he not had children. The adoption made clarity a prerequisite for him and his children to freely participate in the life of the extended family. Enrique firmly believes that their life wouldn't be possible in more conservative Southern California, but he needs to be able to move back and forth comfortably to sustain the kind of family he wants to have.

"We're as Much a Family as Any Other Family"

Not all fathers identify their families of orientation as models for their own lives as gay dads. For some of the men, conscious decisions about being "gay families" shape their ideas about family composition, even as some of the images they deploy seem to depend on conventional family configurations.

For Javier Vélez and his partner, Nate Sherman, claims of family status loom large as issues of activism. I met with Javier one day in his office at the San Francisco social service agency where he works. As we will see in chapter 5, Javier describes dramatic changes in his life after their adoption of Diego and Graciela, seeing the children as a force that made coming out mandatory to good parenting. At the same time, however, some of the decisions the two men have made, particularly to adopt a second child, reflect an attempt to recreate a kind of family existence they both remember from their youth.

> What happened was that once we got Diego, and we had him for, like, nine months, we, well, I wanted to, well, initially we were open to any gender, any race actually, it didn't matter what we got. And once we had a boy, I said to Nate, "I really want to have a daughter now that we have a boy. I would like some female energy in the house." And I also think that with, certainly we can share, we have enough to share. And we said we could have another child, and if we're going to do it, let's do it now while I'm at home versus going back [to work] and then doing it again. And also, I figured it would be nice for Diego to have a sibling. If we could have two children, obviously they would have family memories together—Christmases and holidays and these sorts of things—and it would be nice for them to have that to share, their family.

But even as Javier hoped to provide his children with some of the experiences attributed to traditional families, being a father led him to change his ideas about how to have a meaningful life. His new emphasis on making himself visible as a gay, Latino father and on acknowledging the feminine traits that parenting aroused in him was crafted as sharply different from his upbringing in a traditional Latino family. He saw himself as having to overcome his lifelong expectations about gender if he was to succeed as a father. For Javier and Nate, these commitments are inflected with anger over their lack of access to the privileges of other families.

> After we had the kids . . . we had to do, like, wills and power of attorney for illness and possible stuff, just to make sure that we were covered that way, which is the stuff that you automatically get if you are married and you're heterosexual. We feel that we have chosen for our family unit to be married for inheritance, for the children, for each other. . . . I have to do my taxes as a single person, I actually have to do it as a single parent. So that feels discriminatory. But also, we're as much a family as any other family over there, and why can't we have the same, under the law, the same protections, the same privileges, and the same responsibilities and the same consequences?

He goes on, describing the ramifications of this discrimination on their experience buying a home: "We bought a house [and] I had to write a letter to the loan officer about why I stayed home for six years, and what I was doing. If I was a woman raising a child, they wouldn't have questioned why I was staying home. And I felt really invaded there, because it was just private information that I felt I shouldn't have to share. The system is set up, certainly it's not supportive of same-gender people applying for loans."

To make their family status clear, the two men plan to change their last names so that the entire family will share a single surname, with Javier and Nate using their original surnames as middle names. This would make their family status clear, he explains, "to mark us as a family, that we're married."

Issues of family also penetrate their interactions with other gay people. Javier describes the frequent hostility he has encountered from gay men and also reports an instance in which Nate was called "a breeder": "Sometimes with gay guys we'd be, like, in a store talking to them with our kids hanging off our chest in a Snuggli, and it would be forty-five minutes before they would say something about the kid, like, 'Is that your child?' They wouldn't even address the elephant in the room, they wouldn't talk about it. And if they did, it was like, 'What the hell are you guys doing?'"

Like many other fathers, Javier describes losing many friends who couldn't get used to the constraints parenting imposed on social life.

> People are use to calling you and saying, "Hey, let's go somewhere," and you dump everything and you move. And with our kids, of course you can't do that and of course, little by little, you start losing your friends and then you start associating with people with their own children, and then the whole basis of friendships is that. Some people, I felt that, well, I don't want to say jealous, like, "I don't want to be around you guys," because we represented too much stability because of our relationship, and with the children, it was too formal, too structured, too traditional, too I-don't-know. And it seemed threatening to them somehow. And we didn't feel comfortable being around them because of that.

Even so, the two men have maintained some of their old friendships with gay men.

> We did manage to retain a few single gay men who are now uncles. One of them is also a grandpa, because he said, "Your kid has too many uncles, so I'll be a grandpa." And that's Grandpa Jack and Uncle Ed, because Ed didn't want to be a grandpa. And so we did retain a few, those we've been friends with for many years. And of course, it's also been realizing that when you're gay or lesbian or bisexual or transgender, you become a family, you really are starting to, you

are, you have this script, and this is the great thing about our family—we don't
have to follow anybody else's pattern, anybody else's script. We write our own,
and we create our own family . . . and all of a sudden they become an auntie or
an uncle or a cousin or somebody, but we make a family. We're not related by
blood, but we're related by the spirit and by other things.

Javier's use of the term "family" reveals a complicated interplay of
competing definitions, associations, and ideals. On one level, as we shall
see in more detail later, he understands his family as having allowed him
to get in touch with a feminine side of himself, allowing him to function
as a "mother." He also invokes the images of holiday celebrations as the
occasions that constitute critical moments in the definition of a family.
Having a family gives meaning to holiday celebrations that they don't seem
to have otherwise; holidays have the power to continue old traditions and
generate new ones, but they can only play that role when they emanate
from a real family.

The authenticity of family can also be symbolically rendered in surnames, which is why Javier and Nate plan to change their names in a strategy that recalls that of the Pearls (whom we met in chapter 3). But their
decision is based as well on their activism as they intend it as a way of
demanding access to the rights associated with family status—tax benefits,
inheritance, and a kind of cultural legitimacy and visibility. So what seems
like an accommodationist move looks more complicated when one considers the logic that motivates it.

On another level, Javier feels strongly that their family puts them in a
tenuous position vis-à-vis the gay community. Being parents leads them
to be treated as outsiders by many gay men, even as some gay friends
have found a way to maintain connections by reinventing themselves as
"uncles." It is this ability to call upon kinship terms that Javier sees as a
special advantage of gay life, i.e., being able to craft kinship on the basis of
"the spirit." But the fact that the imagery of these novel family forms is securely framed in the language of kinship brings us back to the traditional
family as a rich source of cultural expectations.

Claiming Family

The stories presented in this chapter reveal a number of ways that gay
fathers use ideas of "family" to organize ordinary experience and to make

sense of their objectives as parents. In some, fathers carefully adhere to definitions of family that are in many ways conventional, i.e., that are explicitly modeled on their own families of procreation. In these instances, the men, like Randall and Trent, explain their desire to have children in terms of their yearning for a family of their own, a goal that will forever elude them unless they have children of their own. In other words, the very definition of "family" in these constructions is reproductive; one's membership in any other sort of "family" doesn't count as one's own. Continuing connections with parents, siblings, and other relatives doesn't count; neither does being in a long-term relationship, even when the larger constellation of kin recognizes it and includes the spouse in family activities. This understanding is familiar from the common language used to discuss reproduction: "Do you plan to start a family?" means "Do you intend to have children?" One simply can't have a family without being a parent in a unit that includes children. These fathers' stories are founded on their understanding that the family is a natural formation, but not one that can occur in the absence of children. As we saw in chapter 3, the men regard their yearning for family as something that resists explanation—it's simply natural—even if the ability to form a family demands careful planning and action.

What stands out in these narratives is that fathers not only see children as a defining attribute of a family, but view the alternative—not having a family—as profoundly unsatisfying. This may be because having children is regarded as a particularly worthwhile part of life, but it also reflects a notion that without establishing a family, one remains forever confined to a kind of superannuated adolescence. Having a family and achieving adulthood are mutually defining, in this discourse, and (despite the alleged cult of youth in our culture) aging without achieving adulthood is understood as somehow inadequate. In his memoir of seeking fatherhood, Jesse Green, reflecting on the birth of his brother's son, explains his concerns, "On a twigless branch of the family tree, merely an uncle, I would never achieve that kind of adulthood; I'd just keep aging. My hair might fall out, my gums might retreat to the bone and beyond, but all it would make me was old. Without a child you were always a child: a hanger-on, an exile, a zero" (1999, 96).

In other words, having one's own family constitutes a kind of achievement for which there are no substitutes. As Andrew Cherlin (2004) has argued, forming a family in the U.S. has begun to serve as a foundation for marriage, rather than the reverse, as couples struggle to demonstrate that they have arrived at a state of full maturity before entering into a formal marriage. His data show that couples often defer marriage until the solidity of the relationship has been fully revealed, generally by the longevity of the relationship and its financial stability, as well as by the arrival of children. In like fashion, Kathryn Edin and Maria Kefalas (2005) have shown that low-income, unmarried mothers, often publicly vilified as sabotaging or devaluing marriage, actually hope to marry eventually, but not before they have overcome various obstacles to full citizenship, many of which are material, e.g., secure employment and home ownership. In this context, being parents can be a precondition to marriage, if not predating it then providing the evidence that the marriage has produced a family and is thereby worthy of celebration. Historian Nancy Cott (2000) has demonstrated the multiple links that exist between marriage and citizenship in American history. Having children ratifies a marriage as no other marker can, making clear to the world that a family exists. I would argue that for the gay fathers whose stories I heard, having a family may be a more critical marker of citizenship than establishing a committed relationship ("marriage"), serving to delineate maturity, the ability to continue and contribute to tradition, and, as we shall see in the next chapter, a kind of moral solidity not readily accessed in other ways.

Having a family, in the sense of having children, also can open up and enrich connections to one's blood relations. Even reluctant grandparents—those who have long histories of homophobia, those who look askance at reproduction through assisted procreative technologies, or those with questions about adoption or racial difference within a family—seem to rise to the occasion when actual grandchildren make their appearance. The rapprochements that children can broker are not uniform, and don't always succeed, but some of the narratives in this chapter speak dramatically to their possibility. Connections with family also offer a pathway toward building on traditions, carrying them on and having the right to transform them to reflect the formation of new family units. That these are tied to biologized notions of kinship, as they are in Enrique's notion of sharing Latino identity with his children, resonates with the way American families construct relatedness out of ethnicity, race, or predestination.

At the same time, the connection with family that children produce can connote a fidelity to history and a way to claim a place in one's community. Like some of the strategies I documented for lesbian and gay commitment rituals (Lewin 1998), having children offers a way to position oneself as entitled to tradition, custom, or ethnic heritage. This is particularly mani-fested in Tyrone and Thomas's story. Although they exist in a social world composed mostly of other black, gay men like themselves, the model for parenthood they put forward is solidly rooted in the childrearing practices and values of their families. They have no need to invent new ways to fa-ther Damian; the blueprint exists in the story of their own childhoods.

For some other men, like Peter and Ben, fatherhood situates them in a larger kinship constellation but also in a moral universe of things that are important. This is another version, certainly, of the association be-tween family and adulthood, but it has particular poignancy when the op-posite of "adult" and "responsible" is implicitly (or explicitly) "the gay male thing." We will see in chapter 5 that the mandate to do good, to be responsible citizens, to contribute to the world can be realized through parenthood, particularly when one chooses to be a father to a child who might otherwise be neglected or mistreated.

And in still other cases, like that of Javier and Nate, images of family play a contradictory role in men's understandings of how they ought to go about organizing their own lives. While they depend on seemingly tradi-tional devices, like shared surnames, as a way to make their family's status concrete and visible, they also see that strategy as profoundly subversive, a way to make demands in a system that unjustly excludes them. Javier's response to parenting was to distance himself from his conventional Latin upbringing but also to embrace some of its features, particularly the as-sociation of caring with the role of the mother. At the same time, however, Javier has also been inspired to activism since becoming a parent, and as we shall see in chapter 5, understands his family as the engine that drives his commitment to social change.

Because family is so deeply naturalized, it is particularly difficult to observe the range of meanings attached to it when one looks only at nor-mative, ordinary (i.e., married heterosexual) families. It is the families thought to be on the margins: those that must struggle to gain recognition, those that must manipulate—and sometimes outwit—legal and techno-logical obstacles, those that feel themselves to be precarious in any way that most clearly reveal the strategies that underlie the process of family formation and continuity. It is difficult to grasp the meaning of genetic connection when one looks only at families formed through straightfor-ward biological means; we need to turn our attention to those who make use of assisted reproductive technologies to see how such connections are actually understood. In like fashion, the ways in which family formation

sparks concerns with traditions and a desire to play a role in their continuity are most powerfully expressed among those who have to assert their
claims forcefully if they are to be heard. Those on the margins may share
the desires of those on the inside, but every assertion of inclusion must be
articulated with far greater precision if it is to succeed.

CHAPTER FIVE

Do the Right Thing

It ought not be surprising that fatherhood can be the foundation of a moral stance, a way of positioning oneself on the side of the good guys in the world, but this is rarely the first thing that leaps to mind when one considers fatherhood in the abstract. As we saw earlier, fatherhood is more securely anchored in popular imagination to a kind of masculine achievement, a good one without doubt, but still not directly linked to the formation of broad moral claims. In this dominant conception, fatherhood differs markedly from motherhood, so often conflated with goodness, altruism, and nonviolence. The Virgin Mary, the archetypical figure of maternal purity and selflessness, cannot be imagined in a masculine form, though of course there are many images of masculine generosity and moral stature that might come to mind. As we have seen, some recent, postfeminist conceptions of fatherhood have stressed the ways that fathers can benefit emotionally from closeness to children, but the man who takes the "daddy track" is still viewed with suspicion and assumed to be somehow emasculated.[1] These discourses of paternal commitment place greater emphasis on the benefits men can derive from involved fatherhood than on how their devotion contributes to children's development. In other words, elaborated paternal bonds tend to be imagined as beneficial but not strictly essential to the formation of successful childrearing environments.

But many of the fathers I spoke with put forward understandings of their paternal experience that gave a central role to the moral authority one can draw from being a father. In many cases, men situated this in stories about how being a father compelled them to be honest about their identity in the face of constant challenges to recognition of their position as gay men and gay fathers. Over and over, I heard stories about gay fathers being read as heterosexual in public places, assumed to be "helping" their wives by "babysitting." Even when both partners were out with their child, heterosexuals tended to see them as a father and his friend, filling in for the child's mother. While coming out in every such instance can be exhausting and sometimes doesn't seem worth the trouble,[2] many of these fathers understood honesty as a parental obligation. Enrique Morales, whom we met earlier, subscribed to this view, explaining that having children radically changed his relationship to his parents and to the wider heterosexual world. He told his parents from the beginning that he intended to raise his children in an "out family, a gay-identified family." His mother, in particular, had always been reluctant to fully accept his homosexuality, and particularly avoided hearing about his relationships. At some level, Enrique mused, his parents saw him as less adult than his brothers.

> So I told them at one point, "I'm no longer willing to be apologetic for my life to you. You need to stop calling me and saying, 'Why don't you move down here? Why don't you do this and that?' You need to realize that I'm a grown man, I have a family. My family is just as valid as my brother's family. Yes, there's no wife in this family. Yes, we don't have the same look. But it is as legitimate a family as my brother's and I don't feel that you give me that." And I don't think they did. I think they still saw me as my younger brothers at the time who were still single.

Enrique suspected that making this sort of stand wouldn't have seemed as vital had he not adopted his children. He wants them to be proud of who they are and the family they are growing up in, and can't see any way to do that without being consistently and unambiguously out. Particularly since his children had a difficult start in life—taken away from a drug-addicted mother—giving them a solid sense of self-worth is a major part of his job as their father. Concealment and shame cannot possibly contribute to that process.

Narratives such as Enrique's that situate honesty as a central feature of personal morality also draw on wider discourses about coming out that have circulated since the early days of gay liberation. These basically hold that both outright lying about being gay and the more passive dishonesty that comes with passing as straight by not correcting heteronormative assumptions are at least morally suspect—if not clearly reprehensible—both because such deception obviates the need to change popular misconceptions about gay people, and, probably more importantly, because it requires a gay person to disown the very essence of his/her identity. Liberationist understandings of coming out are deeply rooted in the assumption that sexual orientation is the most critical truth about one's being and that coming out enables a kind of existential honesty that is both morally cleansing and politically transformative. These views have obviously been central to debates about outing closeted persons, particularly if they are celebrities, and have shaped a range of liberation agendas from Gay Pride celebrations to demands for civil entitlements. The HIV/AIDS crisis, for example, is widely credited with transforming the face of gay America by making the sexuality of those afflicted with the disease a matter of public record along with the often stirring stories of personal courage that the epidemic called forth.

Enrique's narrative also implies that he has drawn a parallel between the situations of gay families and those who are members of ethnic minorities or other stigmatized populations. He draws on a discourse of group pride as an antidote to discrimination, indicating that such pride can be instilled at home and that teaching self-acceptance is an important aspect of good parenting. By framing the issue this way, he suggests that group identity can be asserted as a matter of moral strength, and that the family can be a bulwark against a hostile world.

The Moral Careers of Gay Fathers

Being a parent, whether one thinks of that condition as being decreed by the laws of nature, mandated by tradition, or driven by the desire to strengthen kinship bonds, can be usefully thought of as the foundation of a moral career. From one perspective, the product of one's parental efforts offers a basis for judging how well one has done one's job. Though popular discourse is more likely to blame mothers than fathers for childrearing outcomes that are less than optimal, when men take on primary responsibility for childrearing, they also can expect to be held accountable for how well their children turn out. Parenting offers a chance to produce a person whose impact on the world will go far beyond one's individual reach; that is, the good that might be generated extends in directions not fully predictable.

My use of the term "moral career" in this chapter is drawn from *Asylums*, Erving Goffman's classic work on the lives of psychiatric patients. Goffman defines "moral career" broadly as "the regular sequence of changes that career entails in the person's self and his framework of imagery for judging himself and others" (1961, 128). He sees the usefulness of the term in its "two-sidedness": "One side is linked to internal matters held dearly and closely, such as image of self and felt identity; the other side concerns official position, jural relations, and style of life, and is part of a publicly accessible institutional complex. The concept of career, then, allows one to move back and forth between the personal and the public, between the self and its significant society" (1961, 127).

In Goffman's formulation, the constitution of the self "resides in the arrangements prevailing in a social system" (1961, 168), as individuals' lives change. In the case of mental patients, Goffman speaks of their lives before institutionalization and the ways they adjust their identities as they move through the psychiatric institution. It is not coincidental that moral careers in this account are crafted in the context of the shame attached to mental illness; they are, indeed, a key strategy for managing the "spoiled identities" generated by stigma, as Goffman has detailed in his classic work *Stigma* (1963). I argue that analogous forms of identity management emerge in the personal narratives of many gay fathers, reflecting the complicated dance they must perform around seemingly conflicting elements of their subjectivities. These patterns reflect the compromised citizenship of gay men in the U.S., to be sure, but also speak to the cultural conflicts these men must negotiate as they fashion themselves as fathers.

Like the stigmatized individuals Goffman describes in his work, the elaboration of paternal virtues that appears in gay fathers' narratives shows "that oscillations may occur in his support of, identification with, and participation among his own" (1963, 38). These oscillations, which I will attend to in this chapter and in chapter 6, make clear that the assessment of who, exactly, is defined as "his own" may fluctuate as parenthood makes available affiliations and identifications not otherwise readily accessible. As they become fathers, gay men may find that they can be counted as ordinary members of families and as citizens in a way usually connected to developmental markers of marriage and family only available to heterosexuals. There are some marked differences, however, between Goffman's formulation and the narrative strategies used by gay fathers. Goffman's account traces a developmental path that allows mental patients to manage occupying progressively more stigmatized positions. The gay fathers whose stories I will present ground their parental careers in moral terms and thus are able to distance themselves, at least in part, from sources of stigma and consequently to achieve a sort of upward moral mobility that resembles the more common meaning of "career."

Parenthood, and most particularly motherhood, is understood in American culture (as in many others) as a condition that should engender selflessness and altruism. As we saw earlier, these sentiments are usually framed as progressing "naturally" from the biological or social dimensions of reproduction, but anxiety about whether they are, in fact, reliable is reflected in various sorts of sanctions that cultures have established to insure adherence to these ideals. We saw, for example, in chapter 2 that indications of overlap between familial love, whether parental or conjugal, and profit or financial advantage, are severely stigmatized in U.S. culture. Concern with the welfare (however that might be defined) of one's child motivates the parent, in this construction, to perform acts of transcendent goodness, none of which are calculated to bring benefit to the parent. A parent willingly gives up comfort, financial security, and personal safety to assure the wellbeing of the child; all thoughts of personal advantage are supposed to be removed from parental decision making. Indeed, allegations that parents do not put their children's welfare first constitute a potent moral condemnation that no excuse can mitigate.

Some scholars have pointed to breeches that have occurred in this apparently seamless system in particular cultural settings or historical periods, suggesting that maternal altruism may not be as "natural" as is claimed. Anthropologist Nancy Scheper-Hughes, for example, has written persuasively of maternal behavior she characterizes as "benign neglect" that she observed in the impoverished favelas of northeast Brazil, where malnutrition and infant mortality both reach catastrophic proportions. According to her interpretation, pervasive and extreme deprivation drives mothers to calculate whether or not a particular child will survive; minimal maternal investment is made in children deemed too weak or passive to surmount these pressures. She argues that mothers thus prepare themselves to manage relentless loss and also husband their meager resources in a strategy that might, at least, pay off for a few of their children (1992).[3]

These insights notwithstanding, the dominant perspective in the contemporary U.S. is that motherhood and maternal devotion are universals driven by nature. Indeed, the intense revulsion that explodes when mothers are shown to be demonstrably cruel or neglectful provides eloquent testimony to the depth of popular commitment to a belief in a natural maternal instinct. The outcry over recent cases in the U.S. of mothers who were convicted of killing their children is particularly evocative in this regard. Both Susan Smith in South Carolina and Andrea Yates in Texas murdered their children, though the circumstances of each case differed dramatically. Andrea Yates was portrayed as mentally ill, even psychotic, which drew considerable sympathy to her situation and eventually led to her acquittal on mental-health grounds in a second trial. She also appeared to have been under the thumb of a controlling husband who had demanded obedience to his plans for the family, including her homeschooling the children and continuing to have babies even after physicians recommended against it. In contrast, Susan Smith emerged from media coverage as a sexual predator, eager to dispose of her children so that she could more easily pursue an extramarital affair (Korbin 1998; Meyer 2001).

Public outrage has taken a similar form when newborns are killed or discarded by young mothers who often claim to have been unaware of their pregnancies. Anthropologist Anna Tsing examines a number of these cases, arguing that the extent to which such "bad" mothers display shame along with a visible desire to accept institutional guidance has much to do with the disposition of their cases (1990). In other words, their crimes are not only considered in their concrete details but in terms of the adherence of women (or girls) to norms of passivity. It is not unimportant that the range of acceptable behavior for young women facing unplanned or out-of-wedlock pregnancies has historically differed along racial lines. Historian Rickie Solinger (1994) shows how in the years prior to *Roe v. Wade*, pregnant white teenagers were expected to relinquish their babies for adoption, thereby demonstrating readiness to go back to their normal lives, essentially cleansed of their sin. In sharp contrast, black teen mothers had to keep their babies, as they were regarded as having no value in the adoption market. This racialized discourse of motherhood extends, of course, into popular understandings of poverty, welfare, and single-mother families, all imagined (inaccurately) to be dominated by morally weak black women (Gordon 1998; Mink 2002; Quadagno 1996; Roberts 1998).

The moral calculus of good and bad motherhood is brought to bear not only on demonstrably cruel parents—those who intentionally injure their children—but on those who must weigh competing constraints in determining their path as parents, making problematic decisions in the process.

The popular literature is replete with examples of public outcry about mothers who leave their children unsupervised or who pursue apparent personal gratification while being entrusted with their children's care. The targets of this attention are often poor women, usually single, who must juggle childcare and employment with meager resources, sometimes with tragic consequences (Hays 2003). A similar discourse of blame surrounds situations where motherhood is undertaken for presumed financial gain, as is regularly alleged by some conservatives in the case of mothers who receive public assistance (Hancock 2004; Reese 2005). Sexuality is particularly suspect in this context, particularly with respect to maternal motivations; the expectation that good mothers ought not to be sexual beings typifies the tone of mothers' experience with the system of family law, from contested custody cases to determinations of child welfare.[4] In other words, demonstrable neglect need not be asserted; any behavior, however minor, that can be interpreted as placing some priority ahead of maternal duty can be cited as evidence of "bad" motherhood.

Lesbian mothers—stereotypically viewed as excessively focused on their own sexuality—have felt the sting of surveillance most intensely, but many other mothers whose behavior seems not to conform to some implicit standard of altruism (often inflected by class) may find themselves fighting to keep their children. Some commentators on contemporary motherhood in the U.S. have noted the myriad ways that motherhood continues to be posed in opposition to work, even as the majority of mothers of young children are now in the labor force (Garey 1999; Gerson 1986; Stone 2007).[5]

Professional women are particularly wounded by such assumptions, despite the fact that many of them are financially able to provide high-quality care for their children while they are working. Sociologist Sharon Hays used a photograph on the cover of her book *The Cultural Contradictions of Motherhood* (1996) that encapsulates the conflict: a woman is split vertically down the middle. Her right side is wearing a business suit and holding a handbag and a newspaper; her left side is dressed casually and she carries a toddler on her hip. In the book, Hays details the ideology of "intensive mothering," which demands that women jettison commitments to professional and other concerns outside the home and focus entirely on their maternal obligations. The contemporary form of this ideology, based on the moral discourse of "the angel in the home" that permeated nineteenth-century images of mothers, still depends on the notion of the home as a location that remedies the moral corruption of the public domain.

Devoting oneself to mothering is, thus, a moral imperative even more than a theory of child development.

Other cultural commentators have also documented the ways that ideologies of motherhood extol maternal self-sacrifice and excoriate mothers whose "selfish" choices are seen as amounting to child neglect. In her popular book *Perfect Madness*, journalist Judith Warner (2005) writes passionately about the institutionalization of what she calls "the motherhood religion." According to her reading of this "creed," fear of maternal over-involvement has given way to pervasive anxiety about women not devoting themselves sufficiently to the care of their children. Academics have played a leading role in proliferating these fears, with child-development specialists being particularly active in promoting theories that bolster them. Whether these are labeled "attachment theory" or "bonding," these ideas hold that the mother must be constantly available to her child during a crucial period of bonding. Failure to do so, or to do so with sufficient (but immeasurable) dedication is said to result in catastrophic psychological damage to the child (Arney 1980; Eyer 1992).

The intensity of the ongoing controversy over maternal employment has given way, according to some sources, to a conflict dubbed "the mommy wars" that pits employed mothers against stay-at-home mothers and childcare providers. The class-inflected antagonism built into this clash intersects ironically with the mutual dependence of employed mothers and childcare providers, but is also fueled by acrimony over basic values. Do greed and ambition lead employed mothers to sacrifice the welfare of their children? Are stay-at-home mothers ignorant and lazy? Does motherhood demand selflessness, while fatherhood includes no such expectations? Both researchers and popular authors have weighed in on these debates. Media coverage of elite mothers who decide to abandon high-powered careers to become stay-at-home mothers adds to the hostilities, as few of the articles reporting these decisions consider the economic resources of husbands as key elements of such choices (Lewis and West 1996; Marneffe 2005; Nelson 1991; Peskowitz 2005; Steiner 2006). In recent years, both scholars and popular commentators have become fascinated by the phenomenon of mothers who relinquish good jobs in order to stay home with their children, apparently extracting a moral lesson from this seeming repudiation of feminism (Belkin 2003; Stone 2007). This interpretation is amplified by the conventional explanations such mothers offer for their decisions—that they are not replaceable as primary caretakers and that they enjoy being a constant part of children's development. It takes more probing questions to uncover the roles inflexible employers and inattentive husbands play in leaving women few options other than to stay home (Stone 2007).

Ideas about the moral dimension of motherhood have other roots as well. Because children are popularly assumed to have started life without blame or moral defect, association with them also allows one to experience a kind of purity not accessible in other ways. I have shown elsewhere that mothers often emphasize the innocence and authenticity of children in explaining why being close to them can impart some of these same qualities (Lewin 1993). Indeed, for women who have restricted access to activities that might confer public recognition, one might argue that motherhood, seen both as reproduction and socialization, can impart dignity to lives that otherwise seem to lack luster. Raising the next generation is demonstrably important as few other accomplishments are, and women's specialization in this endeavor can thus be the source of claims of moral worth.

What about Fathers?

The discourse of altruism and instinct has been far less developed in ideologies of fatherhood. Fatherhood, as we have seen, tends to be construed as appropriately performed outside the domestic arena and to demand physical separation from, rather than constant interaction with, children. So whereas (particularly middle-class) women who leave their children to earn a living are suspected of neglecting their maternal obligations, fathers who fail to do the same thing are reproached. Fathers, including those who no longer live with their children (and perhaps rarely see them), are most centrally charged with providing ongoing economic support. If their performance in this arena flags, they are condemned as parasites and "deadbeats" (Mandell 2002).[6] Indeed, one of the prominent themes in the design of welfare reform (officially the Personal Responsibility and Work Opportunity Reconciliation Act of 1996 [PRWORA]) has been to force both present and absent fathers to better support their children. The related discourse of the marriage-promotion movement has advocated marriage as a solution to (among other things) the economic problems of poor women and their children (Waite 2000).

Images of fathers who do not meet financial or emotional obligations to their children proliferate in the literature and in popular media. Though debates about the actual extent of paternal irresponsibility are ongoing, the fact that many men who divorce either meet their support obligations erratically or not at all has been well established (Arendell 1988; Fineman 1991; Kurtz 1995; Weitzman 1985). Indeed, the failure of many men to make child support payments or provide other forms of support has been held up as a major reason for many formerly married women having to rely on public assistance. As the numbers of children born out of wedlock has continued to grow, those fathers allegedly join the ranks of the irresponsible, at least in the popular imagination of how welfare dependency comes into existence. This discussion highlights the extent to which fatherhood is conceptualized in our society as an economic role. Paternal involvement with day-to-day childrearing is considered a good thing—indeed, single mothers are assumed to be unable to provide the benefits of such relationships, another purported source of their inadequacy—but the conventional obligations of fathers often end with their paying the bills.

I contend in this chapter that gay fathers find themselves entering into a different sort of paternal discourse from expected patterns for men, one that more closely resembles a maternal model. Most centrally, gay men who seek fatherhood must feel and display levels of urgent commitment; their performance of paternal devotion is motivated in a way routine fatherhood rarely is, at least conventionally, and the intensity of their feelings is a crucial determinant of their success in presenting themselves as deserving of parenthood. Once they become fathers, the care they deliver combines stereotypically maternal (domestic) and paternal (public) roles; for those who become "stay-at-home dads," this care may mirror more closely patterns of maternal behavior. But even as they make these commitments, few of the fathers I interviewed felt comfortable labeling themselves "mothers." With exceptions that I will detail below, they understood "mother" to be a designation that could only be applied to women; viewing themselves in that light would demand shedding their gender identity as men. Given popular stereotypes of gay men as effeminate gender deviants, most of these men resist any designation that would support such images.

But even with their hesitation about claiming maternal identity, fathers were able to access discourses about goodness that are usually associated with motherhood. The notion that caring for children calls for moral attributes not usually visible in men, or that parenthood demands ethical choices men might otherwise be able to avoid, is pervasive in these narratives. For many of these men, fatherhood brings the best in them to the surface, whether that involves honesty about being gay or shifting their focus to their families from what they characterize as the fleeting pleasures of "single" gay life. In these contexts, fatherhood facilitates a language that ranks gay life as frivolous and morally ambiguous (if not just bad), seemingly strengthened by the virtues children help them to access. As we shall see, fathers commonly frame their experience of goodness as a process that takes place over time—a moral career, in Goffman's terms—that enables them to distance themselves from stigmatizing elements of gay (i.e., "spoiled") identity.

"The Day I Burned the Closet"

Javier Vélez, whom we first met in chapter 4, speaks evocatively of the moral growth he felt he experienced as a result of becoming a parent. As we have already learned, he and his partner of fifteen years, Nate, have adopted two children. Javier came to San Francisco from Central America; Nate is U.S.-born and white. Shortly after the two men got together, Nate started to talk about wanting to have children. Javier couldn't imagine any way that would be possible, taking it for granted that "society will not let you get away with this." Despite this, he explains that he was finally the one who began to push for them to adopt.

> I started thinking and remembered that when I was twelve or thirteen, I was thinking already that if I ever have children, I would like to adopt, I don't want to have my own children. I have a very deep sense of why bring more kids into the world when there are obviously plenty of kids that already need homes and affection and education and all that? And I didn't feel the need to see myself continuing. And from the family that I had around me, it was a very selfish thing to do, that the people who were parenting had this kind of fixation about having someone just like them in this world.
>
> ELLEN: Just like them in terms of biological?
>
> JAVIER: Yes, in a biological way, and that just didn't seem like a good reason to have a child. So I started reclaiming those feelings again and realized that, you know, you've been playing someone else's tape. Society wants to tell you that you can't be a parent because you're gay and then I started looking around and realized that, hey, there are a lot people out there who shouldn't be parents for many reasons—societal reasons, cultural reasons, religious reasons, people who weren't prepared to be parents. And then I started noticing that there are people in society who are married and they don't have children, and how other

people treat them, and the kind of abuse they're exposed to because they aren't parents. So with pressure like this, a lot of people have become parents not being qualified, and not even having good intentions, but feeling like, "Boy, I better do this or else." And I realized that, wow, I can do a better job. And so I started reclaiming those feelings and realized that, well if I have those feelings . . . , why would I want to deny myself the chance to explore another dimension to my being a human being. Why am I going to say no to that, just because someone else says that I shouldn't?

ELLEN: What was it about being a parent that appealed to you?

JAVIER: Well, I think basically since the procreating part of it wasn't there for me, it was a sense of sharing wealth—and I mean that in the broadest sense, sharing a home, sharing the love, sharing the material things and the knowledge. And one of the things that I've come to realize by being a parent . . . is that our children do not belong to us—they belong to themselves. And our job as parents is to provide the environment so they can learn and they can be successful human beings, and so that's what I see my role as. Being a parent, someone who can provide the support for another human being in order to be a human being. So I don't think of my children as mine, or that they need to be like me. I think my role is to promote them to be the best human beings they can be by whatever means that is. So I take to parenting from that point. We have a very stable home. We have certainly enough affection to share and we were willing to share that with someone who already was fortunate enough to come into the world. And I think we do a pretty good job of that.

Javier and Nate went through a long process of figuring out how to become parents and finally, about three years into their relationship, decided to do serious research on parenthood. First, they simply stopped anyone they saw on the street who looked like a gay or lesbian parent to ask them about their experience. They then attended seminars for gays and lesbians considering parenthood sponsored by a local organization. Through those, they learned about the various kinds of adoption procedures and, in particular, about the high cost of private and international adoptions, which they quickly decided were far beyond their means. Given these constraints, they decided to explore public adoption, so Nate called the Department of Social Services to find out about the programs they offered. Javier explained, "When Nate was on the phone with them, they asked him, 'Are you white or are you a person of color?' And he said, 'I'm white.' And they said, 'Well, bye.' And he was like, 'Wait a minute, my partner is Latino,' so they said, 'Well, do you want to come tomorrow?'"

Javier understood this response in terms of ongoing debates about trans-racial adoptions, with the National Association of Black Social Workers, in particular, having taken "a vehement stand against the placement of black children in white homes for any reason" in its 1972 position statement (Bremner 1974, 777–80). "Because I was a person of color, we got into the program. And available to me were full Latino children, or biracial Latino children, white, or other children." The agency was open to working with gay couples and with single men and women; since Javier was Latino, the fact that Nate was white was not an impediment to adopting a minority child.

The next step in the process was for the two men to take a ten-week training class on parenting, after which they were certified as foster parents. Although the class was time consuming and repeated a lot of material both men already knew, Javier and Nate agreed that they were glad it was required. As Javier told me, "I found it a great thing to do because now I agree that anyone should go through a parenting class before they become a parent, to think about what they're doing, how they're doing it. I mean, we have licenses for driving, for many things, and actually this is something that should be done so that someone will have at least a clue of what they're getting into. Most people don't. They just do it—'I water, they'll grow.'"

Their son, Diego, who is Latino, was placed with them when he was five months old, though it took another year and a half for the adoption to become final. They had decided that they wanted an infant, reasoning that the problems a child in "the system" would probably have would be more readily addressed if they started early. Nate's experience as an elementary school teacher convinced him that their child would have a better chance of developing normally under these conditions, and they also sought the advice of a friend at Stanford who does research on children who have been exposed to drugs.

Once plans to have Diego move into their home were finalized, however, the situation became complicated. The foster mother, who cared fulltime for a number of children, was horrified to discover that Diego's placement would be with gay fathers. Although she had never before sought to adopt any of her foster children, she suddenly announced that she wanted to adopt Diego. She called her attorney and the Department of Social Services, creating such an uproar that Javier and Nate had to go to court to obtain custody. Even after that, they experienced hostility from case workers that Javier describes as "homophobic."

They were laughing and pointing at us, and acting very disrespectful. At this point, we had gone through so much already, and, having to deal with all this on the day that we're picking up our child, it was really difficult. And anyway, we walked home with him, and the moment we walked through the door, closed the door, the full impact of our decision really hit us! You know. What have we done! Because from now on, this baby is yours and you're responsible for his life, so it really hits you.

Javier describes the process he and Nate went through as they learned how to be parents. They were particularly worried about putting Diego in a daycare facility where direct adult interaction with the children would be minimal. They had clear ideas about the importance of reading to children, talking with them, and providing intellectual stimulation. During Diego's first summer with them, Nate was able to provide a lot of hands-on parenting before he returned to his teaching job in the fall. Javier explains,

I'm forty, by the time we got him, and at forty I thought I knew myself, and all of a sudden becoming a father hit me like a ton of bricks in so many ways. Number one, being a gay man, realizing that we internalize things, with all the homophobia you get, that as a gay man I always wanted to be masculine and that being a parent, I was going to have to appeal to the so-called feminine traits like intuition and nursing a child and being a mom because actually I ended up staying home for six years. We didn't plan this and we thought we had a plan, but as we started looking for daycares, we realized that no one was going to give our child the kind of care that we could.

This period of "mothering" their son led Javier to rethink everything in his life, including all the ideas about parenting and gender he remembered from childhood. Unlike many of the men whose stories appear in chapters 3 and 4, who sought to recreate childrearing practices they recalled from childhood, Javier's experience as a father led him to jettison familiar wisdom and to seek completely new approaches to raising his son. Tradition couldn't provide him with answers that made sense to him. Unlike nearly all the other fathers I spoke with, he spontaneously described himself as being a "mom" with "feminine traits," a radical departure, in his view, from his childhood in Central America. Indeed, his readiness to interpret his new life as "feminine" seemed to be eased by his sense of himself as a gay man (in the stereotypical profession of interior design) who might have easier access to these traits than other men. In Javier's account, the moral content of fatherhood was closely linked to its association with motherhood. He understood his years as a stay-at-home dad to have constituted the equivalent of a maternal career, and the spiritual benefits he drew from this experience were in part drawn from his immersion in a nonmasculine gender role.

> In my previous life, I was an interior designer and I had done that for, like, thirteen years. Which is also again a part of my redefining myself because all of a sudden I became mom, and you know, I was questioning, like, "Who am I now?" I left my profession, so what am I going to be? What am I going to do? And that, I think that the part that really hit me was finding myself having to embrace what I had considered to be, like, feminine traits, which was the nurturing, the parenting, the reading to and really connecting with the child. And sometimes I would just cry holding my child before putting him to bed, I used to rock him after we read and all that and before we put him in the crib, and I was thinking to myself, "Gosh, my dad never did any of this with any of us at all," because in my culture, parenting is left to the mother. I think that in most countries, the parenting is always left to the mother. The bathing, the changing clothes, all of that is left to the mom. And this is the beautiful part about parenting—the connecting, but you're also getting up at three o'clock in the morning, all the stuff that goes on with the child. This is what connects you as a human being to that person. And parents, fathers traditionally, have sort of put themselves out of that equation.

Being a gay father, particularly one who cared for his children, Diego and later Graciela, during the day Javier was exposed continually to the assumptions of other people about how family life is, or should be, organized. Because people constantly assumed he was straight because he was with children, he decided it was essential that he confront those assumptions, even taking pains to wear a pink-triangle pin or other insignia to make sure it was clear that he was gay.

> I always feel like being gay is a special gift and that by being this way, my job is really to help other people understand that we're actually human beings. And I think that parenting, well, we're now forced to interact with people as a parent, and the first day that I went to the supermarket with my kid, the cashier said to me, "Oh, your wife left you with your kids today." And I just thought, gosh, there's a whole bunch of assumptions in that one sentence, and just the tone of voice, and I really had to think, really quick, like, what am I going to say and how am I going to say it? Because here is my kid listening to what I'm saying,

and my response was, "No, I'm not married and my children have two dads." And of course she left it go just right then and there. But that was a very crucial point for me because, it was like from this moment on, I can never go back into the closet, and I know that as gay people we often find it very convenient and sometimes it's for safety reasons, to jump back in the closet when it is convenient to do that. So by not saying anything or by answering in the way that we know people want us to answer, like not telling the whole truth. And we've been made experts at this over the years. But with my children, I realize I can't do this anymore—they're listening to me and they're going to know that I'm lying and not telling the truth, that I'm covering. And I just can't do that anymore, from now on I have to completely be out. And today I refer to that as the day I burned the closet, or actually, my children burned it for me.

Javier's realization about his ability, as a gay, Latino father, to educate people about sexuality and also to contribute to his community had a dramatic effect on his life.

I started participating in town halls for parents . . . going into high schools and talking about what it is like to be gay and a parent and Latino. And I started working with HIV groups in the community, doing all kinds of different things with different groups in terms of work in the community.

ELLEN: Had you done that before?

JAVIER: I had never done that before. I was kind of the person that my sexuality was, you know, it was my own business and no one else's. And I came to realize that sexuality is as important as anything else because unless you say, "I'm here," then people are going to assume that you're heterosexual. And especially being Latino and being a parent and being gay, you know, every time I was doing this, I realized there are a lot of people out there who couldn't go, for whatever reasons, couldn't come out of the closet or couldn't be out. So then I was a voice for them, I was a visible point. And many times I felt used like a token in all of this, but I tried to use that to my advantage. For me it's an opportunity to be represented, for my people to see me there and say, "Hi, we're queer, we're part of the equation." And being able to have a voice and be a part of the decisions. I became part of the Lesbian and Gay Parent Association, our first thing was workshops, questioning the parents—"Should we come out? Should we not? Should we tell the teacher? Should we not?" Because we realized that a lot of parents were struggling with that, in terms of whether or not it's okay to be out at school. That was our first workshop, to deal with these issues. And the next step, something happened at this particular school that happened to have a GLBT parent group. And this was a public school, and they were having difficulties with homophobia. And these two girls, they did something—they went to the principal and asked if they could go around to the classrooms and talk about their moms, and the teacher said, "OK, you can do that."

After his six-year stint as a fulltime parent, Javier felt that he had to move into a job that would enable him to continue the politically engaged direction he had taken as a fulltime parent. His activist work dramatically transformed his notion of what he should do with his life, making his old life seem shallow and insignificant. He now works for an agency that assists immigrants, many of whom are members of sexual minorities and face issues of HIV and AIDS.

It has changed my priorities, it has changed my focus in life, it has changed everything about me. When I came to San Francisco, I was aiming to climb the corporate ladder—my goal was to open a big architectural firm, and I wanted to go to the top. And now I realize that that's not where it's at. That, really, there are other things in life that are more important. And I know that not every gay or lesbian person that becomes a parent has a life-changing experience, but this is what it did to me, you know, and it has really made me an activist. Ten years ago, if you said, "You'll be an activist," I would have said, "You're nuts!" And now that's what I do.

He feels strongly that "being gay is a gift," a tool that has enabled him to uncover the best parts of himself. Because his daughter Graciela has learning disabilities, he explains that he has learned a great deal about children with physical and mental challenges. This new awareness leads him to view everyone he meets with greater tolerance.

[I realize] that no matter what the outside is like, inside there's a human being, and the same way that I was saying about being gay, those of us who are gay—well actually those of us who are different, in one way or another—we are creatures of change, we make other people question what is normality, and that's really what we are about. And so having children, being gay is a gift, that's another way of being different that brings about social change, just by interaction and living your life and moving through the world.

Javier's narrative situates fatherhood as a key element of his moral career along several different dimensions. On one level, it changes his

relationship to the rest of the (straight) world, as it constantly presents
him with concrete examples of heteronormativity that he must negotiate.
His choice to confront the assumptions of others whenever they occur
is morally grounded; he sees himself as setting a good example for his
children and also as teaching those who mistake him for a straight father
that families come in other forms than what they expect. That objective
is part of a longer-range political project that he sees as a central moral
obligation. Being a parent also gives him enhanced access to a series of
moral strengths—for example, the ability to be more sympathetic to many
kinds of difference. In other words, being gay and being a parent together
produce what he experiences as a heightened tolerance for others, an absolute ethical achievement of which he is extremely proud.

Meeting Societal Obligations

But the moral dimensions of fatherhood can be defined in other ways
that also emphasize group loyalties and wider issues of social justice. In
these narratives, fatherhood emerges as a vehicle for solidifying more general moral commitments. This was particularly marked in the narratives
of black fathers and in the stories told by some white men who adopted
black children from the foster care system. Otis and Jermaine Hunter are
working-class black men who live on Chicago's Southwest Side. Otis works
as a medical technician and Jermaine is studying to be a paralegal. Their
daughter, Chantal, now twenty years old, came into their family as a transgender teenager whom Otis had seen hanging out on the street with what
Otis describes as "a bad little group of people."

OTIS: I didn't like . . . the way, you know, they were going. So I just picked Chantal
     out of the crowd 'cause I seen a lot in her and didn't feel that she needed to be
     in that crowd.
ELLEN: What kinds of things was the crowd into?
OTIS: Drugs, prostitution, fraudulent things, things of that nature. And I just seen
     a lot of potential in Chantal. And I just picked her out of the crowd. She was
     fifteen at the time.

Otis made a serious commitment to Chantal based on his perception
that there was something special about her that made it important to get
her off the street. As he explained, "She is just such a doll and she . . .

just have a good demeanor about herself. And I just knew." His decision to rescue Chantal led him to undertake the formal procedures to become certified as a foster parent. Chantal moved from her family's home to Otis's apartment. Most importantly, as Chantal describes it, Otis made it possible for her to begin to understand herself as a person seeking to make a gender transition, enabling her to feel comfortable with her gender transgressive personal presentation for the first time in her life. After Chantal and Otis had been a family for about two years, Otis met Jermaine and he joined their family. By the time I interviewed the Hunters, Chantal had moved into her own apartment nearby and was studying to become a medical technician, like her foster father. Although he never legally adopted Chantal, and she maintains connections with her biological family, she has chosen to be known by his surname. It's clear that she has flourished as Otis's daughter. She describes him as "my angel."

Lawrence Lock, whom we will meet again in chapter 6, adopted two gravely disabled brothers after first serving as their foster parent. As we shall see, Lawrence's motivations for becoming a parent are complex, driven to some extent by the fear and guilt being gay generates for him. But he also believes in doing something "important" with his life, other than seeking what he sees as frivolous pleasures in the company of other gay men, and making sure that his sons Darryl and Marcellus can move toward achieving as much as their disabilities will allow is a powerful motivation.

Lawrence is white and the brothers are African American. Darryl, the older boy, was three years old when he suffered major brain damage after his mother's boyfriend threw him across a room and then choked him. The younger brother, Marcellus, witnessed the assault and though he was not yet three had to give a statement to the police. Darryl's injuries have left him permanently handicapped with motor-skill deficits, impaired vision, and only minimal abilities to learn language. Now a pre-teenager, he remains in diapers. Marcellus's disabilities, in contrast, are more emotional than cognitive or physical.

Although Lawrence formed an intense commitment to the brothers soon after they were placed with him, he only considered adoption after the state had permanently terminated their mother's parental rights, a move that he believes doesn't reflect her real parenting skills. Because she continued to defend her boyfriend after he assaulted Darryl, however, the state has determined that she cannot have her parental rights restored. Her boyfriend was never prosecuted. But even after Darryl and Marcellus became available for adoption, Lawrence was reluctant to move ahead without their explicit agreement. Once they had given it, he asked them whether they wanted to retain their original surname or be adopted with the name "Lock." The boys chose to take his name.

Part of his commitment to the brothers, then, is to try to maximize their sense of autonomy and control. He explains that once they were removed from the custody of their mother, they lost any sense of having real choices about any aspect of their lives. This element of parenting has particular moral resonance for Lawrence; besides making it possible for the boys to do better than they ever would have being shuffled around the foster care system, he sees his mission as one that focuses on endowing them with true agency. An essential part of this commitment is realized in his respect for the boys' mother, maintained despite the fact that she is no longer in their lives and probably never will be again. Although it was her boyfriend who committed the violent act that led to their removal from her custody, Lawrence insists that she was basically a good mother who was betrayed by circumstances beyond her control. His respect for her is grounded in his sensitivity to the difficult conditions she faced as an impoverished single mother; he sees her as a victim of a larger system of injustice as much as her sons are.

Creating Justice

Other men also frame their decision to become fathers as a matter of fundamental moral obligation, linked in many cases to their religious faith. Tyrone Landon and Thomas Palmer, whom we met in chapter 4, share strong religious commitments. Once the two men decided they wanted to be parents, they knew that the only way they would consider adopting was through the foster care system. As black men, they felt duty-bound to parent a child who would otherwise languish in the "system," and they are keenly aware of the numbers of children in that system who are African American and male. These are the children who are regarded as "hard to place" with prospective adoptive parents, most of whom are white and who overwhelmingly prefer to adopt infants or very young children.

Black boys, especially those who are no longer infants, are unlikely to be placed with adoptive parents and run the risk of spending their entire childhood in foster homes or institutional settings such as group homes. Not surprisingly, these boys are at high risk for virtually every sort of negative outcome one can imagine: crime, drugs, poor performance in school, and the like. Tyrone and Thomas originally hoped to adopt two brothers, but didn't find any available at the time they were looking. "We were a little bit frustrated with what we were seeing with sets of brothers that were available at the time so we prayed about it and we talked about it and decided to release looking for brothers and look for single children to create a family," Tyrone explained. Creating a family, as we have seen, was centrally linked to having children for them, and the path to achieving this goal had to be determined through prayer.

In a strikingly similar story, Randall Johnson and Trent Williams, whom we also met in chapter 4, spoke of sharing an awareness of the plight of African American boys in the foster care system and articulated an intense commitment to helping at least one such child find a home. While the political dimension of this concern cannot be underestimated, both men were inspired by their religious faith to take action. None of this can be separated from the men's understanding of what it means to form a family. One's family is where faith and duty are articulated and enacted; it is the site where the most central aspects of those commitments are performed, starting with raising a child.

But for Randall and Trent, having a child also connects them with the larger goals that they see shaping the meaning of their lives. Randall's account of his spiritual focus is spoken with considerable passion.

RANDALL: It's important to me to have a spiritual center. . . . If I don't go to church on Sunday, I feel like I've missed something. That kind of sets the tone for the week for me. It kind of brings me back in focus. What I'm really here for. What life is really about. You could miss that for a while when you work in corporate America. It's all about the dollar, especially when I'm in a conference room with someone, and he becomes confrontational, I have to realize this isn't all my life. Let's really remember what I'm really here on this earth for and how I'm here on this earth.

ELLEN: What are you really on this earth for?

RANDALL: At this point, I think I'm on this earth to create justice. But I think to celebrate life. To celebrate God. To make the world a better place. And that's not always through what I do for a living. That piece of it comes from your house and home and to raise Raymond the way I'd like to raise him. But that's not all that you're about. And going to church every Sunday reminds me that regardless of whether I have this house or a Mercedes, how lucky I am.

Trent's answer to this question about what he's on earth for is more concise. "I'm a serving kind of person. I'm a servant," he said. Both men agree that adopting their son allows them to make the world a better place and to serve God. Randall describes the evolution of their thinking as they moved through the various adoption procedures: "It was more selfish of us, that we want a child to fulfill our lives, to round us out—and after going through the process . . . it really became a matter of helping a child out of what sounded like it could be a really awful situation. Especially black children. We learned that if a black child isn't adopted by the time he's five or six, his chances of getting adopted are cut in half."

In line with their strong sense of social responsibility, they opted for adoption through the foster system, intending to adopt an older black child, probably a boy, who would have a hard time being placed. Getting a child as young as Raymond was a surprise, but they are very happy with him. For Randall and Trent, adopting a child satisfies several priorities. As we saw in chapter 4, his arrival signals the completion of their family unit and articulates their status as an authentic family, something they do not think they can achieve as a childless couple. Because they adopted Raymond through the foster care system, their personal goals converged with their social and spiritual principles, particularly with their commitment to use their resources to help less fortunate members of the black community. Becoming parents allowed Randall and Trent to transcend the spiritual limitations of affluence and to make themselves more substantial citizens.

"Being Present"

It has become almost a truism that the AIDS epidemic fundamentally changed many popular stereotypes about gay men's character, as it also had a dramatic impact on the priorities many gay men used to organize their lives. Most centrally, the epidemic called upon members of the gay community to take on caretaking obligations of the most difficult sort. These caretakers not uncommonly saw friends and lovers through the ravages of the disease and eased their way to death; often they repeated these tasks over and over, sometimes stopping only when they themselves fell victim to AIDS (Andriote 1999; Monette 1988; Shilts 1987). They were almost never rewarded with happy endings; during the period before the discovery of the drug cocktails that later made survival possible, virtually everyone diagnosed with AIDS died. The abilities they had to call upon in order to carry out these duties were rarely ones they had seen in themselves before; they had to summon up qualities of emotional fortitude from invisible reserves. These experiences changed both the men themselves and the perceptions of many around them, adding new images of gay men as gentle caretakers to old ones of frivolous sexual excess.

We met Mark Friedman in chapter 3 and read his account of how he saw fatherhood as having grown out of natural capacities that he understood as always having been a central part of him or as directly related to the values of his Jewish family. Mark describes care of his infant, Abraham, in similar terms, but in this context draws less from his reading of his own personality than on his experience caring for his former partner whom he had looked after during the long course of his having AIDS. During the years after Ted was diagnosed with AIDS up to his death, Mark was suffering from the effects of a serious back injury and was in considerable pain. He never stopped taking care of Ted, but recalls the time as extremely difficult and draining.

Mark explains that their son's birth mother, Audrey, selected him and his current partner, Rick, from among other potential adoptive families because she liked the feeling of warmth and affection that they conveyed in their presentation of themselves. Almost from the time they first met with her, the two men formed a close relationship with Audrey, becoming so close in the weeks leading up to Abraham's birth that it seemed natural for Mark to be the person who played the most intensely supportive role for her at the time of the delivery. He describes to me how he held her hand as she was going through the intense pain of giving birth, and his subsequent elation at being able to be totally committed to the selflessness of caretaking.

She took my hand and I was very comfortable and calm, and the reason why I was so present and so completely present was because I had cared for Ted. In multiple emergency room visits. Keeping him alive. I had been in such dire circumstances and watched him die while holding his hand that I could be present for something that was very painful. And I was able to be present for a period. I was very present during the delivery. I was really aware. It was the closest thing to me giving birth that I ever experienced was Ted dying. And that's not a statement of romanticizing death. It's horrible. Even though he was comfortable, it was more that the caregiving, being present, completely there for somebody else, not being present for yourself.

In Mark's account, caring for an infant calls for much the same sort of total awareness of the other; it's clear that he is inspired and awed by the depth of his commitment to Abraham and by the way this caretaking resonates with his past experience with Ted. He explains that infant care requires much the same consciousness that he had in the delivery room: "I [am] really aware like holding him in the middle of the night that how wonderful it [is] to be a caregiver," he tells me. "There's a whole future to look forward to." Mark's story emphasizes both the feelings associated with selfless caretaking, and an equation he invokes between the care of a dying person and witnessing the arrival of a newborn. He situates this experience at the two most mysterious moments of human existence, birth and death, taking care not to overstep the analogy, but still convinced that his experience could only have occurred given the confluence of these events.

Mark stresses the cleansing power of pain and sacrifice, often mentioning the disabling back problems he had at the same time that he was caring for Ted, and that remained a serious consideration as he and Rick contemplated becoming parents. On the one hand, he explains that his disability makes it inadvisable for them to adopt a child with serious physical challenges, but on the other hand, he describes how they made a commitment to the birth mother to adopt her child regardless of how the pregnancy turned out. While the two men had set forth a list of conditions they considered essential for the birth mother—general physical health, no use of alcohol or drugs—they yielded to their sense that this was simply the right woman as soon as they emerged from their first meeting with her. As he recounts the experience, the decisive factor was their "intuition" that she was the right person to give birth to their future child—even though he also worried that the fact that she was a smoker might increase Abraham's chances of succumbing to sudden infant death (SIDS). Their ability to let go of the need to control every detail speaks to the authenticity they experience in their connection with the birth mother. Mark doesn't see a conflict between the intuitive connection he describes and the fact that the relationship with Audrey has not continued to be particularly intimate in the months since the delivery.

Mark's account is littered with contradictions and inconsistencies. He and Rick had a series of health-related concerns that they intended to investigate before committing to work with a particular birth mother, but those concerns seemingly evaporated in the face of their intuition about Audrey. While Mark explains that, as a man, he can't possibly understand the pain of childbirth, his immediate connection to the event, as Audrey's major supporter, gave him at least indirect access to the experience. Again, he is careful not to equate childbirth with his chronic back pain, but still he feels that his health problems prepare him to empathize with Audrey's pain. By sharing her pain, he is able, in a sense, to give birth to Abraham along with her, thus even more firmly embedding his fatherhood in the realm of nature. By moving in harmony with intuition, he can feel certain that he is not imposing artificial impediments on the connection with both Audrey and, more importantly, Abraham.

Doing Good

Goodness is not an easy virtue to pin down. The stories in this chapter illustrate that there are no absolute indicators of morality in paternal narratives; rather, men must construct them retroactively as they seek to make sense of their parental experience. As we have seen, morality is deeply implicated with nature, as the men seem to express a certainty that nature directs one toward paths of goodness, or that whatever bears the stamp of nature must, ipso facto, possess moral worth. The ways in which virtue is enacted in these stories are diverse, reminding us, again, that goodness is not absolute but can only be claimed through acts of interpretation.

Javier's story illustrates the use of a series of markers of goodness—honesty, public service, rejection of material gain—as central components of what it has meant for him to be a father. Fatherhood propelled him toward absolute candor about his gayness, a stance that helped him to gain pride in who he is, but that he also hopes has broad effects on others. On one level, his honesty elevates his paternal performance, as he teaches his children the importance of refusing to dissemble and of taking pride in their family. Failure to remain open would constitute a betrayal of his children's trust. On another level, by being open he is able to educate the larger community: "I always feel like being gay is a special gift and that by being this way, my job is really to help other people understand that we're actually human beings." Javier's personal need for honesty, then, enhances his ability to undertake the public service that has become central to his life since becoming a father.

Fatherhood has also made Javier a better person, he believes. After his period at home with his children, he realized he could not return to his former career as an interior designer; the idea of devoting his life to mere appearances, to a career that is fundamentally about surfaces, became repugnant. His commitments to his children put him in touch with the nurturing side of his personality, and also helped him to understand that his identity as a gay person has import beyond the boundaries of private life. In other words, he explains that the goodness that caretaking and connection with children opened up for him as a father had to carry over into the rest of his life. He thus moved from choosing work that had to do with superficial concerns (decorating) to work that actively helps others, in this case immigrants and people with HIV/AIDS. Javier is clear about how he got to this place in his life: "I know that not every gay or lesbian person that becomes a parent has a life-changing experience, but this is what it did to me, you know, and it has really made me an activist," as he explains.

Many of Javier's insights are echoed in the story Enrique tells, particularly in terms of how parenthood demands absolute honesty in relationships with one's children and with others. Being a father moved Enrique to demand that his parents recognize his adulthood and respect the legitimacy of his family. This enacts virtue in that he believes that he cannot be a good parent and not take this stance. His paternal obligations and his intimacy with his children elicit the best in him, leading him to take risks (i.e., being more candid with his family) that eluded him before he became a father. Goodness emerges from relationships with children in a sort of feedback loop: his children influence him to be more honest and his honesty is part of what he owes his children.

Goodness is inflected in still other ways in other stories. Lawrence Lock, for example, has been able to provide a home for two boys who otherwise might have languished in the foster care system, perhaps a minor intervention on a societal scale, but one that has enormous import for those involved. Beyond this, having children has enabled Lawrence to do something good that was not accessible without children. In this reading, living on one's own and pursuing one's own pleasures appear to be utterly without moral significance. A shift toward the altruism required for a parent, especially of children who have been mistreated, pulls Lawrence out of the predicament of selfishness. We will see in chapter 6 how intimately this struggle is connected to conflicts over what it means to be gay.

African American fathers, in particular, are likely to invoke larger issues of community responsibility as they explain how they went about becoming fathers. For Otis Hunter, rescuing Chantal from the downward spiral of life on the street has been an act that makes a difference in the world, albeit on a small scale. Tyrone and Thomas were similarly inspired, as black men, to adopt children through the foster care system. While they don't feel able to make interventions that would address all the levels of racism that determine the fate of black foster children, their commitment to adopt one child, and possibly more children, is at least a start. Spiritual forces have particular influence in shaping the direction they need to take, as they explain the role of prayer in setting them on the path to adoption.

Trent and Randall are even more explicit in looking to prayer and spirituality as the source for their decision to be fathers. In words that resonate with Javier's story, they situate both fatherhood and spiritual wholeness in opposition to material acquisitions. In their case, the spiritual benefits of fatherhood can be acquired without jettisoning their well-paid jobs. As Randall explained, "I think I'm on this earth to create justice . . . to celebrate life. To celebrate God. To make the world a better place." All of those virtues can at least be approached by changing the life chances of a child in the foster care system. Even if "it was more selfish of us, that we want a child to fulfill our lives," doing good on this level stands as a moral counterweight that compensates for the personal benefits that also accrue to the couple.

Finally, Mark's story shows us how fatherhood draws on a larger discourse of altruism, creating a psychic space in which one can achieve an absolute expression of goodness. One's own being no longer matters when one is charged with the care of a dying person, or of an infant. Mark puts his experience as a father into the larger narrative of the AIDS epidemic. This was a time when gay men rose above the limitations of their own desires to care selflessly for lovers and friends, even in the absence of hope that they could possibly recover. Fatherhood is a more hopeful enterprise, certainly—"There's a whole future to look forward to," as he puts it—but the feelings of absolute selflessness are very much the same.

These stories, then, reveal ways in which gay fathers can constitute their experiences as stages in a moral career, promoting images that enhance their views of themselves and that also enable them to act on the larger world in a beneficial way. As we shall see in chapter 6, the search for a way to take moral action is not unrelated to the fact of the fathers' gayness. Self-sacrifice, in this context, becomes the vehicle for seeking self-actualization. Though the qualities they aim to enhance already exist within them, purposeful action is needed to allow them to emerge. These moral commitments are enacted in the context of a more general assessment of gayness as morally wanting; these men are speaking to those voices as much as they are reflecting on their own need to claim goodness.

CHAPTER SIX

"We're Not Gay Anymore"

I was enjoying a pleasant Sunday brunch in the Oak Park, Illinois, home of Paul O'Hara and Keith Michaels while their two sons, Jordan and Christopher, ran in and out of the living room. The two men, both white and successful professionals, had adopted the two African American boys, ages two and four, through a private agency when they were infants. The spacious home was clean and orderly, but the boys' energy spilled out of their playroom at regular intervals. Whenever they invaded the "grown-up space" in the living room, one of the men would herd the boys back into their own area. We had been chatting for a while about how they went about adopting the boys and how parenthood had affected their lives. Reaching for a bagel, I asked, "Has becoming parents changed what it means to you to be gay?" Paul and Keith exchanged a knowing look and then Paul said, "Oh, we're not gay anymore. We pick our friends by what time their kids' nap time is."

I discussed earlier the hostile responses elicited by the efforts of gay men and lesbians to establish claims to having valid and authentic family lives. We have seen that such opposition emerges both from the antigay (often religious) right that seeks to exclude gays and lesbians from marriage and family and also from queer activists who disparage gays and lesbians they judge to be accommodating to conventional values. These antagonistic responses to gay fatherhood have concrete consequences, apart from the discursive violence that they do to gay men as they struggle to establish and maintain their families. I'd like to outline some of these here and suggest some of the ways that gay men negotiate around the obstacles presented by both kinds of opposition.[1] Following recent work by Elizabeth Povinelli (2001), I will frame gay fathers' cultural difficulties as problems of "incommensurability." Povinelli uses approaches from the philosophy of language that understand incommensurability as a kind of linguistic indeterminacy, i.e., "a state in which an undistorted translation cannot be produced between two or more denotational texts." This leads her to pose more general questions about how "the inconceivable [is] conceived" (2001, 320). Expanding on these concerns, Tom Boellstorff (2005), writing about the predicament of gay men in Indonesia who also identify as Muslim, examines how individuals facing such dilemmas devise strategies for making their dual identities intelligible or "grammatical" to themselves and to the various constituencies with whom they interact.

Like others who occupy social positions defined as inherently contradictory, gay fathers must seek to establish both cultural visibility and moral legitimacy if they are to carve out space within which to raise their families. Among other tasks, they must negotiate around assumptions that their families present subversive challenges to wider family values (from the right) and that their desire for family reflects craven accommodationism (from the left). Despite the wide political differences and divergent moral foundations between adherents of these positions, their arguments are eerily similar. They essentially claim that being married and/or being a parent is something that only heterosexual people ought to do; both views look to nature for ratification. Gay men and lesbians, in these constructions, are properly positioned outside what are commonly understood to be mainstream social institutions; any efforts they might make to breach the boundaries between the margins and the center constitute an offense against their true natures. Queerness is conflated with generalized subversion; variability in its meanings or in the specific behaviors associated with it is not credited with being authentic.

We saw earlier that gay fathers face particularly challenging obstacles in their quest to become or, for formerly married fathers, to remain parents. For gay men who wish to become parents, demonized images of gay male sexuality may fuel the fears of adoption gatekeepers. The procedural pathways to adoption are complex and time consuming for all prospective parents, but in many cases only children whom heterosexual couples are unwilling to adopt—nonwhite, older, disabled—are made available to placement with gay fathers. International and private adoptions are also cumbersome, and they are also extremely expensive. Surrogacy is a complicated process, both medically and interpersonally, and exacts even higher financial investments. All of these paths may require second-parent adoptions by the partner of the primary adoptive parent, a legal process that is not universally accessible and that adds further investments of time and money even before parents confront the expenses involved in raising children.

In other words, the challenges gay fathers encounter have to do both with finding a way to become fathers and with managing continuing relationships with children. Though the specific features of these difficulties are distinctive, both draw on the same prejudices about gay men and children: that they are morally unfit to parent and that parenthood is intrinsically incompatible with homosexuality. And gay fathers may continue to face problems even after becoming parents as people with whom they come into contact disparage them in various ways.

"All the Very Normal Sort of Things"

Russ Anderson and Jason Williams live in a townhouse in a Chicago suburb. After they had been together for about five years, they began to discuss having children. Jason, who is African American, was especially skeptical about whether they could become adoptive parents. He suspected that gay men simply wouldn't be allowed access to adoption and also wondered whether it would be fair to bring a child into a family without a mother or into a family with two fathers. But Russ, who is white, described parenting as something he had always wanted to do, and while he had never considered embarking on parenthood as a single man, or thought specifically about how a gay man might manage to become a father, he felt strongly that they should try. They briefly considered having a child with a surrogate, but once they discovered the cost of such procedures, decided that only adoption would be feasible. In an effort to bring Jason around, Russ brought home numerous articles from psychological and other academic journals, all of which indicated that there is no long-term negative impact on children who grow up with same-sex parents. Once Jason had been convinced that there was nothing unethical about pursuing fatherhood, they took another step: joining a group for gay and lesbian couples who wanted to become parents. Attending this group further helped to demystify the process that lay ahead. As Russ explains, "We met other normal people. Very normal couples who wanted children. And they were talking about how they were going about it and looking for doctors . . . and looking for lawyers and looking for hospitals. And just all the very normal sort of things that a couple would need to be doing. It helped a lot."

Meeting other gay and lesbian prospective parents not only made parenthood seem accessible, but provided them with practical information about how to proceed. They learned, for example, that international adoption would be out of reach for them financially, but that as an interracial couple they would be viewed preferentially for a domestic adoption of a black or mixed-race child. Referrals from the group helped them to find a private agency that specializes in precisely these kinds of placements, matching pregnant women with adoptive parents, and, when birth mothers agree, finding children for same-sex couples. Advice from other group members also helped Russ and Jason navigate the thicket of bureaucratic procedures that all adoptive parents face: home visits, foster parent licensure, and (for those adopting across racial boundaries) a class on transracial adoption specifically targeted at the white member of the couple. They also learned about the specific legal barriers they would have to negotiate, most crucially relating to second-parent adoption.

Probably most central, however, to what Russ and Jason gained from belonging to the prospective parents group was a sense that their desire for a family was "normal." The other people they met in the group seemed to have similar values to theirs and were trying to become parents for the same sorts of reasons: primarily the desire to count as a "family." As time went on, members of the group achieved their goals and moved on, proving that the obstacles presented to gay parenting were not insurmountable. The support Russ and Jason received in the group also made the changes that parenthood would make in their lives seem more manageable. Believing that parenthood required more child-friendly living arrangements, they moved from the city to a suburban area where they could more easily find a house with a backyard and have access to highly regarded public schools. They began to stay home more in the evenings—largely to save money for the expenses of adopting—but gradually found themselves less interested in bar-hopping and gay nightlife, which had, in any case, become less accessible from their new location. Their move to the suburbs also coincided with their joining a local Episcopal church, and once the adoption was final they began to form friendships with other parents they met in the neighborhood, through play groups or daycare. Very few of these new acquaintances were gay. While they claimed that their view of themselves as "gay" had not changed, the daily rhythms of life had clearly situated that identity in a very different context. Indeed, Russ and Jason not only became parents, but essentially reconfigured most features of ordinary life, a shift that was facilitated by their discovery that gay parents could be "normal." Once they found that they could live in this new way, it was also clear that they would be able to manage not only the practical, but also the moral challenges they understood to be intrinsic to fatherhood.

Being a Father, Becoming Gay

For some men who became gay after having fathered children in a marriage, the incommensurability of gay and paternal identities emerges in the course of trying to establish themselves as gay men, and particularly as they seek out sexual and romantic partners. Joe O'Reilly, a divorced father in his early forties who lives in a Chicago suburb, has struggled to maintain a close relationship to his two children while also experiencing the social and emotional dislocations of coming out. Many of our conversations focused on disappointments he had experienced in relationships with men and particularly on the vicissitudes of dating, much of which he negotiates via the Internet.

Joe and his former wife have joint custody of their two children, ages six and eight, and he is committed to playing a very active role as a parent. This means that Joe cannot even contemplate living anywhere other than the suburban community where his wife also lives, with his living arrangements and work schedule carefully planned so that the children's school placement and daily lives do not require geographical dislocation. The divorce, which followed an intense personal struggle and several years of intensive psychotherapy, has left him struggling to manage his financial obligations to the children while also trying to sustain an active social life. The process has not been easy. The first man he dated claimed to love children, but once the children were actually in his life, became impatient with the constraints they imposed on their time and freedom. Joe has had similar experiences with other men as well.

> Sometimes I've found [boyfriends] sit and brood because they don't want to not be the center of attention and there's drama involved and there's attention involved and there's time and there isn't enough to go around with kids. . . . A lot of men that I have started to see, they thought they could [share me with the

children], and they thought it was an interesting idea . . . and then . . . couldn't after the reality set in terms of my time [and] . . . who I devoted it to. Nobody wanted to play effectively second best, and although I never looked at it that way, because for me that was apples and oranges—the love for your children is very different from the love you have for a partner or someone you expect to spend your life with—but that was the effect in that it was divided affection and it wasn't satisfactory.

Joe's anxiety about trying to manage life as a gay man along with his commitments as a father, and particularly his deep desire to settle into a stable, committed relationship, were sharpest when he talked about his efforts to find "Mr. Right." One man, in particular, resented having to move to the suburbs to live with Joe and chafed whenever time with the children conflicted with plans he had made. Joe described him as someone whose relationship with his own blood relatives was minimal. He explained, "He had a very sort of negative idea about family. You know, his family was his friends." While his financial obligations to his former wife have left him with little disposable income, the economic pressures of fatherhood pale in comparison to the logistics of dating, particularly as he now seeks to meet men on the Internet. When should he reveal the fact that he has children? Would a partner resent the time and attention he devotes to his children? Is it appropriate to bring his children to gay events, like the annual Pride Parade, and to introduce them to his gay friends? Can he establish himself as a gay man in the same way that men who don't have children seem so easily to achieve? Most pointedly, do basic definitions of fatherhood and gayness collide in ways that make them unmanageable?

Elusive Gayness

Other gay fathers are more directly engaged in renegotiating their identities in ways that seem fully to accept the discursive distance between gayness and fatherhood. But while these men understand being gay and being fathers as contradictory domains, they do not necessarily ground these understandings in the same definitions or undertake the same sorts of strategies to manage them.

For Lawrence Lock, who lives in a working-class Chicago suburb, and whom we met in chapter 5, becoming a parent was framed in counterpoint to the painful realization that he was gay. He is white, a deeply religious man who grew up and was educated as a Southern Baptist but was ousted as music director of a large Baptist church when he came out to his pastor. It had been his lifelong dream to be a father, but he feared that he might be gay, which in his view would preclude fatherhood on moral grounds. "So I remember praying *constantly* for God to change the way I felt about men," he told me, until at the age of thirty-three he could no longer deny his feelings, realizing that God could no more make him straight than "turn me into an elephant." Still, relationships never seemed to work out for him. He described himself as "no good at this relationship-with-adults thing," a realization he reached after a series of "dysfunctional" relationships. Uncomfortable with gay bar life, the only kind of collective gay life he knew about, he reached the decision that he should instead seek out parenting as an appropriate vehicle for his need to "love somebody." He began by becoming certified as a foster parent and caring for a number of children who had been removed from their families because of neglect or abuse.

The two African American brothers he adopted, both seriously disabled, were initially placed with him as foster children. He feels strongly that he has been called by God to parent these boys, becoming animated as he details their progress since they came to live with him and his intense connection with them. Being the boys' father has enabled him to do something "important," rather than "wasting [time] on entertainment things," things that, in his words, "just don't matter anymore." Among those "things" is clearly being gay as more than an abstract identity. Further, now that he has two children, he believes that the likelihood of his making a romantic connection is even slimmer, explaining that, "If you tell a gay man that you have two children at home it tends to stop conversation."

Some gay fathers' narratives point to parenthood as a condition that imposes particular spatial, temporal, and material constraints that limit their ability to engage in indexical "gay" activities. In this view, "gayness" becomes reconfigured as one set of daily practices that is replaced by another, the new set more child oriented and rooted in domesticity and social responsibility. One suburban Chicago father, Len Olson, told me that the difference in what gayness means to him since he and his partner adopted their son, now three, in Guatemala, can be summed up in reference to opera attendance, an activity that was once central to their lives. He said that now, if they're lucky, they might get to one or two operas each year. They used to purchase a subscription for the entire season of Chicago's Lyric Opera, and Len clearly sees opera attendance as an activity closely associated with gay identity.[2]

Now that Len and his partner, Richard Parsons, are parents, however, going to the opera has become a difficult chore, requiring a substantial financial outlay for tickets, dinner, parking, and babysitting, costs that compete with the many other expenses they face as a family. It also means going to bed late, problematic for the chronically sleep-deprived parents of a toddler. Beyond this, now that he has adult, i.e., parental, responsibilities, going to the opera just doesn't seem as important as it once did. At the same time, however, he recalls opera attendance almost nostalgically, as a memento of a past life.

"We've Joined Another Club"

What counts as a "gay" pastime, however, emerges in these accounts as far from uniform. In some men's narratives, particular activities were identified as "gay" because they were done in the company of other gay men, rather than because they involve stereotypically gay behaviors. I spent one evening in the suburban Chicago home of Chris O'Neill and John Stone, the parents of three-year-old twin girls born through gestational surrogacy, who described the desire to have children as something that they had once assumed was simply impossible. Chris described the long process that led to his becoming comfortable with his gay identity after years of feeling lonely and different. "I thought that being a gay parent would be yet again an isolating experience. I finally had found this big community, a community of people that I've had a lot in common with—a gay community—then to take this next step would be isolating."

But not long after beginning their relationship, the two men began cautiously to investigate parenthood. They attended workshops at a gay clinic and were encouraged by the fact that gay men and lesbians in their friendship circle, and particularly two men who lived in an adjoining townhouse, had become parents or were considering doing so. While becoming part of a community of gay fathers was not necessarily what Chris and John visualized, knowing other gay parents gave a face to the desire they experienced, and a gay face at that. Their eventual move from Lakeview (the Chicago neighborhood popularly known as Boys Town) to suburban Oak Park also turned on their knowledge that gay and lesbian families were a well-established part of that community, that some of their friends with children had already moved there, and that their daughters would not have to bear the burden of being the only such children in their school or neighborhood. Living in Oak Park, they reasoned, would not force them to choose between being parents and being gay.

The birth of their daughters (through surrogacy) strengthened their relationships with other gay and lesbian parents, but, to their surprise, it also created the basis for friendships with straight parents. Soon after they moved to Oak Park the two men met a straight couple with children about the same age as their daughters. When they learned that they both had subscriptions to the same theatre series, they decided to order their tickets for the same nights so that they could go together (and share a babysitter). Still, children loom large in this relationship and are clearly what makes the friendship work. Chris explained, "It's the common interest thing. . . . We rattle on and on and on about the kids."

These changed social connections make clear that parenthood alters the connection of identity to daily practices and activities. For men like Chris and John, being gay is now a condition embodied in their relationship and in their personal histories rather than in specific interactions with a community or immersion in gay-oriented or gay-populated pastimes. That is, it is who they are rather than what they do. Paradoxically, this means that they sometimes feel that being gay has become a less central part of ordinary consciousness, but also that it is sometimes more salient. John reflects, "I almost feel like *more* gay because I'm not in a gay neighborhood, and in many social situations, I'm the only gay person there." But Chris notes that the process sometimes goes in the opposite direction.

> I'm less aware of being a gay man now that I'm not doing all of those things, like having the *Will and Grace*–type banter with your friends . . . , people acting queeny . . . to be funny. There's no time for that. When you're living more tightly in the gay community, I think you're far more aware of being gay, of being part of that community. And now I feel less aware of it on sort of a daily basis. I guess I feel like we've joined another club and this club is the club of parents of three-year-old girls.

In this dynamic, gayness seems to be contained both in particular kinds of activities with other gay persons and to be a function of conscious self-awareness in some contexts. But it also emerges in response to perceived hostility or discrimination. It's not needed, it would seem, when no threat is apparent. "What's great to me is that there are so many couples who treat us like normal parents," John explained, almost with surprise.

Thus, although John and Chris don't think that their newfound experience of being "normal" erases their gay identities, they are acutely conscious of the ambiguities parenthood has introduced into their formerly clear sense of being gay men. After years of simply assuming where they fit in terms of a wider community, John and Chris now find themselves examining how it is, exactly, that one knows one is gay. Is it hanging out with other gay men? Is it engaging in camp repartee? Is it intrinsic to being comfortably ensconced with people like oneself, or being aware of one's differences from those with whom one interacts? It seems that being a member of a same-sex couple may not necessarily make one unequivocally gay, at least not under all imaginable circumstances. In other words, how central does gayness have to be on a daily basis to be fully legible to others and to oneself? While fathers like John and Chris have to consider whether being members of the parents of three-year-old girls club qualifies them to continue to claim being gay, their awareness of the ambiguities highlights issues that probably all gay men and lesbians face. How many identities can each of us possess, and how much variation can we accommodate before the boundaries of identities begin to crumble?

"The Social Responsibility Piece of It"

On a frigid January evening, I settled into the comfortable living room at Dennis Caruso and Harvey Stone's Victorian cottage in Rogers Park, an enclave of older homes and apartment houses on the Far North Side of Chicago. When I first met with them, they had completed the process of applying to adopt from Guatemala and were waiting to be summoned Guatemala to pick up the daughter they had been matched with, whose pictures they showed me. Dennis was planning to travel to Guatemala on his own, playing the part of the "single father" that he had been officially labeled for the Guatemalan officials, but he would bring his mother along to help with the care of their daughter.

Dennis, thirty-seven, is a high school teacher in a tough, inner-city high school on the city's West Side, and Harvey, thirty-two, is involved in a start-up software company. Though they come from different parts of the country—Dennis from a small town in downstate Illinois and Harvey from the South—both men trace their backgrounds to stable, large extended families, where the idea of parenthood loomed large as a central element of what life was understood to be all about. Both families had blue-collar backgrounds, but education has allowed both men to live differently from their parents and siblings. Like some of the men whom we met in earlier chapters, Dennis and Harvey connect their desire to be fathers to the values with which they were raised, particularly the image of a fully realized life rooted in raising a new generation and adult identity anchored in being a parent. Dennis, for example, tells me that he can't remember not wanting to be a father, explaining, "Really, for me, I think part of it was having grown up [in a big family], I think it was just hard to imagine not. I think growing up in a family where [being a parent] was the one goal of every single person in it." This was so important to him that even when he came out at about age twenty, he insisted on believing that he could still be a parent. While he acknowledges that he was probably "programmed" to want to be a parent, his desire for a child feels central to his identity: "I always believed. Part of it was, like, rooted in defiance. . . . I will be able to do this if I want. I mean, I'm not going to let being gay not let me do something that I've thought about and that I think I would like to do. So part of it was in reaction—like that's part of the reason that got me thinking about it."

Having children was something that both men assumed they would do. The question they wrestled with was not *whether* they would eventually take this step, but *when* they would seek to become parents. The formation of their relationship, nine years earlier, started the discussion in earnest, though Dennis thinks that the fact that Harvey was five years younger meant that he wasn't really ready to think concretely about parenthood at the start of the relationship. Dennis tells me about the process: "It was always something I thought I would want to do. And then when Harvey and I met, it becomes a very different story when you can actually start imagining yourself with this not imaginary person, but here is this person. I can imagine *us* actually having a child."

In other words, becoming a father wasn't something that occurred to Dennis in the abstract or as an individual venture. Part of the image that drove his desire was the idea of a family as one in which two parents, settled in a home, move toward having a child. Unlike the trajectory in his own family, however, where his mother started having children at the age of nineteen, Dennis's plan was influenced by having achieved a level of education that emphasized a slower entrée into full adulthood. The responsibility of children is best reserved, in this version, until after parents have established careers and figured out who they are as individuals, or as Dennis puts it, "being able to develop as a human being."

But becoming parents means more to Dennis and Harvey than the cul-
mination of a process of maturation. They are careful to make clear to me
that they see their decision to adopt a child from Guatemala as something
linked to their sense of "social responsibility." Elaborating a theme that was
central to chapter 5, the two men speak about their understanding of parenthood as more than a source of personal gratification. Harvey explains:

> I think another part of the wanting to be parents that has developed over time
> for us is kind of the social responsibility piece of it. And I think it's probably
> a common thing. Well, I know it's a common thing because I've heard it from
> a lot of other potentially adoptive parents, where because, for whatever rea-
> son—you're gay, biological reasons, whatever—you can't have kids and you
> visit this possibility of adopting a kid, there's all the other stuff we just talked
> about, where for whatever reason in our lives we want to have kids. But there
> then becomes this piece, for us, especially in the last five years, it's like, we've
> worked hard. We have a great life, and resources, and this nice thing going, and
> what a cool thing to share with a kid that might not otherwise get that. So that
> starts to enter into it. There's over and above all this other stuff, maybe this want
> of doing good. Not that that's always there, but I think it increasingly becomes
> kind of like, at the end of the day.

Here Harvey associates ideas that focus on doing good and on following
a pattern based in family tradition, but that also locate that impulse at some
distance from being gay. Like other men whose stories we heard earlier, he
makes clear that he sees the desire to share the good things in life with a
child who might otherwise not have access to such advantages. But he also
understands this urge as distinct from being gay, as something he and Dennis have in common with other potential parents, particularly those who,
like them, cannot achieve simple biological reproduction. Parents who are
gay or who are infertile have to think in a more deliberate and morally
explicit way about the process on which they are embarking. They have to
do this because the course that leads to successful adoption demands self-
reflection and exposes the couple to intense scrutiny by a host of adoption
gatekeepers. No step on the route to adoptive parenthood is automatic;
one must publicly expose one's motives and have them evaluated by those
who will decide on one's right to adopt. While he acknowledges that heterosexual couples can more easily convince these gatekeepers of the authenticity of their desire, he believes that the examination mandated for all
makes it necessary to think through one's motivations.

At the same time, the theme of social responsibility is linked, albeit reactively, to their being gay, even as they both take pains to explain that it is something they share with other prospective parents. Dennis tries to make their decision-making process more transparent.

I was just going to add that not only that social responsibility, that's all in there. But another one that we talked about, and I think I remember one of the moments where we were kind of in this "Do we or don't we, do we or don't we?" And the case I was making to Harvey was at the end of the day, at the end of our lives, do I want to say, "Wow, we had some great trips to Key West, and wasn't the Pottery Barn fabulous when we furnished our house, and wasn't my garden cute?" I mean, is that what I want the essence of my life to be? Yes, there was career and friends, and all that stuff that was important, but then there's also that bigger legacy that's important. When you think about importance, it ties to social responsibility and making a difference and growing and raising this hopefully happy, and well-adjusted, and productive, and caring human being. Because we're short on them in many, many, many instances. And so, I don't know, that goes on, too, it has gone on in the decision.

Dennis contends, however, that this thinking isn't related to being gay. Because he came out in the mid-1980s, he says, "I kind of missed the show tunes, Key West all the time, White Parties, because I came out in the middle of the AIDS epidemic, I was terrified to have sex, terrified to have a relationship. I was sure I was going to die. When I say things like this, really I don't consider us to be part of that gay world. We have gay and lesbian friends. But this is our life, it's not 'gay.' "
Harvey elaborates on this theme.

That's our big joke. We're always going through, like, "When do we start the gay life?" Well, there's laundry, then we go to the grocery store, and then we get up for work, and then we rent movies, and we have some friends over for dinner, and we buy a good bottle of wine once in a while, and got a new cat. And we love to do that. Because, what's this gay thing? But at the same time, it gets into identity issues with us in terms of, like, that whole set of White Party, muscle boy, gym boy. That subculture is something that really doesn't appeal to us on a lot of levels.

As they talk more about how they conceptualize their lives, both men suggest that maintaining a clear "gay identity" can be burdensome, forcing them to play roles that feel contrived and inauthentic, and thus blocking their access to experiencing who they really are. Dennis is particularly emphatic about this, using an account of the kind of gay life he led before he met Harvey to illustrate his point.

> I was down in Boys Town. My life was very—my primary friends were gay men for a period of time, and I got older and started working and doing work I liked and I think as I started becoming who I am versus, okay, I've moved, I'm gay, I've moved to the gay neighborhood, and I have to assume an identity. And I think as I grew up and started saying, well, wait a minute, now I have to have my own identity and develop as the person I am, that our lives are more balanced now. Where we have this, this is our life, that this is the kind of people we are.

Harvey adds to his description, trying to give me a sense of how they see themselves, and how they organize their lives.

> I think as we both matured as gay men, finding authenticity and real down-to-earth people has been a huge thing to us. We have this joke where we're like, it's why do we have so many lesbian friends? We find [in them] so [much] more of what we consider, like, [an] authentic, down-to-earth quality that we value in friends. . . . Part of this is about authenticity. Back to your point about what really is important in our lives. And this becomes one of those ways that both of us want to measure our importance to the world. And this is part of a life well-lived for us, that we would have this connection.

While Harvey and Dennis are careful to avoid disparaging gay life specifically, it's clear that their construction of "a life well-lived" is situated at some distance from a particular image of gay life that they clearly share. They mention White Parties repeatedly, a reference to the circuit party world associated with reckless sexuality, extravagant drug use, and squandering money in traveling from scene to scene (Carrington 2006; Share 2006), but also a coded allusion to all of the elements of "gay life" from which they try to distance themselves. Regardless of whether this image is accurate, they imagine the world of circuit parties as one that emphasizes superficial physical attractiveness, i.e., hours spent in gyms, frivolous partygoing, and casual, probably anonymous, sex.

All of these pursuits contrast in fundamental ways with the high value they both place on the centrality of their relationship, their desire to achieve full adulthood and self-realization through the process of raising a family, and their focus on mundane details of daily life (laundry, grocery shopping, and the like) that give their lives substance and meaning. Their accounts also underscore the continuity they see between their core values and those they attribute to their families, despite the fact that they have distanced themselves both geographically and socially from these same families.[3] At the same time that Dennis and Harvey put considerable energy into extricating themselves from long-term family involvements by seeking education far from home and settling in Chicago, they now embrace a sentimental account of themselves as engaged in a process of recapitulating deeply held family values.

Dennis and Harvey's accounts of how they envision propelling themselves into "a life well-lived" and into an existence that enhances "social responsibility" are enmeshed with their opposition to a particularly visible kind of gay life. Drawing on some of the most pernicious images of gay frivolity, they call attention to the mundane routines of their ordinary lives—laundry, grocery shopping, gardening—as manifestly contrasting with "gay life." "When do we start the gay life?" Harvey asks, only partly in jest. That they so easily categorize the tasks that frame their lives as not part of "gay life" reveals in stark relief how thoroughly Dennis and Harvey's understanding of "gay life" and stereotypes that pervade U.S. culture intersect. Though they take care to align themselves and their desires with ordinary people, not necessarily gay, their insistence on doing so indicates that the path to moral achievement that they imagine—a path that includes forming a stable family and becoming parents—cannot be undertaken in a "gay" moral universe.

"It's Hard to Be Spontaneous"

For many men, the distance between the lives they led as gay men before they had children and the pressures on them as parents is so great that they find it difficult to make their childless friends understand. This often means that their way of connecting with their old gay social networks changes dramatically, particularly as they must plan every excursion from home carefully in advance. Peter and Ben, whom we met in chapter 4, reported consistent problems reconciling their old friends with the new realities of their lives. When I returned to visit with the two men, several weeks after the bris of their second son, they described some of the adjustments they had made now that they had two children. Material arrangements were falling into place. They had purchased a new home, an enormous Victorian house across the street from their townhouse. The new house would require substantial remodeling and the process of gutting it and building the new interior was already underway. The nanny who had been working for them since the first baby's birth was staying on and they had managed to have the boys accepted at the preschool run by the large Reform synagogue just down the street. This preschool is always inundated with applications and has a long waiting list, but they think that perhaps they owe their quick acceptance to their "specialness" as a gay family.

Having the nanny available for babysitting has meant that the two men get to have one night off a week, which they usually spend having dinner with friends and perhaps attending a play or the opera. While they have kept up connections with friends they had before becoming parents, they can't be as spontaneous as they once were and realize that some of the invitations they used to get to various kinds of social events haven't been coming as frequently. Ben suspects that some friends who don't have kids aren't sure how to indicate whether children are welcome or not. "They don't want to be put in the position of saying, 'Kids aren't invited.' . . . There's the issue that if [someone] invites us, do you presume that children are invited if he doesn't say anything? Or do you presume that they're not invited?"

Despite the fact that their nanny makes it possible for them to maintain some sort of social life, Peter and Ben are conscious that their relationship to their former circle of friends has changed considerably since they first became parents. Ben explains,

In all honesty, I think before our kids, we were at the epicenter of a lot of gay circles, like this whole world and our lives were just plain, well, anybody could count on us for any benefit—call Peter and Ben, they'll donate if it's a good cause, they'll be there, they'll be table captains. If it was a trip somewhere, call Peter and Ben—they'll come. Whatever. I think we were liked and counted on by a lot of people. And we were integral members of this social scene. And I don't want to say that we've dropped out of it entirely because I don't think we have—like I think Chris and John [their former neighbors] have a different take on this whole thing, and they're totally different. They moved to Oak Park, they changed their jobs, so it's totally changed. . . . I don't think our focus has shifted as much as theirs, for example. But, you know, whether we're 70 percent and they're 100 percent, it's still a huge change. You can't help it. Every night, we have to be here with the children. And the people we are friends with, sometimes they just don't get it. Like they can't just call this afternoon and say, "Let's go to a movie tonight." That's just not a possibility. You know, we have to plan days in advance, schedule the babysitter, you know, the whole thing.

ELLEN: Does that feel like a loss to you at all?

BEN: It kind of does. Sometimes it does. I think it's hard to be spontaneous. It's virtually impossible. And we would do anything before. If somebody said, "Do you want to go [out] tonight?" we'd go. I mean we were—we would do things. Or, "Do you want to go to New York this weekend?" we'd go. Seriously, we'd go. It's not a big deal.

ELLEN: So is it only the babies, the scheduling part? Or do you feel like you don't want to spend your money the same way?

BEN: Well first of all, there's not as much money to spend.[4] And, you know, our friends without children don't understand—you have no choice but to be here. I'm so exhausted right now that just the thought of being there and comforting somebody else is exhausting to me. But you have no choice. These children, they need you. What are you going to do? Schedule your kids?

Some of Peter and Ben's friends still don't begin to fathom the time and attention that young children need and how much the care of an infant, in particular, makes other kinds of activities simply impossible. When they first got home from California with the new baby, they were overwhelmed with his needs plus those of their toddler, and despite help from the nanny and Peter's sister, they were exhausted. While they were in California, they were able to give almost no attention to their jobs, so they were also struggling to make up what they had missed during that time.

PETER: [When we first came home] the baby was up all night. We literally did not sleep for, like, two weeks. And friends were, like, calling and wondering what was going on. And they really had this kind of selfish thing. And we were really out there—we were sleep deprived, feeling pressure and feeling stress from everywhere. And I had to work at the same time and Ben had to work. And everyone was wondering what was going on. And it was really too much. Finally, the baby is a month old and we're invited to this brunch. And one friend takes me aside and says, "I need to talk to you. I'm really concerned about you." It was almost like an intervention.

BEN: Seriously. All of our friends said, "We've been talking and we're concerned about you because we don't hear from you. And we're concerned about you, and I've been taking yoga and I understand that it's really important to get in touch with your inner feeling, whatever." And I was like—do you understand that I'm up all night changing diapers and trying to feed this kid and not sleeping and trying to function? I wish I could take yoga and get in touch with my feelings right now, but I can't. . . . And all of that is great, but I have a new child, this baby, and maybe you should consider that. We're just trying to get through the day!

At the same time, some of Peter and Ben's friends were far more supportive. Ben explains,

But in contrast, we did have friends who got it, who totally got it and just said, "Tomorrow night we're bringing over dinner—and we're just going to drop it off, we're not even going to stay. We're just going to drop it off."
ELLEN: So were these friends who have kids?
BEN: Yes. They got it. Every night we'd order in, and I didn't even feel like ordering in or dealing with people. But somebody who says, "I'm bringing over dinner, just heat it and enjoy it, and there's enough for leftovers," they're such a blessing. And then there were those other people who were like, "I never see you." The difference is people being sensitive to our situation, and then other people being so self-focused and, like, basically what they're saying is, "I'm not getting what I need from Peter and Ben," as opposed to saying, "You guys need to not worry about dinner for a night."

When I ask Ben whether any of their friends who are not parents have begun to understand their new priorities, he tells me, "Some have. Very few, but some have. You have the gay male thing there, the gay man, and there's a lot of stuff."

ELLEN: What kind of stuff?
BEN: You know, the priority of getting to the gym and looking good and going out. And then the restaurants, and then this and that. And it's just such an antithesis of what we're doing. We're just trying to make it through the day and make sure these kids are both okay.

It is clear that having a second child places a great many more constraints on Peter and Ben than they experienced when they only had one son. Even with their nanny and access to preschool for their toddler, even with Peter's family close at hand and sometimes able to provide babysitting, even with their high incomes, and even as a couple who both take on parenting duties, on some days they are simply overwhelmed with managing all the needs of their young children. They are often sleep-deprived and exhausted from juggling infant care and their jobs, so the insistent demands of some of their gay friends for their attention pose an added strain they are unwilling to accept. They readily explain their friends' lack of understanding as "the gay male thing," by which they refer to a broad complex of behaviors and interests centered on the self and one's social life. While they try to avoid being judgmental about their friends' priorities—which resemble those they once had—they clearly situate their own concerns in a different, implicitly more adult and responsible, dimension.

Making the Invisible Visible

The gay fathers whose narratives I've presented all speak, in one way or another, to a problem of managing the conflicting demands and cultural requirements of fatherhood and being gay men—a problem that resembles the incommensurability of ungrammatical utterances. Each of them devises a strategy—and sometimes more than one strategy—that will allow him to frame his existence in a form that is legible and intelligible to others and to himself. Fatherhood requires gay men to consider various kinds of incommensurability: palpable conflicts between the social orbits of parents and gay men without parental obligations; issues of recognition in a variety of social settings coded as appropriate to "families" or to "gay men," but rarely both; questions of priorities when these contradictory identities trespass into distinct sites characteristically occupied by one or the other. The contradictions they must negotiate are rarely as simple as "gay" versus "father": professional, class, race, and other identities and commitments intersect with and moderate the sharpness of that single opposition.

These fathers all offer accounts that define gayness and fatherhood as conflicting along a number of dimensions. At the same time, however, the ways in which they imagine these discontinuities suggest that basic beliefs about identity are only a small part of the process they use to classify themselves. They sometimes frame fatherhood and gayness as opposing moral universes, but at other times as temporal and spatial domains that rarely intersect, embedding being gay in patterns of social interaction, in specific moral domains, in personal development, or as a form of self-awareness. Each of these understandings connects to parenthood differently; each presents distinct challenges as men attempt to reconcile specific ambitions, goals, emotional and moral priorities; and, further, each changes after the arrival of children in the men's lives.

Are these fathers still gay? They certainly all identify with the term and were willing to participate in research that focused on gay fathers. Even as Paul and Keith claim that the label "gay" no longer pertains to them, they are active in a Chicago-area network of gay parents, taking the lead as the organizers of family events and helping to maintain e-mail connections among members. Joe understands the simultaneous conditions of fatherhood and gayness as contradictions that will need careful management if he is to find a partner who will care about his children. For Len, gayness is embedded in his personal history, deeply part of him even as parenthood has submerged aspects of its public expression. John and Chris manage to live in two worlds, maintaining close friendships with other gay fathers but also finding that their connections have expanded in unexpectedly satisfying new directions. Lawrence, in a different strategy, conceives of his move into parenthood as a moral and ethical choice, one that doesn't erase his being gay—that is, after all, an identity that is God-given—but that allows him to acknowledge it without losing the opportunity for a satisfying family life.

In a different twist on Lawrence's attempt to trade the clear virtues of fatherhood, particularly for children with serious developmental problems, for the morally compromised self-indulgence of gay life, Dennis and Harvey position the tame rhythm of domesticity as more appealing than the ephemeral pleasures of being gay. They situate themselves in opposition to a particularly toxic image of gay male existence, the White Parties. Posed against the frivolous and forgettable entertainments of the circuit parties is what they characterize as "authentic" and "down-to-earth"— the daily round of cleaning, shopping, and cooking, along with an effort to embody long-standing family values. Interestingly, they emphasize the importance of lesbians in their social network, implicitly invoking the reputation of lesbians as less sexually driven and less stylish than their gay male counterparts. Russ and Jason's strategy has much in common with Dennis and Harvey's, though their discovery of "being normal" is enacted through their experience of fitting in with the other parents they have met in their suburban community and in the church they joined.

These narrative fragments speak to a range of complications in the articulation of gay identity in a population whose legitimacy is often challenged both by opponents of gay rights and by queer-culture fundamentalists. That gayness and fatherhood are widely understood to be contradictory domains is eloquently demonstrated by the near total absence of these men from scholarship in lesbian and gay studies. Paul and Keith, who told me they were no longer gay, playfully drew on a definition that foregrounds patterns of association as the foundation of sexual identity: since they pick their friends according to their children's nap times rather than through common interests in gay culture, they must not be gay anymore. By socializing with other gay fathers, John and Chris find a way to mitigate this contradiction, but wonder whether being gay depends on being in the midst of other gay people or being isolated in a heterosexual setting. Len and Lawrence, along with Harvey and Dennis, embrace a moral domain that ironically draws on some of the same stereotypes that homophobes employ: the notion that there is something immature and frivolous about gay life and that parenthood demands priorities that are both more adult and more unselfish. At the same time, their accounts differ in terms of how focally sexual behavior is implicated in gay identity. Len has a partner but he situates gayness symbolically in a pastime associated with gay men—opera attendance. Lawrence is single; he contrasts the depth of his bond with his sons with the superficial world of the gay bar, a world he assumes is hostile to parents. Harvey and Dennis, it seems, have simply declared "gay life" something so inauthentic that they cannot imagine attempting it, while Jason and Russ have found themselves far from their earlier gay lives, almost as an accidental benefit of becoming parents and embracing a new way of life in the suburbs.

All of these accounts underline identity as a process rather than as a stable personal attribute, a label that changes meaning from moment to moment, dependent on both social and discursive context. These men sometimes invoke gay identity as intrinsically part of them; at other times they frame it as chosen, and at still other times see it as a label imposed on them. I argue here that gay fathers are aware that parenthood destabilizes their gay identities, and that their approaches to the incongruities the two statuses pose help us move toward more precise definitions of what gay identity actually might be.

Despite the fact that all of the men must contend with similar sorts of cultural contradictions, their solutions to the dilemma are strikingly different. These divergent strategies reflect distinctive normative readings of their statuses, but are also informed by the actual turns their lives have taken since they became parents. Their accounts indicate an active process of making sense of their situations, a process that sometimes hinges on reinterpretation of events, and sometimes requires them to adjust their images of what being gay should entail. In other words, they are engaged in an active process of negotiating and renegotiating their experience, resisting the conventional wisdom that gay men can't be parents, but also subscribing to some of the very preconceptions on which such wisdom is based. They must be energetic cultural strategists, constantly reconsidering how (and whether) they can still be "gay," and what version of gayness they can access. In a sense, they are not only claiming the legitimacy of their status as fathers, but redefining what it means to be gay, sometimes within the boundaries of conventional understandings and sometimes in new ways they devise themselves.

CHAPTER SEVEN

Corrective Lenses,
or Revisioning Yuckiness

All I knew about Philip Rothstein before we met in 2002 was that he had been investigating surrogacy as a single man. The other Chicago dads who mentioned his name to me thought that taking on parenthood, particularly through surrogacy, but without a partner's support, indicated an unusual dedication. We met in his Lakeview townhouse, meticulously decorated in an art moderne style that perfectly fit the house's horizontal lines. "I'm pregnant," he announced, when I asked about his interest in fatherhood. "We got pregnant with triplets," referring to himself and the surrogate. I was struck by the intensely embodied quality of Philip's account, and wanted to know more about what it would feel like for a man to be "pregnant."

ELLEN: When you say you're pregnant, do you *feel* pregnant?
PHILIP: Sometimes.
ELLEN: In what way?

Philip's gaze shifted toward his belly as he thought about a response.

PHILIP: I feel myself changing. Definitely. I feel myself thinking for more than one.
ELLEN: Can you give me an example of that?

PHILIP: Well, I think about the future and providing. Definitely. That's first. That's what I think about. While I'm pregnant, you know, what am I going to provide, not only financially, but emotionally, spiritually.

He continues,

So I'm just growing in a different direction now. And that doesn't mean that I don't still have my single side, and you know. But I just feel that now that I'm pregnant I'm just growing in a bit of a different direction.

ELLEN: Does that feel good?

PHILIP: It feels wonderful, like I'm just in a different chapter of my life. I'm thirty-seven, I feel grounded and secure. I feel emotionally stable, financially, I guess, as secure as I can be at this point. And ready. Like I wish it would happen tomorrow. I mean not really ready-ready, but as ready as I can be. Who's really ready?

Philip asserts that he always wanted to have children, presenting this desire as something that had never *not* been a part of him, that is, something he can't remember having to make a decision about. He grounds his account both in nature, i.e., the desire for fatherhood is intrinsic to him, and in family, as he links this impulse to his experience in his natal family. He explains, "In the back of my mind, I've always wanted to be a father because I grew up seeing my parents and just, you know, living in a family environment hoping one day to do the same." But when he first began to think that he might be gay, he worried that parenthood would be impossible, that there would simply be no way to do it. The fear that he would lose out on something so central to his self-image led him to resist being gay for some years, though he finally came out when he was almost thirty. "I don't know that I've ever *not* thought about being a dad. I grew up thinking one day I'd have a family. There was a brief period of time that I didn't think it was possible. When I finally came to terms with being gay, I wasn't sure that it was possible to be a dad. . . . I didn't think it was possible without being married. I didn't know."

Gradually, he came to realize that being gay might not be an insurmountable obstacle to fatherhood. With the help of a therapist, he came to some conclusions about how his gay identity intersected with other parts of his personhood.

When I decided that it was going to be time for me to come out, I saw a therapist. And we worked on sorting everything out, which is what you do in therapy.

And once we sorted everything out, we determined that *my gayness was not going to define me.* . . . Being gay wasn't going to get in the way of fatherhood for me. It was just an aspect of my life. I'm a man with a mission, so to speak. You know, it's a yearning to reproduce, and it's possible.

Beyond this personal revelation, Philip's model for how to become a father came not from gay friends or contacts in the gay and lesbian community ("I didn't have a wide circle of gay friends"), but from his family. He grew up in a Chicago suburb and has remained close to his parents and siblings. His sister and her husband had fertility problems and ended up having twins with a gestational surrogate, a process he followed closely as it was unfolding. He realized that he could do something similar in order to have his own children, and raised the question of having children with his long-term partner.

While this was going on with my sister and even before, I brought up to my partner that this is something that I would like to do. I didn't know how to do it. But then while my sister was going through this, I kept discussing it with him. And this is something that he ultimately chose not to participate in. And so we split up.

ELLEN: So you split up explicitly because of that?

PHILIP: No, there were other issues that I don't need to discuss. They don't have anything to do with children. But he just felt that he has nieces and nephews and that's enough for him. And they enriched his life. And they do enrich his life greatly. And they're very near and dear to him. And as a gay man he just didn't see himself in a role as a parent. And I respected that. He didn't respect, I guess, the fact that I'm . . . he felt that I was, which I was I guess, ultimately choosing a life with children over a life with him. I wanted both. We were together seven years. And I started on this journey, having children, about a year and a half ago.

Once he and his partner had split up, Philip decided he needed to find a house that would be big enough for children, and, if all went well, a future partner. He purchased the three-bedroom townhouse even before the pregnancy began, systematically putting in place all the conditions he felt would be necessary once he had a family. The house is in the heart of Boys Town, less than a block from Broadway, the main shopping street of Lakeview, where a supermarket and other stores are conveniently located. Because he started the process expecting to be a single father, he imagined that ease of shopping would be vital and that he would need a third bedroom to accommodate the fulltime help he would need. The house is also walking distance from his office, which will facilitate his coming home for lunch or for any emergencies that might arise.

Philip followed his sister's lead in pursuing surrogacy, but he also explains how important it was to him to have children that were biologically his "own." He never seriously considered any way of having children other than surrogacy because of his belief that he had something within him that would be worth passing on. This meant starting with a newborn. "And coming from me. I mean, my genes. I just felt like I had something that was good, and I want to give to my children something that's great. My own. I just wanted to. That's my first choice."

Philip was less able to control all the financial exigencies that becoming a father through surrogacy can entail, though he saved carefully for the costs he anticipated. But the process proved to be much lengthier than he had expected and the expenses have been escalating. There were three unsuccessful attempts before the current pregnancy, using a different surrogate and egg donor, and each egg retrieval and IVF attempt has been costly. Since the surrogate is carrying triplets, he is paying her a higher fee than originally planned, about $40,000, and he must travel to California, where she lives, for each medical procedure in which he wishes to participate, particularly ultrasounds. To meet some of these unexpected costs, Philip has started a second job on weekends selling real estate, supplementing his salary as a healthcare administrator. The only way for him to "economize" was on ova: he decided he really could not afford Jewish eggs, even though he would have liked his offspring to be Jewish on both sides. That would have signified "balance, for me. And harmony. There's so much you don't know about an egg donor, even though you try, you only know what's on paper and what's given to you. The comfort level for me would have been greater." Nonetheless, he managed to locate an egg donor who has two Jewish grandparents, apparently not enough Jewishness to drive up the price (and also not enough to make the offspring Jewish at birth).[1]

Philip's comments about family and his perceptions of his natural inclination to be a father resonate with stories told by fathers we have met in previous chapters. But central to these perceptions about himself is another theme, one that separates gayness and fatherhood, and locates fatherhood in the part of himself not defined by gayness. On one level, Philip understands his yearning to be a father as something deeply rooted within him. Once he discovered that "gayness doesn't define you," he felt freed to pursue parenthood. The implication is that gayness may not be similarly located deeply within his nature.

But even after disengaging his desire for fatherhood from his gayness, he still holds out hope that he will find a long-term relationship. He sees his desire for this, like that for parenthood, as rooted in his basic character, telling me that he is "a partner person." He explains what he means by this: "I just have a lot of love to share. I just like being part of a unit." But when I ask him whether it will be difficult to find a partner once he is a father, particularly of triplets, he agrees that it probably will be.

> The reality is when you're having one baby, it's a lot of work, and a lot of your—all of your—nonwork time is devoted to that one baby. But with three? Where do you find time? What do you give? When you're involved with somebody for four years and you've cemented a relationship, you can pull from and leave some in reserve with your partner. I don't know. I'm just going to have to leave it up to fate. I'm very open. And I've been dating. I don't tell people right away that I'm pregnant, because I just don't know that that's appropriate.
>
> ELLEN: What happens when you do tell them, or when do you tell them?
>
> PHILIP: Lately I've told a couple people. And I don't know. The relationship just hasn't grown or gone anywhere. But I don't know that that's necessarily because I'm pregnant.
>
> ELLEN: Are people surprised when you tell them that?
>
> PHILIP: I think a lot of gay men are surprised and a little bit in awe.

Philip's social life as a gay man has moved into a transitional state as he contemplates the birth of the triplets, and he finds himself calculating when he can share this information. At the same time, he has had to economize significantly in preparation for his family, and this has affected the way he lives as a gay man. When I ask him whether he's had to cut back on spending, he exclaims:

> PHILIP: Oh, my god, yeah. Less trips to Barney's.[2] My gosh, my spending's been cut! My budget has been trimmed! No more shoes. I really have cut back. I have to be less selfish. You know, when you're single and you're alone, you can do most things that you want for yourself. And then you just have to stop and think of somebody other than yourself. And I have to do this right away, because, you know.
>
> ELLEN: So have there been really dramatic changes?

PHILIP: I've dramatically cut back my spending. And I'm trying to become more domesticated. The meatloaf . . . [He gestures toward the kitchen, where the aroma of a meatloaf in the oven is unmistakable.]

ELLEN: So you do a lot more cooking?

PHILIP: I do a lot more cooking. I do a lot more cooking.

ELLEN: Did you used to eat out more?

PHILIP: I did. And I used to go out more socially, like to bars. Which I still do every now and then. But instead now I'm trying to increase my social circle of people similar to me. I'm making a more concerted effort to meet people more like me, so that, I don't know. Just because, I guess. I want to learn more about them and what they're going through. And how this is affecting them.

ELLEN: So more like you, you mean other dads?

PHILIP: Yeah, or other people that want to do the same thing that I want to do. Because ultimately I think it will help me make decisions for my future. I want to bounce things off these people. You know, my parents and my family are supportive. *But they're not like me.* And so, since I found out that I'm pregnant I'm trying to find and meet more people like me.

Philip's desire to find more "people like me" has solidified new relationships with other gay fathers and has strengthened his resolve to join organizations devoted to gay parenting issues. His friendship with two other gay dads, Ben and Peter (chapters 4 and 6), who are his neighbors, is important to him; he describes them as being "like brothers," and through them, he has met other gay dads, people whose goals he sees as close to his own. The image of growth, evocatively tied to pregnancy, frames his perception of how he is developing as a person.

ELLEN: So do you think this is going to make you a different sort of person than you were as a single gay man?

PHILIP: Definitely. Definitely. I think that the whole experience has strengthened me. It has strengthened me. I think it prepares you to deal with failure. Loss. Hardship. And this is something that I can hopefully pass on to my children. How to deal with circumstances in life.

Philip's story touches on virtually all the themes that I've discussed in the preceding chapters—consumption, nature, family, goodness, and the uncomfortable intersection between being gay and being a father. His journey to fatherhood has involved him in the procreative market place, with costs for genetic material and surrogate services expanding into buying a new house and contemplating hiring fulltime help. The escalating expenses have required him to think carefully about his priorities, with the choice of not-quite-Jewish eggs as a careful form of economizing. The costs have also forced him to be more careful about spending on "selfish" things—clothing and eating out are the examples he mentions—and to center his life more domestically. He sees the procreative process and his future life as a father as the foundation of a kind of moral maturity, as he lets go of the self-indulgent spending habits of a single[3] man and settles into a more thrifty domestic life with old-fashioned dishes like meatloaf symbolizing a new simplicity. His changing consumption patterns coalesce in a picture of family-centered life that will nurture his basic nature; this trajectory is supported by his firm belief that gayness does not define him. But fatherhood and domesticity, like gayness, have to be performed if they are to be convincing, so Philip has devoted more than a little energy to putting the symbols of family life in place.

Philip understands his parental yearnings as driven by nature, as a fundamental part of who he is, and by his location in a close natal family. His concern with nature also emerges in his commitment to have children using his own genetic material; he seems to feel that this urge to recreate one's family line is a fact of life that requires no explanation. In other words, Philip's commitment to fatherhood is largely supported by an acceptance of "nature" as the force moving the project ahead, an explanation that is simply obvious and taken for granted. According to this construction, gayness is located at some distance from family, possibly as something artificially imposed on top of one's basic character. Philip takes some pains to reject what he calls selfishness, including much of what he understands as gay in this category. Gayness, in his calculation, is most clearly enacted in consumption activities (shopping at Barney's) and in time spent away from home (eating out). Fatherhood, now framed as natural, is performed by economizing and eating in, activities that connote a kind of moral responsibility, not easily accessible when one is pursuing the life of a single gay man.[4]

Making Space for the "Yucky People"

The preceding chapters have brought the existence of gay fathers into focus, offering us a glimpse of the complex details that make up their personal narratives—their accounts of how and why they became parents, how they have navigated around the obstacles they have faced, and most important, what these experiences tell us about their understandings of themselves. Gay fathers, as I have noted, confront a phalanx of practical challenges surrounding their desire to bring children into their lives, challenges that require financial calculation, but also careful consideration of how to present and perform themselves in the worlds of adoption and assisted reproduction.

As daunting as these obstacles may be, gay fathers must also negotiate a set of cultural exigencies that punctuate their every move. On the one hand, in a culture that gives scant recognition and respect to same-sex couples and has only grudgingly decriminalized homosexual behaviors, gay men who wish to be fathers must manage the suspicion and hostility they are likely to meet as they explore adoption and assisted reproduction. Once they have achieved parenthood, they may continue to confront ignorance and sexism from those who think men, and especially gay men, cannot or ought not to be parents. While they may reasonably expect to encounter hostility in interactions with the mainstream heteronormative world, they also painfully learn that gay men and lesbians may be as likely to hold them at arm's length as those more obvious opponents. As I have emphasized in this book, gay men who seek to establish families through fatherhood must handle the skepticism of the gay communities they thought they belonged to, often reflected in inflammatory discourse produced by queer activists and scholars.

These are not just intellectual problems; the doubts the activists and scholars articulate are grounded in normative assumptions about the opposition between "family" and "queerness." That these normative assumptions echo the very same views that fuel homophobia is ironic, but perhaps not unexpected. Queer ideas and so-called mainstream beliefs are more deeply interwoven than either group would like to acknowledge. Opponents of gay and lesbian family rights firmly believe that what they see as the hypersexual and transgressive nature of same-sex relationships sullies the virtues they associate with marriage and family. This view helps explain the seeming illogic of the Defense of Marriage Act (DOMA): how can keeping people from marrying "defend" marriage as an institution? The answer lies in the cultural trappings of marriage, and by extension parenthood, as imbued with a sort of transcendent purity, as untouched by motivations deemed to be crass or materialistic. Never mind that the history of marriage and reproduction has much to do with securing economic advantages and populating a productive work force.

But virtually the same views, albeit framed in terms of a different set of priorities, characterize the position I have called (for the sake of simplicity) "queer fundamentalism." In this case, however, the direction that pollution is thought to flow is seemingly reversed. These adversaries believe that the purity and altruism they attribute to marriage and family will seep into the character of queer people, contaminating homosexuality by making it less transgressive and less culturally particular. Taking a hint from the right wing, they have framed the struggle as a culture war between convention and transgression, viewing these two impulses as incommensurable. Such convergences between the views of putatively opposing political positions are less uncommon than might be thought. Anthropologist Faye Ginsburg (1989) demonstrates dramatic overlaps between the "procreation stories" crafted by both pro-choice and anti-abortion activists in Fargo, North Dakota. In her recent study of the political debates surrounding surrogate motherhood in the U.S., sociologist Susan Markens (2007) describes similar findings. Those who oppose the legalization of surrogacy contracts and those who have worked to legitimize such arrangements both draw on similar ideological positions grounded in conservative constructions of gender and parenthood and a concern with "the plight of the infertile," coupled with anxiety over what they view as the commercialization of reproduction.

Both forms of opposition may prompt gay fathers to bifurcate their understandings of gayness and parenthood, resulting in sometimes unexpected definitions of which parts of their divided selves are construed as more authentic and "natural." Nature is commonly invoked as a way to explain yearnings and activities that stand in seeming contradiction to queerness. Whether queerness is then coded as "unnatural" is not clear. Fathers like Tony and Jeff Pearl (chapter 3), for example, understand the desire to procreate biologically to be a simple human urge that requires no special explanation. Their status as fathers links them to generational bonds that otherwise might have been elusive and helps them to forge relationships across the gay-straight divide. Both capacities are naturally human, so this reading of their new ability to cross boundaries implies that gayness before children might have been limiting and might have distanced them from fundamental connections.

For Matt Parker (chapter 3), fatherhood is something that he sees as having just sort of happened to him, without explicit planning, so he is inclined to view everything that has since occurred as simply preordained: "I always say that there's a purpose, so there must have been some reason he [his first son] came home that day." The end point for him has been to be a single father of three, to have a social life largely made up of soccer games and juvenile movies, and to have intensified his already close relationship with his natal family. He sees this as appropriate, both because he has been able to provide a warm home life for children who would otherwise have languished in the foster care system ("I'd rather have a child of Malcolm or Karim's age and stabilize their life than a baby"), and because it is appropriate to a man in his late forties. When I ask about whether he thinks he will settle down with another partner, he responds, "I'm forty-eight. I don't feel like I need to anymore." His judgment that future romance is unlikely is based not only on the fact of his parenthood ("With kids the traditional reaction I get is, 'Oh, this is wonderful.' They'd kind of dig being a parent. And that will usually last a day or two and then it's like, 'Can't you get a sitter for that kid?' "), but on his chronological age. Aging is inevitable and seen as supremely natural, dictating what is appropriate and interesting at its own relentless pace.

In many of these accounts, the force of nature is mysterious, revealed as such because it is not consciously preplanned. Andrew Spain's story (chapters 2 and 3) exemplifies this understanding of the natural as something that defies explanation. The realization that he should pursue fatherhood, which he describes as having come upon him out of the blue after seeing an ad in the *Chicago Reader* ("It was like a neon sign"), simply emerged from an ineffable source that he instantly recognized as being the right thing for him. His emphasis on the lack of conscious planning involved in the basic decision suggests that he imagines forethought as somehow impure, sullied by suggestions of consumption or personal advantage, almost outweighing the careful strategizing he proudly describes having undertaken to get the child he recognized as his own. It seems that maneuvering in service of something that has mysterious roots doesn't undermine the fundamental naturalness of his commitment to this particular child.

This reliance on nature to excuse unexpected behaviors operates in precarious harmony with the other typical invocation of nature: as an explanation for being gay in the first place. The simultaneous geneticization of self and family thus ensnares gay fathers in a perplexing contradiction, though they rarely seem to engage with it directly. Can your DNA explain your sexuality as well as your desire to be a parent? Are both directions equally natural? Can nature, in other words, charter both conventional and transgressive behavior?

The dichotomization of gayness and family emerges in these pages as a key element of how fathers account for themselves and their decisions. It some instances, as we saw in chapter 6, parenthood lifts men out of their location in gay life, however they conceptualize that, offering them a chance to move beyond what they perceive as the moral and social drawbacks imposed by being gay. Some fathers are amazed that other people treat them as "normal," that they can fit into communities they had assumed would disparage them; in some instances, they perceive this as a source of pride, while other men I interviewed are ambivalent about its long-term meaning.

At the same time, however, it is not unusual for fathers to declare their new lives as parents to be morally superior to being gay—less selfish, more adult, more constructive. These men often disparage gay life as frivolous and lacking in real significance, as does Lawrence Lock (chapters 5 and 6). Lawrence understands his decision to parent two severely disabled boys as something God brought him to, in part to help him resolve the moral dilemma presented by being gay, but also to provide him with a vehicle for all the love he had to offer. He explains that fatherhood has allowed him to do something "important," rather than "wasting [time] on entertainment things." The implicit link between "entertainment things" and his understanding of what gay life is all about, heavily influenced by his experience of bar life, reveals a belittlement of gayness as spiritually empty.

In a similar strategy, Dennis Caruso and Harvey Stone offer an account of a search for authenticity, a desire to be "down to earth" that puts their lives at odds with the artificiality of the White Party and associated gay pastimes. While achieving the kind of solidity they seek doesn't require parenthood, becoming fathers can clearly facilitate their ability to be socially responsible in a way they associate with long-term family loyalties and being located in a community broader than the gay world they question.

In the case of some fathers, like Len Olson, gayness is recalled nostalgically, as something linked to an iconic gay pastime—opera attendance—that is no longer a central part of his life. Opera is simply too expensive, too time consuming, and too tiring to be a frequent activity for Len and his partner now that they are the parents of a toddler. It doesn't seem as important as it once did now that they have other things to focus on. But it lives on as a memory of what it was like to be gay on a full-time basis, recalled much as one might ponder any of one's youthful exploits, a remnant of a time before the arrival of major responsibilities. Again, the implication here is that gayness and parenthood are sharply at odds with one another, practically but also morally.

In still other instances, the presumed disconnect between fatherhood and gayness provides the punch line for an ongoing gay dad joke. Paul O'Hara and Keith Michaels (chapter 6) wryly comment on their present lives as being defined by "kids' nap time," knowing full well that their status as gay has not been simply erased by fatherhood. They are both activists in gay parenting organizations, involved in planning get-togethers and networking for gay and lesbian parents, and in taking stands on issues they see as important for their families. Paul and Keith are acutely aware of their precarious social standing, and of the tenuousness of their links with nongay parents. They are also alert to their problematic status among gay people who are not parents, and their quip about no longer being gay resonates with bitterness at the fact of their exclusion.

That some of the fathers construct gayness as not only incompatible with fatherhood (as Joe O'Reilly explained in chapter 6), but as morally inferior to it, suggests that these men are not only responding to definitions of queerness as antifamily, but have steeped their identities in toxic conceptions of gay life. That is, they seem to share assumptions pervasive in the antigay world that gay life is frivolous, self-indulgent, and ultimately meaningless, assumptions that are only partially restated in the writings of some queer scholars and activists. These narratives depend heavily on associations between consumption and gay life, assuming that a never-ending search for entertainment or for high-quality shopping is a fundamental engine of queer existence. As Jesse Green wrote it in his memoir of gay fatherhood, "Without a child you were always a child: a hanger-on, an exile, a zero" (1999, 96).

These dichotomous readings of "family" and "gayness" are not the only cultural challenges gay fathers face. Gay and lesbian people who are working class or poor (or sometimes just middle class), who are not white, and who maintain connections with social and cultural institutions outside the confines of "queer life" all risk erasure in a system that confounds sexual difference and affluence (Badgett 2001; Maskovsky 2002). Gay and lesbian family studies has not been the only field that has been banished to the category of "yucky" in the calculus of queer fundamentalism. Religion and spirituality have received less attention than they should, apparently based on the same sort of assumptions that have pushed gay and lesbian family life to the margins.[5] It is noteworthy in this context that many U.S. denominations have been roiled by controversies over their treatment of

gay members, their position on gay weddings and commitment ceremonies, and their stance on gay and lesbian clergy. Some of these struggles
appear to have the potential to cause major denominational rifts, perhaps
the most intense since Northern and Southern Protestants split over the
issue of slavery around the time of the U.S. Civil War (Gaede 1999; Grenz
1998; Hartman 1997; Siker 1994; Wink 1999). Despite how far-reaching
these controversies have been, however, serious discussion of them has
been limited, in large part, to religious-studies scholarship, studies that
focus on particular denominational issues, and personal commentary.

Along similar lines, political conservatism among gays and lesbians has
been decried by queer scholars, but has rarely inspired serious investigation. The existence of the Log Cabin Republicans (an organization of gay
Republicans), the doctrinal variations among lesbian and gay activists, and
the formation of the Independent Gay Forum (supported by such gay conservative icons as Bruce Bawer, Andrew Sullivan, and Jonathan Rauch)
are all in the peripheral vision of queer fundamentalists, brought forward
occasionally for purposes of criticism and then consigned to relative ob-
scurity (Duggan 2003). But such commentary rarely considers whether
gay and lesbian conservatism might deserve examination as something
other than betrayal.

The location of lesbians and gay men in so-called mainstream communities—small towns, suburbs, or urban neighborhoods not identified as
gay ghettoes—has also received less equitable examination than it merits,
even as geographers like Gary Gates and popular writer Neil Miller have
documented the wide distribution of lesbian and gay populations in what
are perhaps unexpected locales (Fellows 1998; Gates and Ost 2004; Howard
2001; Miller 1989).[6] And although there have been some studies of aging
among gay people, including personal memoirs, and there has been activism directed toward providing gay-friendly geriatric care, older gay men
and lesbians rarely receive the attention their numbers mandate, particularly as members of the baby boom reach their later years (Kimmel, Rose,
and David 2006). These (partial) erasures reinforce stereotyped views of
gays and lesbians as young, urban, white, affluent, frivolous, politically lib-
eral, and religiously uninvolved, even as those of us who study "the yucky
people" are well aware of how limited such stereotypes are.

What does it mean to be gay or lesbian in these circumstances? The works
that have looked at some of these populations—rural residents, working-
class gays, gays of color (Carrington 1999; Fellows 1998; Hawkeswood
1996; Miller 1989)—point to a way of life that is sometimes bifurcated into

"gay" and "nongay" elements, and sometimes comfortably integrated. What the research does show is that living in bounded gay communities with little involvement with nongay worlds is enabled in large part by privilege (Maskovsky 2002), although research on the most marginalized and impoverished queer populations—street fairies, transgender prostitutes, and others who refuse or are unable to accommodate to the straight world—suggests that intensely ghettoized existences may also be linked with poverty (Newton 1972; Valentine 2007), not only for gay, lesbian, and transgender adults, but for youth (Gray 1999; Peacock 2006; Peacock et al. 2001). Many gay men and lesbians cannot afford to live in high-priced gay neighborhoods, need to maintain solidarity with kin to manage day-to-day obligations, and experience themselves as having complicated identities and loyalties. Those gay men who become (or remain) parents exemplify the need to breach boundaries on a constant basis. They have no choice but to confront the issues I have addressed in these pages: does parenthood demand transferring loyalties to "nongay" domains, and if so, do gay fathers experience such shifts as dislocating or stressful, or perhaps as gratifying? What might it mean to suddenly have something significant in common with neighbors who are parents, or to have formerly tenuous kin relations blossom into true affection and support? What sorts of numbers of gay fathers might constitute a "critical mass" that would alter all of these meanings?

As we have seen, such shifts are not undertaken in the absence of more pervasive values, and not surprisingly, gay men are as likely as anyone else to ascribe moral superiority to activities and relationships viewed as nongay (or nonsexual). This seems to be especially true when these nongay activities have to do with parenting. In their accounts, fathers emphasize how parenting brings out their best qualities, allowing them to access their capacity for selflessness in ways rarely possible (though the AIDS epidemic also called for many of these virtues to be expressed). When men become parents of children otherwise discarded by the system, those devalued and despised because of their age, race, or health status, they feel that they are doing something quite beyond simply acquiring a family—they are serving the wider society. The kind of love the fathers of the conventionally unlovable bear for their children reverses the value systems that measure children in terms of how much they approximate some standard of "excellence." They subvert the wider culture of consumption far more explicitly than through confrontational queerness. And beyond this, they deal a fundamental blow to the exclusionary binaries that have confined gay and lesbian people to what is for some a barren ghetto. The expectations for rebellion that confine this ghetto lose their allure for men who have plunged into what they experience as the real-life business of parenting.

Of course, all these judgments are artificial constructions. Being a father is not concretely superior to attending the opera; having an all-gay social circle is not intrinsically more outrageous than hanging out with other parents whose children are the playmates of your children. Nor is attending a school picnic fundamentally more conformist than participating in a protest, particularly if one's inclusion in the former event only recently became feasible. Engaging in queer political protest is important, but so is working with your neighbors to get a traffic light installed at a dangerous intersection. The moral evaluations that attach to all these activities and that rank them are no more authoritative than a preference for tortillas instead of bread, wine instead of water, or classical music over country western. The meaning of any of these activities, or of any cultural preferences, is not embedded in the material of the behavior, but in the intentions that shape it.

Lessons from Gay Fathers

Do the struggles of gay fathers bring into focus ongoing issues facing families in the United States? First, the concerns gay fathers have expressed in these pages speak to the ongoing salience of the family as a moral universe that embodies fundamental values and alliances, but one that cannot be automatically accessed. Choosing the side of family allows a stance in support of long-term commitments, an allegiance to history, a protest against superficial fads or self-indulgence. Whether or not any of these public virtues has any actual connection to parenthood—and I would insist that none of them necessarily do—they are read in that way by citizens at large and by many gay men along with them, as they are, indeed, by the queer activists and scholars who have positioned themselves at odds with gay and lesbian family aspirations. At a moment when being gay is invoked in popular discourse as a code for irresponsibility, profligacy, and selfishness, gay fathers and gay men who aspire to fatherhood can stake a claim to a different moral terrain just by declaring their desire to parent. Whether there are wider audiences that are listening to these claims is another matter; the controversies that continue to rage over gay and lesbian family forms suggest that there is no consensus over the ability of people who are openly nonheterosexual to achieve the virtues of parenthood in the same way that (presumably) heterosexual married couples are simply assumed to be able to do.

Beyond this particular contentious debate, however, the emerging visibility of gay fathers suggests a need for significant rethinking of what we mean by "mother" as an identity and by "mothering" as an activity, as well as of the connection of "mothering" to the shape of gender as a cultural system. This is not a new discussion: feminists in the second wave, as was noted earlier, have developed a cottage industry of sorts in the business of predicting what would be needed to undermine the conflation of "woman" and "mother," thereby sabotaging the foundations of gender as a system of inequality and injustice. In many different contexts over the last four decades, we have heard pleas for men to take their rightful place in the business of childcare, to reveal their hidden abilities as nurturers, and to accept the impediments such commitments might erect to full competition in the (more prestigious and economically rewarding) public domain. As we learned in chapter 1, efforts to make parenting more egalitarian have had only mixed results; the connection between motherhood and the devalued domestic domain remains firm even as alternatives to gender dichotomies have been proposed and promoted to various constituencies.

But here come gay fathers, yearning for a chance to raise a child from infancy, to rescue a child from the dead end of the foster care system, to offer a child from a third-world country an opportunity to live a more privileged existence, to sustain a relationship with a child from an earlier heterosexual union, or to struggle to create a child from their own genetic material. These are certainly not the only men in the U.S. who have sought to achieve these objectives, but the fact that they launch their quests from the position of being gay men or gay couples deserves particular attention. Are they more able to articulate their desire to be parents because of their distance from conventional sexual subjectivities? Do their efforts represent a protest against gender constraints? Or, as some queer critics would argue, are they just trying to fit into a world that will never actually accept them?

The accounts that have filled this book point to something less dramatic as the source of gay men's new prominence as parents, something that adds up to neither accommodation nor resistance. Gay men's desires for parenthood seem to derive from their solid connection to the larger culture, a connection, I would suggest, that has never been completely absent even when it appeared to have been definitively severed. What do gay men seek in parenthood? We have seen again and again that they are struggling to define themselves as authentic members of families, that they are seeking ways to incorporate themselves into compelling accounts of natural processes, and that they are examining ways to carve out moral careers that contradict images of gay people as lacking in virtue and altruism. Because of their central connection to the values that are key motifs in U.S. culture, they draw on some of the same assertions that are characteristic of the wider scene: they conflate gayness and selfishness, they see adulthood as stymied in the absence of children, they assume that they cannot make true contributions to the society without propelling another generation into existence.

These associations are not evidence of homophobia or wholesale surrender into the hands of conventional society, much as some might identify them as such. They are, rather, evidence that gay men are now, and have always been, part of the larger story. What has changed, it seems, is their ability to act on their involvement and articulate their citizenship. So in this sense, the struggle for family, the yearning to constitute a unit that extends back in history and forward into unimaginable futures is a locus for the expression of citizenship. It is an arena in which claims are made, even when that arena will also host contests requiring strength and skill, contests that will sometimes be won and sometimes be lost.

Gay fathers' narratives emerge in the preceding chapters as multilayered accounts that can simultaneously tell several stories. Some of the threads that the men weave into their accounts are strategic, meant to tell the interviewer (myself) what they think I should know about them, about parenthood, or about the larger world. They may be intended to draw attention to their moral strengths or may instead seek to elicit sympathy for their vulnerabilities and misfortunes. Alternatively, they may embody performances of various qualities: irony, intellectual acuity, political principle, or belonging to some specific group. Some of the stories emerged in a context of intimacy and sharing; some assumed distance based on my difference from their positions in the world. On the one hand, as a lesbian who has built my career on writing about lesbian and gay family issues, some fathers saw me as a sympathetic figure, someone who would readily understand them. But others, no doubt, saw me as different in critical ways from themselves: I am much older than almost all of the men I interviewed; I am a woman; I am white and Jewish and speak with a distinct New York accent. And most importantly, I am not and never have been a parent. I can only guess how any of these attributes shaped the content of the narratives I recorded or the motivation of the men to want to share their experiences with me.

At the same time that the struggle for families speaks to larger demands for full citizenship and visibility, and that this struggle incorporates values that are central to the wider culture, it also reveals fault lines in the society. Family formation is a process that involves choices, even when such choices are implicit and defy expression. Those seeking families make decisions that enhance their acceptance of nature as the arbiter of when they shall be parents and that lead to reproduction having specific forms and distribution. Gay men and lesbians are not the only Americans who face obstacles to parenthood. Infertile people whose resources allow them access to technological assistance also must struggle to become parents. But less visible are the difficulties faced by the poor, by persons of color, by immigrants and others whose economic and/or racial situations make their family aspirations less central to national priorities, who are unlikely to be given access to assisted reproductive technologies or to adoption.

In other words, reproduction is everywhere a stratified process (Ginsburg and Rapp 1995), not only because of larger patterns of social valuation, but because of the racialized desires that underpin efforts to reproduce. Gay men, like other potential parents, imagine their families in terms of what they will look like and strategize to form families based on the particular visualization of "family" that they decide to pursue. All of these processes are necessarily implicated in wider patterns of consumption, whether the mechanisms have to do with promoting or preventing biological reproduction, or whether they have to do with accessing various modes of adoption. No one is exempt from these impulses, even when they fail to notice their influence on the decisions they make or on outcomes that seem to emerge without conscious decision making. Gay men and gay fathers share in these contradictory processes, and in so doing also share in the broader sweep of American culture at the start of the twenty-first century.

Notes

Prologue

1. Robson refers here to the many pungent feminist critiques of marriage from both the first and second waves of feminism. There was also a "free-love" tradition that paralleled first-wave feminism espoused by such figures as Victoria Woodhull and Emma Goldman (Goldman 1970; Goldsmith 1999; Passet 2003; Woodhull 2005).

2. See also Giddens (1993, 2002) on the notion that gay people are more likely than heterosexuals to be "pioneers in exploring the new world of [democratic] relationships and exploring its possibilities . . . [because] gays weren't able to depend upon the normal support of traditional marriage" (2002, 64).

3. Since many gay fathers I interviewed were motivated to move to suburbs after they had children, I can only assume that men with children didn't register as "gay" in his search for subjects.

4. The figure of the outlaw is sometimes valorized as the supreme icon of American individualist expression. The ways in which the mythology of the outlaw, along with other solitary heroes who are imagined as flourishing in the frontier, emerge as cultural insignia are discussed in Richard Slotkin's seminal work (1973).

Chapter One

1. Just before completion of this book, a story about a "pregnant man" got prominent play in the media. An appearance on *Oprah*, videos available on YouTube and other Internet sites, and magazine coverage all presented the story of Thomas Beatie, a female-to-male transgendered individual who had retained his female reproductive organs despite undergoing a sex change. When his wife was unable to conceive, he suspended testosterone treatments, resumed his female reproductive cycle, and was able to become pregnant through donor insemination.

While this story is not particularly remarkable from a biological point of view, Beatie's characterization as a pregnant man was presented in a way that suggested a process both miraculous and bizarre (Beatie 2008).

2. This episode calls attention to a wider pattern that appears in custody and other disputes between former lesbian or gay spouses. Couples have available to them discourses that either denaturalize the status of a partner as not being a "real" parent, or, like Meehan and Dysarz, trade on assumptions about gay couples engaging in violent or pathological sexual behavior. See, for example, Liptak 2006.

3. The examples from anthropology are almost too numerous to choose a citation, but some interesting treatments include Carsten 2000 and Schneider 1984. Historians, too, have written prolifically in this area. See, for example, Coontz 2005; Shorter 1975.

4. Recent historical research has documented these patterns, particularly the tendency of many lesbians and gay men to lead "double lives" that involved marriage and parenthood. These family arrangements were the foundation for later custody battles and activism on the part of lesbian mothers and gay fathers as early as the 1970s.

5. While concerns about legal rights in the absence of same-sex marriage continue to preoccupy many gays and lesbians, many now perceive battles for gay rights as having been won, making such events as gay pride parades far less relevant than they once were (*Economist* 2007).

6. It is worth noting that these assumptions about gay men and HIV/AIDS contrast with equally unjustifiable assumptions about lesbians having no risk for the disease. Whether these assumptions reflect a tendency to desexualize lesbians (and other women), or whether other dynamics underlie them, they have the effect of detracting from efforts to provide HIV/AIDS services and education to lesbians.

7. These generalizations do not apply to the enslaved portion of the U.S. population, where fatherhood and motherhood were configured very differently (Gutman 1977).

8. This is just one strand of the numerous feminist critiques that took up the issue of gender inequality in the family. Famously, many writing in the early years of the second wave called for the abolition of the family or for women to remove themselves completely from reproductive and domestic labor. See, for example, Firestone (1970) and Barrett and McIntosh (1982). In an influential discussion of gender stratification, Mary O'Brien (1981) argued that men's alienation from reproduction lies at the heart of men's oppression of women. Early cross-cultural studies by anthropologists argued that reproductive and childrearing responsibilities gave rise to women's exclusion from high-prestige, and possibly dangerous, economic activities (Brown 1970); others have framed the issue in terms of the symbolic associations of women and "nature" (Ortner 1974) as the consequence of the bifurcation of space into domestic and public, with domestic space being de-

voted to childcare, among other tasks. Being located in the domestic sphere, in this accounting, prevents women from establishing extradomestic alliances essential to gaining political influence (M. Z. Rosaldo 1974).

9. Ideals of "shared parenting" as a way to undermine gender inequality have circulated in both popular and academic domains since the 1970s. One of the first major phrasings of these ideas in feminist writing is that of Nancy Chodorow, who argued that the personality patterns associated with conventional gender divisions—particularly those marked by women exhibiting more intensely nurturing behavior than men—could be traced to the fact that women are "everywhere" the primary socializers of children. Using a psychoanalytic framework, later criticized for referring narrowly to an idealized white and middle-class Western family, she argued that this configuration repeats itself in each generation and that only a major change in the dynamics of childrearing, i.e., one that moved men into primary caretaking roles, would offer an opportunity to interrupt the cycle, inexorable though it seemed to be (Chodorow 1978).

In another influential and often-cited work, philosopher Sara Ruddick (Ruddick 1989) argued that motherhood is best thought of as a set of practices that give rise to what she called "maternal thinking," a set of preoccupations that emphasize the nurturance and protection of children. Because of their concern with the survival and growth of their children, women—as mothers—are particularly inclined in Ruddick's view toward nonviolence and the pursuit of peace. While this perspective was read as essentialist by many critics, and as class-based by others, Ruddick was careful to connect these inclinations to maternal practices rather than personalities, hence suggesting that men could be equally peace-oriented if only they became primary providers of maternal care (Ruddick 1989). Neither Chodorow nor Ruddick proposed specific strategies for drawing men into the day-to-day business of childrearing, or even for making such activities more attractive to men, although a purposeful interruption of prevailing patterns seemed to be essential to disrupting the conventionally gendered parental practices they criticized.

10. Ehrensaft's work was echoed in a well-known study by Arlie Hochschild with Anne Machung, *The Second Shift*, which documented the resilience of conventionally gendered patterns of domestic labor even among couples who claimed that their arrangements were egalitarian. In the families Hochschild and Machung studied, equality proved to be a label attached to particular patterns rather than a literal account of how time and effort were allocated, with the desire to claim equality being more predictive of normative claims than observable behavior (Hochschild 1989).

11. In earlier research on formerly married mothers, both heterosexual and lesbian, I found that a marker of successful motherhood was provision of an engaged father (Lewin 1993).

12. Child custody conventions have not always assumed that mothers are the most appropriate custodial parents. As they have evolved, they have proven to

be a sensitive indicator of other social and economic processes and particularly of women's status in any particular historical period (Mason 1994).

13. A 1993 ruling by the state appeals court in Florida held that the ban could be justified because homosexual parents are unlikely to be able to give heterosexual children sound dating advice.

14. National Adoption Information Clearinghouse, Cost of Adopting [updated Aug. 2, 2000], available at http://costs.adoption.com/articles/the-costs-of-adopting-a-factsheet-for-families.html#intro, accessed December 11, 2008.

15. See http://adoption.about.com/od/financialmatters/a/domadoptcost.htm, accessed July 10, 2007. As of this writing these costs could run as low as $5,000 but sometimes as high as $40,000.

16. "The guidelines include a requirement that applicants have a body-mass index of less than 40, no criminal record, a high school diploma and be free of certain health problems like AIDS and cancer. Couples must have been married for at least two years and have had no more than two divorces between them. If either spouse was previously divorced, the couple cannot apply until they have been married for at least five years. In addition, adoptive parents must have a net worth of at least $80,000 and income of at least $10,000 per person in the household, including the prospective adoptive child. Parents can be as old as 55 if adopting a child with special needs" (Belluck and Yardley 2006).

17. The costs for such adoptions in 2005, according to the U.S. Department of State, ranged from $17,300 to $45,000, with expenses to parents averaging $27,000 (http://travel.state.gov/family/adoption/country/country_389.html, accessed July 10, 2007).

18. All of the overseas adoptions except one were undertaken in Guatemala; one man adopted a child from Russia.

19. There is now a substantial literature on reflexivity in anthropology that takes up this issue in detail. See, for example, Behar 1997; Ruby 1982; Salzman 2002; Turner and Bruner 1986.

Chapter Two

1. This was also a theme in some of the stories gay men and lesbians told me about having commitment ceremonies or weddings. These ritual occasions were often seen as markers of achieving full adulthood (Lewin 1998). Judith Halberstam (2005) frames the association between queerness and adolescence differently, arguing that "queer subcultures offer us an opportunity to redefine the binary of adolescence and adulthood" (161) in ways that allow for "the refusal of adulthood and new modes of deliberate deviance" (174). From this perspective, not being regarded as fully adult appears as the outcome of an affirmative strategy. Historically, however, the linkage between homosexuality and immaturity has been cast in

less benign, indeed pathological, terms. As Jennifer Terry documents in her study of scientific and medical understandings of homosexuality, a recurring theme has been the notion that homosexuality represents "arrested development" or some other type of psychosexual immaturity. The rationales behind these theories vary. Freud's perspective was that "sexual pleasure not ultimately oriented toward reproduction represented immaturity" (Terry 1999, 60). Some later psychiatric theories equated homosexuality with promiscuity and, as such, saw it as "an immature refusal on the part of the subjects to settle down and take on the responsibilities of adulthood—that is, stable marriage for the purposes of reproduction" (Terry 1999, 248). All of these approaches normatively situate homosexuality as indicative of immaturity "measured against the ideal endpoint of a healthy maturation process: adult reproductive heterosexuality, comprised of complementary male and female partners, preferably sealed in a bond of marriage" (Terry 1999, 275). These views prescribe marriage and reproduction as the only appropriate path to achieving recognizable adulthood; the fact that gay men and lesbians tend to be preoccupied with this issue—even sometimes embracing "immaturity" as resistance—ought not to be surprising.

2. See Gail Landsman (2004) on disabled children as "lemons."

3. An influential approach proposed by Nancy Chodorow (1978) tried to resolve the question of why, given all these drawbacks, women want to be mothers, locating the engine that drives "the reproduction of mothering" in universal psychodynamic patterns. These conclusions have been controversial, both because of their failure to consider material forces that might be involved in configuring families and because of their foundation in the experience of Western, middle-class women. But the question of motivation remains compelling, perhaps more so as developing procreative and adoption technologies have complicated reproductive decision-making processes, making them more explicit and largely robbing reproduction of the accidental component that has been so long part of how it is conventionally imagined.

4. An abundant popular literature dealing with adoption and assisted reproduction is animated with themes that illustrate the collision of emotion and consumption in the process of becoming a parent. The authors of many of these works report a heroic process of overcoming adversity, gaining the sought-after result, and, in essence, living happily ever after. They highlight the importance of personal resilience, dedication to testify to the struggle to form a family as a search for the "right" child, even as whatever child is acquired is nearly always understood to embody the child they were meant to have (Aizley 2003; Green 1999; Orenstein 2007; Savage 1999). An analysis of this genre of personal narrative goes far beyond the objectives of this book; suffice it to say that authors share preoccupations with discerning the role of fate in the final resolution of their search for a child, thus imbuing the entire process with an aura of mystical preordination. The assumption that "things happen for a reason," to quote a popular saying that has come to be

a cliché, situates the entire venture beyond the reach of human intervention, and thus indisputably natural.

5. Figures from the Evan B. Donaldson Adoption Institute indicate that nonwhite families in the U.S. are more likely to adopt children related to them, often doing so informally or with minimal contact with the legal system. Nonwhite mothers are also less likely to surrender unwanted children for adoption, though white mothers have also become more likely to keep out-of-wedlock children instead of giving them up (Pertman 2000).

6. This is an interesting reversal of the widespread preference for boys when couples are going through pregnancy with their own genetic material. There has been considerable speculation about the preference for girls in adoption, with at least some indications that girls are expected to be less aggressive than boys and therefore less likely to engage in undesirable or dangerous behavior. These concerns underscore the anxieties that accompany adopting a child who doesn't share the parents' DNA or who might have been traumatized in ways that would foster aggression. A particular apprehension seems to attach to African American boys, who potential adopters fear will be either dangerous or endangered. (See Barbara Katz Rothman 2005, esp. 8).

7. The reluctance of prospective parents who are white to adopt children of color is reflected in adoption statistics, although a growing proportion of adoptions do cross racial lines (Pertman 2000). Despite the large number of nonwhite children awaiting permanent placements, statistics indicate that an estimated 15 percent of the 36,000 adoptions of foster children in 1998 were transracial or transcultural adoptions (Pertman 2000).

These figures indicate that only about 19,000 of the 127,000 foster children waiting for permanent placements are adopted each year. According to the U.S. Department of Health and Human Services's Adoption and Foster Care Analysis and Reporting System (AFCARS 2006), some 581,000 children were in foster care in 1999, the last year for which firm figures are available. Of these, 22 percent, or 127,000 children, had been cleared for adoption. In 1992, the National Center for State Courts (NCSC) gathered adoption totals from a variety of sources, and estimated that 126,951 children were adopted through international, foster care, private agency, independent and stepparent adoptions. The NCSC estimated that stepparent adoptions accounted for 42 percent of all adoptions, and foster care adoptions accounted for 15 percent (Flango and Flango 1995). A substantial proportion of adoptions occur outside this system, including international, stepparent, and domestic private adoptions. But while numbers of international adoptions have grown at a rapid pace, amounting to the largest absolute number among Western countries, they still amount to only about 5 percent of all adoptions in the U.S. (Gailey 2000; Selman 2000).

8. It is also possible for parents who adopt from foster care to apply for state subsidies to reimburse them for one-time adoption expenses (such as court costs

and attorney fees). When children are eligible for federal assistance prior to adoption, that eligibility may carry over after adoption. See "Adopting a Child with Special Needs," Adoption.com, http://library.adoption.com/articles/adopting-a-child-with-special-needs-2.html, accessed December 13, 2008.

9. See Gail Landsman (1999) on the notion that a disabled child is a "gift."

10. Writings, many based in personal experience, on transnational and transracial adoption speak to the intense scrutiny families experience when children and parents do not "resemble" each other. This issue arises, as well, for families formed through gamete donation, and can be a source of considerable anxiety as families move about in public places. See Becker, Butler, and Nachtigall 2005; Orenstein 2007; Register 1990; Rothman 2005.

11. See Carney 2007. The article points out that many newborns are available domestically, but almost solely through the mechanism of private adoption. Costs for such adoptions average $5,000 to $30,000, and 31 percent of parents work with more than one birth mother before securing a child. Half of these adoptions are of white infants.

12. Recent high-profile adoption cases (e.g., Madonna, Angelina Jolie and Brad Pitt) suggest that foreign-born black children have an allure not possessed by U.S.-born blacks who find themselves in the foster care system.

13. The desire of white parents to find a child who resembles them has made Romania, Russia, Ukraine, and other countries in Eastern Europe important sources for children despite the health problems these children have been reported to suffer. As of 2001, Russia was the second-largest source of overseas adoptions to the U.S., surpassed only by China (http://www.adoptioninstitute.org/research/adoptionfacts/php, accessed December 13, 2008).

14. In a provocative discussion of whether the emotional significance of having children resembles that associated with having pets, Nancy Folbre (2001) points out that children do have economic utility on a broader, societal level. That is, reproduction is essential to the health of the economy and to the ability of older generations to be assured of support in their later years. Seen from this angle, not everyone has to have their own children, but everyone benefits from other people having children. While pets may provide most of the emotional benefits one seeks in children, their impact is on their owners alone; they do not produce advantages that affect the larger community.

15. The ways in which pregnant women interpret even ambiguous ultrasound images to be their "babies" have been widely discussed in the feminist literature on reproductive technologies. Such images are commonly treated analogously to photographs, finding their place in family albums and often having personality or other individual features attributed to them (Petchesky 1987; Taylor 2004). They represent the unborn baby, making its personhood more substantial than would otherwise be possible, but they also provide opportunities for consumption as they become treasured objects.

16. In a similar vein, historian Lauri Umansky (1996) observes that both feminist and conservative social critiques demand separation of the wholly emotional domain of maternal love and the contaminated realm of marketplace economic relationships. In other words, intersections of love and money are widely perceived as morally impermissible, and as the source of many ills that afflict family life. Parenthood is not the only familial domain in the West in which financial considerations are taboo; similar sentiments typify responses to both "arranged marriages" and "mail-order brides," both of which are seen as impermissibly corrupted by the desire for material gain, whether such advantage would accrue to the bride, the groom, or their families (Constable 2003; Khandelwal 2009).

17. This dilemma illustrates the organization of ethnicities into mutually exclusive categories despite many situations that fail to conform to simple dichotomies. (See Newman 2007.)

18. A substantial literature has addressed the issue of whether transnational and cross-racial movements of children lead those children eventually to feel robbed of their heritage and thus uncertainly connected to the markers they might otherwise use to constitute their identities (Dorow 2006; Fogg-Davis 2002; Patton 2000; Rothman 2005). These authors raise the largely unanswerable questions of whether adoptions that span these differences are morally questionable because they were enabled by commercial processes, or because only materially advantaged Westerners can undertake them. In other words, do interracial and transnational adoptions embody inequalities to the extent that they are illegitimate on their face?

19. Note that this process parallels the shift of Western economies from production to consumption.

20. As anthropologist Lynda Layne (2004) has shown, consumption becomes a central mechanism for mourning in cases of pregnancy loss, with conventional themes (e.g., butterflies, angels) symbolizing the innocence and spirituality of the deceased.

21. Legal practices vary from country to country. Some countries impose age or sex limitations on those who wish to adopt, or will only work with married couples. Some require children to live in orphanages for particular periods of time before being released for adoption; others keep children in foster homes until their new parents have been approved. The ages at which children may be available for adoption vary widely, as do pre-existing medical conditions they may be known to have, or that may surface late in the process. Not surprisingly, the political and diplomatic considerations surrounding international adoptions can be complicated and capricious, and the process of overseas adoption may come to have political meanings not related to the concerns of hopeful parents. Nor is the process always predictable and orderly. Countries may suddenly change the relevant regulations or impose new demands on adoptive parents, and officials involved in the process may need to be bribed if the adoption is to be completed in a reasonable amount of time. Some countries require adoptive parents to stay for substantial periods of

time or to make more than one visit before completing the legalities, which can impose a substantial burden on the prospective parents (Bartholet 1993; Modell 2002; Simon and Altstein 2000).

22. It should be noted that not only adoption, but most technologies of procreation and reproduction are also differentially priced and thus accessible to different segments of the public. This ranges from the low-cost end of the process, e.g., purchases of products like ovulation predictors, home pregnancy tests, and consultations with physicians, to the high-cost area of assisted procreation and various kinds of medical interventions in fertility, pregnancy, childbirth, and childcare.

23. Jennifer Lee and Frank D. Bean (2004) have examined the continuing rigidity of the black-white color line in the context of immigration and the increasing numbers of Americans who identify as being of mixed racial heritage.

24. These analyses show that the dismantling of welfare services and the escalating economic pressures mothers face in heading families lead them to relinquish their children "voluntarily" as well as to have them removed by the state for a variety of reasons. Poor people, of course, face more intense surveillance than people with higher incomes, so neglect and abuse are more likely to be visible in low-income families. In cases where parental rights are terminated children are, in a sense, reallocated to middle-class and predominantly white parents.

25. According to Spar, in 2002, there were 534,000 children in the U.S. foster care system, 126,000 of whom were eligible for adoption (Spar 2006, 177).

26. Some feminist commentators have lamented the commodification inherent in these transactions, arguing that they inevitably disadvantage poor women and women of color, potentially exploiting their economic need to induce them to serve as surrogates and egg donors (Spallone and Steinberg 1992; Stanworth 1990). They argue that such procreative technologies are bizarre eugenic ventures that devalue those who are infertile and also stigmatize offspring who are less than "perfect." But others, such as bioethicist Ruth Macklin, have taken the position that such commodification, even if "unsavory," is not fundamentally immoral (Macklin 1996). In a market-driven society, Macklin argues, financial interests and income disparities characterize virtually all interactions; singling out commerce in eggs, sperm, and the use of reproductive organs as uniquely deserving of prohibition can hardly be justified.

27. As Signe Howell (1999) notes, another reason that infertile couples in Norway and (some) other countries in western and northern Europe move quickly to international adoption is because of government restrictions on the use of assisted reproductive technologies (ARTs) and surrogacy.

28. As sociologist Rene Almeling comments, female gametes are more highly valued than male gametes in the U.S. genetic marketplace. She traces such evaluations to the "gendered stereotypes about caring motherhood and distant fatherhood" (2007, 337), as well as to the more rigorous medical regime required to

extract ova as compared to the more readily accessible sperm. In other words, cultural images of maternal altruism seem to attach to the commodification of egg donation, thus elevating the value of ova. Perhaps paradoxically, she also reports that the genetic materials of nonwhite donors, whether sperm or eggs, are also more highly priced, in this case because of demand. This system reinforces a biological reading of race, while also immersing the genetic foundations of life in a complicated financial calculus.

29. Laura Mamo's study of how lesbians negotiate various technological regimes to achieve pregnancy carefully analyzes the complex calculations that inform how women choose sperm donors (Mamo 2007).

30. Many of the men I interviewed had worked with a single agency, Growing Generations in Los Angeles, which specializes in providing assisted reproduction services to a gay and lesbian clientele. According to the Growing Generations Web site, "costs for surrogacy generally range between $115,000.00 and $150,000.00, which includes estimated costs for all aspects of the process, including medical, legal, psychological, surrogate fees, egg donor fees (if applicable), medications, insurance, etc." (http://www.growinggenerations.com/financial, accessed December 13, 2008). These costs can be reduced if the prospective parents have an egg donor available from their own personal networks, or if they already have obtained frozen embryos.

31. Egg donors are typically paid fees ranging from $5,000 to $15,000 or more per ovum transfer, though the prospective parents may face other expenses, for doctor appointments, medications, and travel, bringing the total cost much higher than the donation fees. They are more highly valued if they are tall, blonde, and blue eyed, are college graduates, have high GPAs, SATs, and IQs, or, according to one Web site, are "considered stunningly attractive" (http://www.cyberfeminism .net/eggdonor/ed_fleshmarket.html, accessed July 10, 2007). An advertisement placed in a University of Michigan newspaper, for example, said: "Wanted: Healthy, athletic women. Under age of 29. 1300-plus SAT score. Compensation: $10,000" (Robert Samuels, "Baby Business: Wannabe Moms, Dads Court College Coeds," *Detroit Free Press*, September 22, 2005).

32. In recent research with lesbian couples who use gestational surrogacy, Suzanne Pelka found that couples imagine this method as *enhancing* the connection of both women with their baby, as both may be viewed as "biological" mothers. In these instances, one woman donates her ova and is thus the genetic mother and the other carries the pregnancy and is the gestational mother; for these couples, the sperm donor's significance is dramatically reduced in the accounts of the mothers (Pelka 2005). But these arrangements can backfire: in the case of *KM v. EG* in California, KM, the egg donor, had signed a hospital consent form at the time of the donation waiving parental rights. She assumed signing the release was pro forma, but when EG, the gestational mother, ended the relationship, she used the form to bolster her claim that KM had no relation to their twin girls (Belluck and

Liptak 2004). Despite an early ruling in support of EG, in which the court equated the position of KM to an anonymous sperm donor, the California Supreme Court ruled finally ruled in support of KM in 2005 (Liptak 2005).

33. One Web site estimates IVF costs, including "office appointments, [medical fees] . . . , injections and training, FSH tests, estrogen, ultrasound monitoring, hospital retrieval costs and lab fertilization costs. This excludes surrogate's fee per attempt and travel expenses" (http://www.givf.com/financialprograms/pricing.cfm, accessed December 13, 2008).

34. The ups and downs of surrogacy for gay men have been chronicled in a number of memoirs and how-to books (Menichiello 2006; Sember 2006), and in a recent documentary film, *Beyond Conception* (Symons 2006). In her book on assisted reproduction, *Everything Conceivable*, Liza Mundy reports the case of one San Francisco couple in detail (2007).

35. The Internal Revenue Service offers a tax credit of $10,960 for families completing adoptions. Also, some adoption services offer information on how to finance an adoption.

36. These men were engaging in "resemblance talk," described as a serious issue for parents whose children were conceived with donor gametes (Becker, Butler, and Nachtigall 2005; Orenstein 2007).

37. Helena Ragoné's (1994) work on surrogate mothers shows that they systematically downplay the commercial dimensions of surrogacy and see themselves as engaging in largely altruistic service.

38. Egg donors are, of course, not literally "donors" at all. Jewish donors are highly sought after and can command top dollar. The process of donating ova is arduous, as the donor must take large doses of fertility drugs intended to produce hyperovulation and must endure the invasive procedures used to "harvest" the eggs (Derek 2004; Spar 2006).

39. Jewish identity is passed through the maternal line only.

40. This is not to suggest that procreation through "natural" means is free from the taint of consumption. As the essays in *Consuming Motherhood* (Taylor, Layne, and Wozniak 2004) make abundantly clear, procreation and motherhood are deeply entwined with consumption-related practices. Purchasing consumer goods, as well, is a central theme of childrearing in the U.S. (Seiter 1995).

Chapter Three

1. See such works as Michael Pollan's *The Omnivore's Dilemma* (2007) for an account of the ambiguities and downright inaccuracies of this model when applied to food.

2. Such language is particularly marked in the explanations mothers offer for virtually any aspect of their experience, and scholars of gender have long noted

the centrality of nature in accounts of women's reproductive lives. In her classic article, for example, Sherry Ortner (1974) remarks on the tendency of most (if not all) cultures to see women's reproductive activities as deeply embedded in nature and men's productive and political activities as contrastingly part of culture. While she argues that both claims are interpretations, not facts—that the conduct of both women and men necessarily draws on both domains—she proposes that the seemingly universal devaluation of femaleness has its origins in this dichotomy. In a similar vein, feminist theorists from other fields have tended to situate what they claim are women's characteristic inclinations—toward nurturance, altruism, sensitivity to the needs of others—in the natural requirements actual or potential motherhood imposes on female persons (Gilligan 1982; Hays 1996; Ruddick 1989). Whether something invisible (hormonal, genetic, psychodynamic, ethical) in women predisposes them toward caring or whether such impulses result from childhood training is a matter of intellectual taste or doctrinal preference. Either explanation situates the behaviors and emotions connected with motherhood squarely in the domain of nature.

3. The feminist position on nature, however, is anything but monolithic. Other leading theorists have focused instead on the constructedness and complexity of both motherhood and nature in an effort to disrupt conventions that limit women's sphere of activity to reproduction and childrearing. Adrienne Rich (1976) famously argued that motherhood is both an experience and an institution though she also posited a fundamental rift between motherhood and intellectual creativity. Philosopher Sara Ruddick (1989) put forward the notion that motherhood was a set of practices that, in fact, could be accomplished by either women or men, though her vision was limited by the class and cultural boundaries of her own experience. Although she grounded the protective activities she associated with motherhood in specific needs and activities, then, many critics maintain that the image she produced was reductive and essentialized (see, for example, Dietz 1985).

4. In many areas of the country, local television programs highlight available children, presenting them in short segments that emphasize their attractiveness as potential additions to viewers' families. The San Francisco Bay Area's CBS affiliate, for instance, long featured *Brian's Kids*, hosted by newsman Brian Sussman, an adoptive parent himself. The parallel with shopping is hard to miss, though the affective experience draws on different images. Kelly, one of the fathers who appears in the documentary film *Daddy and Papa* (Symons 2002), adopted two boys he first saw on the show, and, like most adoptive parents, quickly began to see them as "meant" to be his. In a particularly moving scene in the film, Kelly describes how one of his sons dreamed that he was wandering about looking for his "home." He went to different houses and knocked, but none of them was the right place. Finally, he came to Kelly's house, and knew this was "his home." Kelly weeps as he tells this story; it coincides with his own understanding of the adoption as intended by forces beyond logical comprehension.

5. As media scholar Lisa Cartwright (2005) has shown, the representation of children from third-world countries as "waiting children" whom Western parents can rescue from squalid futures is a powerful image and one that counters the commercial overtones of much international adoption rhetoric. Along similar lines, Christine Ward Gailey (2000) observes that children available for adoption are nearly always represented as "orphans," even if their parents are still living. This image contributes to adoptive parents' rescue fantasies while obscuring the social and economic conditions that led parents to relinquish their child.

6. But Barbara Katz Rothman (2005) discusses "wrongful adoptions," in which children are returned to the placing agency or the agency is sued, often with allegations that some condition, medical or otherwise, was not disclosed prior to adoption. She suggests that the logic of these cases parallels that of prenatal testing, as prospective parents feel entitled to prescreen the fetus so as to decide whether the pregnancy should be completed or terminated. The assumption here is that consumers should be able to be fully informed about the characteristics of their purchase before completing the transaction.

Chapter Four

1. Ben and Peter realize that they may be the only gay couple anywhere who have formed a family with this particular configuration of sperm and ova.

2. Recent scholarship on assisted reproductive technologies has highlighted the complicated kinship calculations that can enter into particular decisions about egg donors, surrogates, and other options. See, for example, C. Thompson 2005. The two men realized a considerable saving, however, by having their sisters donate ova, and because their sisters are both Jewish, their children will not have to go through a conversion process.

3. Despite this sense of responsibility, Enrique does not feel obligated to seek out his children's older siblings for adoption. Though he has mixed feelings about what to do if their mother has other children in the future, he told me that he couldn't imagine how he could manage more than three children.

4. See C. Thompson (2001) on the way that women receiving egg donations use ethnic or racial labels to classify potential donors so at to enhance perceived genetic closeness. See also Goslinga-Roy (2000) on how racial images become embodied for gestational surrogates.

Chapter Five

1. This term derives from the debate over the so-called Mommy Track, a term used widely in the business world to describe how women's tendency to prioritize

maternal obligations slows their professional progress (Schwartz 1989). Some commentators have bristled at the notion that the difficulties mothers face in the workplace derive from "choices" they have made to make hands-on mothering more important than their jobs; others have suggested that fathers may make similar choices but that they are seen merely as unmotivated workers when they do so (see also Greif 1990).

2. See Sullivan 2004 for examples of this dilemma among lesbian co-mothers.

3. Along similar lines, some scholarship has stressed the unevenness of maternal devotion to be found in the historical record. French historian Elisabeth Badinter contends that mother love is a cultural creation rather than a universal condition (1981). She looks in detail at France prior to the eighteenth century, when more affluent mothers regularly consigned their infants to neglectful wet nurses under whose capricious care many perished. These deaths were not mourned, according to Badinter, as children's lives were not sentimentalized. The "maternal instinct" emerges in her analysis as a particular historical product rather than a biological imperative (1981). Similar findings on pre-Revolutionary Russian peasants suggest that assessments of neglect need to be understood in relation to both poverty and ignorance, even as what physicians considered poor standards of infant care might have been normative in particular settings (Ransel 2005).

4. These themes also emerge vividly in fictional representations of motherhood; novels such as *The Good Mother* by Sue Miller (1988) and *The Fifth Child* by Doris Lessing (1989) take their themes from the dramatic potential of maternal blame and guilt, in one case over the mother's sexual passion and in the other over the existence of a dangerously defective child.

5. Suspicion toward and surveillance of mothers is particularly intense during pregnancy. Concerns about drug use, alcohol consumption, and smoking have led to sometimes draconian measures to keep suspect mothers in line, or to punish them if they stray from what is considered appropriate behavior during pregnancy (Golden 2006; Murphy and Rosenbaum, 1999; Oaks 2000).

6. Some recent literature has questioned this approach, arguing that fathers who fail to meet child support obligations should be understood as "turnips" (as in the adage "you can't get blood from a turnip") rather than "deadbeats" (Mincy and Sorensen 1998).

Chapter Six

1. The material explored in chapter 6 is presented in a different form in "Who's Gay? What's Gay? Dilemmas of Identity among Gay Fathers," in *Out in Public: Reinventing Lesbian/Gay Anthropology in a Globalizing World*, ed. Ellen Lewin and William L. Leap (Malden, MA: Wiley-Blackwell, 2009), 86–103.

2. The ways in which opera has come to constitute a particularly marked cultural arena for gay men have been examined by Wayne Koestenbaum (2001) and Paul Robinson (2002).

3. The idealized references to the solid values of their families break down at a later point in the interview when Dennis refers to the difficulties he faced growing up gay in a "dysfunctional family." His memory of these problems intensifies his desire to be a parent so that he can do better than his parents did at dealing with nonconformity in a child.

4. The assessment of there being less money to spend is clearly quite subjective, as Ben and Peter are able to spend money on remodeling their new house, on a fulltime nanny, and on other amenities out of the reach of many families. Their commitment to spend less money on seemingly frivolous entertainment reflects their idea that as parents they need to be more responsible, to think about financial matters long term, and to conserve funds for the welfare of their children.

Chapter Seven

1. Because Jewish identity is passed matrilineally, the children will have to go through a conversion ritual if they are to be considered Jewish.

2. The Chicago branch of a high-end New York clothing store.

3. Like many lesbian mothers I interviewed (Lewin 1993), Philip equates not having children with being "single."

4. Happily, when I visited Philip again about six months after the birth of his healthy triplets, he had met his partner, Stan, who had moved in and was taking an active role in parenting the children.

5. Although little of this work has penetrated queer scholarship, there is a substantial (and growing) field of gay-related religious studies in addition to more personal accounts of religious/spiritual experience among gay men and lesbians (Perry 1972). There are also quite a few studies that challenge conventional rejection of gayness as sinful or reconsider religious history in light of positive inclusion of homosexuality. There are scholarly works that examine gay religious practice, evaluate the historical foundation of homophobia in mainstream religion, and look at the ways that gay people have reclaimed religion. See Erzen 2006; Jordan 2000, 2005; Shallenberger 1998; Shokeid 2002; Thumma and Gray 2005; and Wolkomir 2006.

6. See Brekhus (2003) for a treatment of gay suburbanites that adheres to the dichotomous model.

References

ABC News. 2004. "A Different Arithmetic: Pioneering Parents Raise New Questions about What Defines a Family." *Primetime Thursday*.

Administration for Children and Families. 2006. AFCARS Report. Washington, DC: U.S. Department of Health and Human Services.

Agigian, Amy. 2004 *Baby Steps: How Lesbian Alternative Insemination Is Changing the World*. Middletown, CT: Wesleyan University Press.

Aizley, Harlyn. 2003. *Buying Dad: One Woman's Search for the Perfect Sperm Donor*. Los Angeles: Alyson Books.

Almeling, Rene. 2007. "Selling Genes, Selling Gender: Egg Agencies, Sperm Banks, and the Medical Market in Genetic Material." *American Sociological Review* 78:319–340.

Altstein, Howard, and Rita J. Simon. 1991. *Intercountry Adoption: A Multinational Perspective*. New York: Praeger.

Anderson, Benedict. 1983. *Imagined Communities*. London: Verso.

Andersson, Gunilla. 2000. "Intercountry Adoption in Sweden: The Perspective of the Adoption Centre in its 30th Year." In *Intercountry Adoption: Developments, Trends, and Perspectives*, ed. P. Selman, 346–67. London: British Agencies for Adoption and Fostering.

Andriote, John-Manuel. 1999. *Victory Deferred: How AIDS Changed Gay Life in America*. Chicago: University of Chicago Press.

Arendell, Terry. 1988. *Mothers and Divorce: Legal, Economic, and Social Dilemmas*. Berkeley: University of California Press.

Ariès, Phillippe. 1965. *Centuries of Childhood: A Social History of Family Life*. New York: Vintage.

Arney, William Ray. 1980. "Maternal Infant Bonding: The Politics of Falling in Love with Your Child." *Feminist Studies* 6(3): 547–69.

Badgett, M.V. Lee. 2001. *Money, Myths, and Change: The Economic Lives of Lesbians and Gay Men*. Chicago: University of Chicago Press.

Badinter, Elisabeth. 1981. *Mother Love: Myth and Reality*. New York: Macmillan.

Barrett, Michèle, and Mary McIntosh. 1982. *The Anti-Social Family*. London, NLB.

Bartholet, Elizabeth. 1993. *Family Bonds: Adoption, Infertility, and the New World of Child Production*. Boston: Beacon Press.

Beatie, Thomas. 2008. *Labor of Love: The Story of One Man's Extraordinary Pregnancy*. Berkeley: Seal Press.

Becker, Gary S. 1960. "An Economic Analysis of Fertililty." In *Demographic and Economic Change in Developed Countries*, ed. National Bureau of Economic Research, 209–31. Princeton: Princeton University Press.

Becker, Gay. 1997. *Disrupted Lives: How People Create Meaning in a Chaotic World*. Berkeley: University of California Press.

Becker, Gay, Annaliese Butler, and Robert D. Nachtigall. 2005. "Resemblance Talk: A Challenge for Parents Whose Children Were Conceived with Donor Gametes in the US." *Social Science and Medicine* 61(6): 1300–1309.

Beemyn, Brett. 1997. *Creating a Place for Ourselves: Lesbian, Gay, and Bisexual Community Histories*. New York: Routledge.

Behar, Ruth. 1997. *The Vulnerable Observer: Anthropology That Breaks Your Heart*. Boston: Beacon Press.

Belkin, Lisa. 2003. "The Opt-Out Revolution." *New York Times Magazine*, October 19, 42.

Bell, David, and Jon Binnie. 2000. *The Sexual Citizen: Queer Politics and Beyond*. Cambridge: Polity Press.

Belluck, Pam, and Adam Liptak. 2004. "Split Gay Couples Face Custody Hurdles." *New York Times*, March 24.

Belluck, Pam, and Jim Yardley. 2006. "China Tightens Adoption Rules for Foreigners." *New York Times*, December 20.

Benkov, Laura. 1994. *Reinventing the Family: Lesbian and Gay Parents*. New York: Crown.

Bérubé, Allan. 2001. "How Gay Stays White and What Kind of White It Stays." In *The Making and Unmaking of Whiteness*, ed. B. B. Rasmussen, E. Klinenberg, I. J. Nexica, and M. Wray, 234–65. Durham: Duke University Press.

Bhabha, Jacqueline. 2006. " 'Not a Sack of Potatoes': Moving and Removing Children across Borders." *Boston University Public Interest Law Journal* 15(2): 197–218.

Blake, Judith. 1968. "Are Babies Consumer Durables? A Critique of the Economic Theory of Reproductive Motivation." *Population Studies* 22(1): 5–25.

Blum, Linda M. 1999. *At the Breast: Ideologies of Breastfeeding and Motherhood in the Contemporary United States*. Boston: Beacon Press.

Bobel, Chris. 2002. *The Paradox of Natural Mothering*. Philadelphia: Temple University Press.

Boellstorff, Tom. 2005. "Between Religion and Desire: Being Muslim and *Gay* in Indonesia." *American Anthropologist* 107(4): 575–85.

Bourdieu, Pierre. 1984. *Distinction: A Social Critique of the Judgment of Taste*. Trans. R. Nice. Cambridge, MA: Harvard University Press.

Bozett, Frederick W. 1987. "Gay Fathers." In *Gay and Lesbian Parents*, ed. F. W. Bozett, 3–22. New York: Praeger.

Brekhus, Wayne H. 2003. *Peacocks, Chameleons, Centaurs: Gay Suburbia and the Grammar of Social Identity*. Chicago: University of Chicago Press.

Bremner, Robert H. 1974. *Children and Youth in America: A Documentary History*. Cambridge, MA: Harvard University Press.

Briggs, Laura. 2006. "Making 'American' Families: Transnational Adoption and US Latin America Policy." In *Haunted by Empire: Geographies of Intimacy in North American History*, ed. A. L. Stoler, 344–65. Durham: Duke University Press.

Brodkin, Karen. 1998. *How Jews Became White Folks and What That Says about Race in America*. New Brunswick: Rutgers University Press.

Bronski, Michael. 1984. *Culture Clash: The Making of Gay Sensibility*. Boston: South End Press.

Brown, Judith K. 1970. "A Note on the Division of Labor by Sex." *American Anthropologist* 72 (5): 1073–8.

Bull, Chris, and John Gallagher. 1996. *Perfect Enemies: The Religious Right, the Gay Movement, and the Politics of the 1990s*. New York: Crown Publishers.

Cain, Patricia A. 2000. *Rainbow Rights: The Role of Lawyers and Courts in the Lesbian and Gay Civil Rights Movement*. Boulder: Westview.

Calhoun, Cheshire. 2000. *Feminism, the Family, and the Politics of the Closet: Lesbian and Gay Displacement*. Oxford: Oxford University Press.

Carney, Eliza Newlin. 2007. "Perception and Reality: The Untold Story of Domestic Adoption." In *Adoptive Families Magazine*, May–June, 36–39.

Carrington, Christopher. 1999. *No Place Like Home: Relationships and Family Life among Lesbians and Gay Men*. Chicago: University of Chicago Press.

———. 2006. "Circuit Culture: Ethnographic Reflections on Inequality, Sexuality, and Life on the Gay Party Circuit." In *Sexual Inequalities and Social Justice*, ed. N. Teunis and G. H. Herdt, 123–49. Berkeley: University of California Press.

Carsten, Janet. 2000. *The Cultures of Relatedness: New Approaches to the Study of Kinship*. Cambridge: Cambridge University Press.

Cartwright, Lisa. 2005. "Images of 'Waiting Children': Spectatorship and Pity in the Representation of the Global Social Orphan in the 1990s." In *Cultures of Transnational Adoption*, ed. T. A. Volkman, 185–212. Durham: Duke University Press.

Castells, Manuel. 2004. *The Power of Identity*. Malden, MA: Blackwell Publishing.

Cherlin, Andrew. 2004. "The Deinstitutionalization of Marriage." *Journal of Marriage and Family* 66(4): 848–61.

Chin, Elizabeth. 2001. *Purchasing Power: Black Kids and American Consumer Culture*. Minneapolis: University of Minnesota Press.

Chodorow, Nancy. 1978. *The Reproduction of Mothering: Psychoanalysis and the Sociology of Gender*. Berkeley: University of California Press.

Constable, Nicole. 2003. *Romance on a Global Stage: Pen Pals, Virtual Ethnography, and "Mail Order" Marriages*. Berkeley: University of California Press.

Coontz, Stephanie. 1992. *The Way We Never Were: American Families and the Nostalgia Trap*. New York: Basic Books.

———. 1997. *The Way We Really Are: Coming to Terms with America's Changing Families*. New York: Basic Books.

———. 2005. *Marriage, a History: From Obedience to Intimacy, or How Love Conquered Marriage*. New York: Viking.

Cooper, Elizabeth B. 1992. "HIV Infected Parents and the Law: Issues of Custody, Visitation and Guardianship." In *AIDS Agenda: Emerging Issues in Civil Rights*, ed. N. D. Hunter and W. B. Rubenstein, 69–122. New York: The New Press.

Cott, Nancy F. 2000. *Public Vows: A History of Marriage and the Nation*. Cambridge, MA: Harvard University Press.

Dalmage, Heather. 2000. *Tripping on the Color Line: Black-White Multiracial Families in a Racially Divided World*. New Brunswick: Rutgers University Press.

DeLaMar, Roy. 2003. "And Babies Make Six; As Their Quadruplets Approach Their First Birthday, Thomas Dysarz and Michael Meehan Are Redefining What It Means to Be a Family in Kentucky." *Advocate* 892 (June 24): 72.

Delaney, Carol. 1991. *The Seed and the Soil: Gender and Cosmology in Turkish Village Society*. Berkeley: University of California Press.

D'Emilio, John. 1983. *Sexual Politics, Sexual Communities: The Making of a Homosexual Minority in the United States, 1940–1970*. Chicago: University of Chicago Press.

Derek, Julia. 2004. *Confessions of a Serial Egg Donor*. New York: Adrenaline Books.

DeVault, Marjorie L. 1991. *Feeding the Family: The Social Organization of Caring as Gendered Work*. Chicago: University of Chicago Press.

Dietz, Mary G. 1985. "Citizenship with a Feminist Face: The Problem with Maternal Thinking." *Political Theory* 13(1): 19–37.

Dorow, Sara K. 2006. *Transnational Adoption: A Cultural Economy of Race, Gender, and Kinship*. New York: New York University Press.

Doucet, Andrea. 2006. *Do Men Mother? Fatherhood, Care, and Domestic Responsibility*. Toronto: University of Toronto Press.

Douglas, Ann. 1998. *The Feminization of American Culture*. New York: Farrar, Straus and Giroux.

Downey, Gary Lee, and Joseph Dumit. 1997. *Cyborgs and Citadels: Anthropological Interventions in Emerging Sciences and Technologies*. Santa Fe: School of American Research.

Duggan, Lisa. 2003. *The Twilight of Equality? Neoliberalism, Cultural Politics, and the Attack on Democracy*. Boston: Beacon Press.

Dumit, Joseph. 2003. *Picturing Personhood: Brain Scans and Biomedical Identity*. Princeton: Princeton University Press.

Duquaine-Watson, Jillian. 2005. "Negotiating Need: Single Mother College Students in Post-Welfare Reform America." Ph.D. diss., University of Iowa.

Duster, Troy. 1990. *Backdoor to Eugenics*. New York: Routledge.

Economist. 2007. "Lexington: Out and Proud Parents." *Economist* 383:58.

Edelman, Lee. 2004. *No Future: Queer Theory and the Death Drive*. Durham: Duke University Press.

Edin, Kathryn, and Maria Kefalas. 2005. *Promises I Can Keep: Why Poor Women Put Motherhood before Marriage*. Berkeley: University of California Press.

Ehrensaft, Diane. 1987. *Parenting Together: Men and Women Sharing the Care of Their Children*. New York: Free Press.

Eller, Cynthia. 1993. *Living in the Lap of the Goddess: The Feminist Spirituality Movement in America*. Boston: Beacon Press.

Elshtain, Jean Bethke. 1981. *Public Man, Private Woman.* Princeton: Princeton University Press.

Erzen, Tanya. 2006. *Straight to Jesus: Sexual and Christian Conversions in the Ex-Gay Movement.* Berkeley: University of California Press.

Ettelbrick, Paula L. 1992. "Since When Is Marriage a Path to Liberation?" In *Lesbian and Gay Marriage: Private Commitments, Public Ceremonies*, ed. S. Sherman, 20–26. Philadelphia: Temple University Press.

Evans, David T. 1993. *Sexual Citizenship: The Material Construction of Sexualities.* London: Routledge.

Eyer, Diane E. 1992. *Mother-Infant Bonding: A Scientific Fiction.* New Haven: Yale University Press.

Fellows, Will. 1998. *Farm Boys: Lives of Gay Men from the Rural Midwest.* Madison: University of Wisconsin Press.

Fineman, Martha Albertson. 1991. *The Illusion of Equality: The Rhetoric and Reality of Divorce Reform.* Chicago: University of Chicago Press.

Finkler, Kaja. 2000. *Experiencing the New Genetics: Family and Kinship on the Medical Frontier.* Philadelphia: University of Pennsylvania Press.

Firestone, Shulamith. 1970. *The Dialectic of Sex: The Case for Feminist Revolution.* New York: William Morrow & Co.

Flango, Victor, and Carol Flango. 1995. "How Many Children Were Adopted in 1992." *Child Welfare* 74(5): 1018–32.

Fogg-Davis, Hawley. 2002. *The Ethics of Transracial Adoption.* Ithaca: Cornell University Press.

Folbre, Nancy. 2001. *The Invisible Heart: Economics and Family Values.* New York: New Press.

Frank, Arthur W. 1997. *The Wounded Storyteller: Body, Illness, and Ethics.* Chicago: University of Chicago Press.

Franklin, Sarah. 1997. *Embodied Progress: A Cultural Account of Assisted Conception.* London: Routledge.

Franklin, Sarah, and Celia Roberts. 2006. *Born and Made: An Ethnography of Preimplantation Genetic Diagnosis.* Princeton: Princeton University Press.

Frykman, Jonas, and Orvar Löfgren. 1987. *Culture Builders: A Historical Anthropology of Middle-Class Life.* New Brunswick: Rutgers University Press.

Gaede, Beth Ann. 1999. *Congregations Talking about Homosexuality: Dialogue on a Difficult Issue.* Herndon, VA: Alban Institute.

Gailey, Christine Ward. 1999. "Seeking 'Baby Right': Race, Class, and Gender in US International Adoption." In *Mine—Yours—Ours—and Theirs: Adoption, Changing Kinship and Family Patterns*, ed. A.-L. Rygvold, M. Dalen, and B. Saetersdal, 52–81. Oslo: University of Oslo.

———. 2000. "Race, Class, and Gender in Intercountry Adoption in the USA." In *Intercountry Adoption: Developments, Trends, and Perspectives*, ed. P. Selman, 295–313. London: British Agencies for Adoption and Fostering.

Garber, Marjorie. 2000. *Sex and Real Estate: Why We Love Houses.* New York: Pantheon.

Garey, Anita Ilta. 1999. *Weaving Work and Motherhood.* Philadelphia: Temple University Press.

Garro, Linda C., and Cheryl Mattingly. 2000. "Narrative as Construct and Construction." In *Narrative and the Cultural Construction of Illness and Healing*, ed. C. Mattingly and L. C. Garro, 1–49. Berkeley: University of California Press.

Gates, Gary J., and Jason Ost. 2004. *The Gay and Lesbian Atlas*. Washington, DC: Urban Institute Press.

Gerson, Kathleen. 1986. *Hard Choices: How Women Decide about Work, Career, and Motherhood*. Berkeley: University of California Press.

Giddens, Anthony. 1993. *The Transformation of Intimacy: Sexuality, Love, and Eroticism in Modern Societies*. Stanford: Stanford University Press.

———. 2002. *Runaway World: How Globalisation Is Reshaping Our Lives*. London: Routledge.

Gilligan, Carol. 1982. *In a Different Voice: Psychological Theory and Women's Development*. Cambridge, MA: Harvard University Press.

Ginsburg, Faye D. 1989. *Contested Lives: The Abortion Debate in an American Community*. Berkeley: University of California Press.

Ginsburg, Faye D., and Rayna Rapp, eds. 1995. *Conceiving the New World Order: The Global Politics of Reproduction*. Berkeley: University of California Press.

Goffman, Erving. 1961. *Asylums: Essays on the Social Situation of Mental Patients and Other Inmates*. Garden City, NY: Anchor Books.

———. 1963. *Stigma: Notes on the Management of Spoiled Identity*. New York: Simon & Schuster.

Golden, Janet. 2006. *Message in a Bottle: The Making of Fetal Alcohol Syndrome*. Cambridge, MA: Harvard University Press.

Goldman, Emma. 1970. *Anarchism and Other Essays*. New York: Dover.

Goldsmith, Barbara. 1999. *Other Powers: The Age of Suffrage, Spiritualism, and the Scandalous Victoria Woodhull*. New York: Harper.

Gordon, Linda. 1998. *Pitied but Not Entitled: Single Mothers and the History of Welfare*. Cambridge, MA: Harvard University Press.

Goslinga-Roy, Gillian M. 2000. "Body Boundaries, Fiction of the Female Self: An Ethnographic Perspective on Power, Feminism, and the Reproductive Technologies." In *Biotechnology and Culture: Bodies, Anxieties, Ethics*, ed. P. E. Brodwin, 1:121–146: Bloomington, IN: Indiana University Press.

Gray, Mary L. 1999. *In Your Face: Stories from the Lives of Queer Youth*. Binghamton, NY: Haworth Press.

Green, Jesse. 1999. *The Velveteen Father: An Unexpected Journey to Parenthood*. New York: Villard.

Greenhouse, Linda. 2005. "Justices Refuse to Consider Law Banning Gay Adoption." *New York Times*, January 11.

Greif, Geoffrey L. 1990. *The Daddy Track and the Single Father*. Lanham, MD: Lexington Books

Greil, Arthur L. 1991. *Not Yet Pregnant: Infertile Couples in Contemporary America*. New Brunswick: Rutgers University Press.

Grenz, Stanley J. 1998. *Welcoming but Not Affirming: An Evangelical Response to Homosexuality*. Louisville: Westminster John Knox Press.

Grier, Katherine C. 2006. *Pets in America: A History*. Chapel Hill: University of North Carolina Press.

Griffin, Susan. 1980. *Woman and Nature: The Roaring Inside Her*. New York: Harper & Row.

Gutman, Herbert G. 1977. *The Black Family in Slavery and Freedom, 1750–1925*. New York: Vintage

Gutmann, Matthew C. 1996. *The Meanings of Macho: Being a Man in Mexico City*. Berkeley: University of California Press.

Halberstam, Judith. 2005. *In a Queer Time and Place: Transgender Bodies, Subcultural Lives*. New York: New York University Press.

Hancock, Ange-Marie. 2004. *The Politics of Disgust: The Public Identity of the Welfare Queen*. New York: New York University Press.

Handel, Nelson. 2002. *Reaching Out: The Guide to Writing a Terrific Dear Birthmother Letter*. Los Angeles: Eastern Edge Press.

Hartman, Keith. 1997. *Congregations in Conflict: The Battle Over Homosexuality*. New Brunswick: Rutgers University Press.

Hausman, Bernice L. 2003. *Mother's Milk: Breastfeeding Controversies in American Culture*. New York: Routledge.

Hawkeswood, William G. 1996. *One of the Children: Gay Black Men in Harlem*. Berkeley: University of California Press.

Hays, Sharon. 1996. *The Cultural Contradictions of Motherhood*. New Haven: Yale University Press.

———. 2003. *Flat Broke with Children: Women in the Age of Welfare Reform*. New York: Oxford University Press.

Hequembourg, Amy, and Jorge Arditi. 1999. "Fractured Resistances: The Debate over Assimilationism among Gays and Lesbians in the United States." *Sociological Quarterly* 40(4): 663–80.

Herrnstein, Richard J., and Charles Murray. 1994. *The Bell Curve: Intelligence and Class Structure in American Life*. New York: Free Press.

Hertz, Rosanna. 1986. *More Equal than Others: Women and Men in Dual-Career Marriages*. Berkeley: University of California Press.

Hochschild, Arlie. 1989. *The Second Shift*. With Anne Machung. New York: Avon Books.

Howard, John. 2001. *Men Like That: A Southern Queer History*. Chicago: University of Chicago Press.

Howell, Signe. 1999. "Biologizing and De-Biologizing Kinship: Some Paradoxes in Norwegian Transnational Adoption." In *Mine—Yours—Ours—and Theirs: Adoption, Changing Kinship and Family Patterns*, ed. A.-L. Rygvold, M. Dalen, and B. Saetersdal, 32–51. Oslo: University of Oslo.

———. 2001. "Self-Consciousness Kinship: Some Contested Values in Norwegian Transnational Adoption." In *Relative Values: Reconfiguring Kinship Studies*, ed. S. Franklin and S. McKinnon, 203–23. Durham: Duke University Press.

Jordan, Mark D. 2000. *The Silence of Sodom: Homosexuality in Modern Catholicism*. Chicago: University of Chicago Press.

———. 2005. *Blessing Same-Sex Unions: The Perils of Queer Romance and the Confusions of Christian Marriage*. Chicago: University of Chicago Press.

Kaplan, Morris B. 1997. *Sexual Justice: Democratic Citizenship and the Politics of Desire*. New York: Routledge.

Katzenstein, Mary. 1995. "Discursive Politics and Feminist Activism in the Catholic Church." In *Feminist Organizations: Harvest of the New Women's Movement*, ed. M. M. Ferree and P. Y. Martin, 35–52. Philadelphia: Temple University Press.

Kaufman, Sharon R. 1986. *The Ageless Self: Sources of Meaning in Late Life*. Madison: University of Wisconsin Press.

Kellams, Laura. 2007. "Group Gets OK on Drive for Foster Adoption Ban." *Arkansas Democrat Gazette*, October 5 (http://www.nwanews.com/adg/news/203380/, accessed December 13, 2008).

Keller, Evelyn Fox. 2002. *The Century of the Gene*. Cambridge, MA: Harvard University Press.

Kennedy, Elizabeth Lapovsky, and Madeline D. Davis. 1993. *Boots of Leather, Slippers of Gold: The History of a Lesbian Community*. New York: Routledge.

Khandelwal, Meena. 2009. "Arranging Love: Interrogating the Vantage Point in Cross-Border Feminism." *Signs* 34(3): 583–609.

Kimmel, Douglas, Tara Rose, and Steven David. 2006. *Lesbian, Gay, Bisexual, and Transgender Aging: Research and Clinical Perspectives*. New York: Columbia University Press.

Klassen, Pamela E. 2001. *Blessed Events: Religion and Home Birth in America*. Princeton: Princeton University Press.

Kleinman, Arthur. 1989. *The Illness Narratives: Suffering, Healing, and the Human Condition*. New York: Basic Books.

Koestenbaum, Wayne. 2001. *The Queen's Throat: Opera, Homosexuality, and the Mystery of Desire*. Cambridge, MA: Da Capo Press.

Kolata, Gina. 1989. "Lesbian Partners Find the Means to Be Parents." *New York Times*, January 30.

Korbin, Jill E. 1998. "'Good Mothers,' 'Babykillers,' and Fatal Child Maltreatment." In *Small Wars: The Cultural Politics of Childhood*, ed. Nancy Scheper-Hughes and Carolyn Sargent, 253–76. Berkeley: University of California Press.

Krieger, Susan. 1983. *The Mirror Dance: Identity in a Women's Community*. Philadelphia: Temple University Press.

Kuper, Adam. 1988. *The Invention of Primitive Society: Transformations of an Illusion*. New York: Routledge.

Kurtz, Demie. 1995. *For Richer, For Poorer: Mothers Confront Divorce*. New York: Routledge.

Lambda Legal. 2004. Overview of State Adoption Laws (http://www.lambdalegal.org/our-work/issues/marriage-relationships-family/parenting/overview-of-state-adoption.html, accessed December 13, 2008).

Lancaster, Roger. 2003. *The Trouble with Nature: Sex and Science in Popular Culture*. Berkeley: University of California Press.

Landsman, Gail. 1999. "Does God Give Special Kids to Special Parents? Personhood and the Child with Disabilities as Gift and Giver." In *Transformative Motherhood: On Giving and Getting in a Consumer Culture*, ed. L. L. Layne, 133–65. New York: New York University Press.

———. 2004. "'Too Bad You Got a Lemon': Peter Singer, Mothers of Children with Disabilities, and the Critique of Consumer Culture." In *Consuming Moth-*

erhood, ed. J. S. Taylor, L. L. Layne, and D. F. Wozniak, 100–121. New Brunswick: Rutgers University Press.

LaRossa, Ralph. 1997. *The Modernization of Fatherhood: A Social and Political History*. Chicago: University of Chicago Press.

Layne, Linda L. 2004. "Making Memories: Trauma, Choice, and Consumer Culture in the Case of Pregnancy Loss." In *Consuming Motherhood*, ed. J. S. Taylor, L. L. Layne, and D. F. Wozniak, 122–38. New Brunswick: Rutgers University Press.

Lee, Jennifer, and Frank D. Bean. 2004. "America's Changing Color Lines: Immigration, Race/Ethnicity, and Multiracial Identification." *Annual Review of Sociology* 30:221–42.

Lehr, Valerie. 1999. *Queer Family Values: Debunking the Myth of the Nuclear Family*. Philadelphia: Temple University Press.

Leonard, Karen I. 1992. *Making Ethnic Choices: California's Punjabi Mexican Americans*. Philadelphia: Temple University Press.

Lessing, Doris. 1989. *The Fifth Child*. New York: Vintage.

Lévi-Strauss, Claude. 1969. *The Elementary Structures of Kinship*. Boston: Beacon Press.

Lewin, Ellen. 1993. *Lesbian Mothers: Accounts of Gender in American Culture*. Ithaca: Cornell University Press.

———. 1998. *Recognizing Ourselves: Ceremonies of Lesbian and Gay Commitment*. New York: Columbia University Press.

Lewis, Deborah Shaw, and Charmaine Crouse West. 1996. *Mother in the Middle: Searching for Peace in the Mommy Wars*. Grand Rapids: Zondervan.

Lewontin, Richard C. 1993. *Biology and Ideology: The Doctrine of DNA*. New York: Harper.

Liptak, Adam. 2003. "Gay Couple Challenges Florida Ban on Homosexual Adoptions." *New York Times*, March 2.

———. 2005. "California Ruling Expands Same-Sex Parental Rights." *New York Times*, August 23.

———. 2006. "Ruling Lets Women Share Rights in Fight over Custody." *New York Times*, November 29.

Lock, Margaret. 2001. *Twice Dead: Organ Transplants and the Reinvention of Death*. Berkeley: University of California Press.

Lowe, Wendy, Jutta Wittmeier, and Carmen Wittmeier. 2006. *Affirming the Birth Mother's Journey: A Peer Counselor's Guide to Adoption Counseling*. Victoria, BC: Trafford Publishing.

Mackie, Marlene. 1977. "On Congenial Truths: A Perspective on Women's Studies." *Canadian Review of Sociology and Anthropology* 14:117–28.

Macklin, Ruth. 1996. "What Is Wrong with Commodification?" In *New Ways of Making Babies: The Case of Egg Donation*, ed. C. B. Cohen, 106–21. Bloomington, IN: Indiana University Press.

Mahon, Nancy B. 1988. "Public Hysteria, Private Conflict: Child Custody and Visitation Disputes Involving an HIV Infected Parent." *New York University Law Review* 63:1092–1141.

Mallon, Gerald P. 2004. *Gay Men Choosing Parenthood*. New York: Columbia University Press.

———. 2006. *Lesbian and Gay Foster and Adoptive Parents: Recruiting, Assessing, and Supporting an Untapped Resource for Children and Youth*. Washington, DC: Child Welfare League of America.

Mamo, Laura. 2007. *Queering Reproduction: Achieving Pregnancy in the Age of Technoscience*. Durham: Duke University Press.

Mandell, Deena. 2002. *Deadbeat Dads: Subjectivity and Social Construction*. Toronto: University of Toronto Press.

Marcus, George E. 1998. *Ethnography through Thick and Thin*. Princeton: Princeton University Press.

Markens, Susan. 2007. *Surrogate Motherhood and the Politics of Reproduction*. Berkeley: University of California Press.

Marneffe, Daphne de. 2005. *Maternal Desire: On Children, Love, and the Inner Life*. Boston: Little, Brown.

Marsiglio, William. 1998. *Procreative Man*. New York: New York University Press.

Martin, Emily. 1995. *Flexible Bodies*. Boston: Beacon Press.

Maskovsky, Jeff. 2002. "Do We All 'Reek of the Commodity'? Consumption and the Erasure of Poverty in Lesbian and Gay Studies." In *Out in Theory: The Emergence of Lesbian and Gay Anthropology*, ed. E. Lewin and W. L. Leap, 264–86. Urbana-Champaign, IL: University of Illinois Press.

Mason, Mary Ann. 1994. *From Father's Property to Children's Rights: History of Child Custody in the United States*. New York: Columbia University Press.

McCracken, Grant. 1988. *Culture and Consumption*. Bloomington, IN: Indiana University Press.

Meeks, Chet, and Arlene Stein. 2006. "Strange Bedfellows: The Institution of Marriage and the LGBT Community." In *Intersections between Feminist and Queer Theory*, ed. D. Richardson, J. McLaughlin, and M. E. Casey, 136–55. New York: Palgrave Macmillan.

Melina, Lois Ruskai, and Sharon Kaplan Roszia. 1993. *Open Adoption Experience: Complete Guide for Adoptive and Birth Families*. New York: HarperCollins.

Menichiello, Michael. 2006. *A Gay Couple's Journey through Surrogacy: Intended Fathers*. Binghamton, NY: Haworth Press.

Merchant, Carolyn. 1980. *The Death of Nature: Women, Ecology, and the Scientific Revolution*. San Francisco: Harper & Row.

Meyer, Cheryl L. 2001. *Mothers Who Kill Their Children: Understanding the Acts of Moms from Susan Smith to the "Prom Mom."* New York: New York University Press.

Miller, Neil. 1989. *In Search of Gay America: Women and Men in a Time of Change*. New York: Harper & Row.

Miller, Sue. 1988. *The Good Mother*. New York: Dell.

Mincy, Ronald B., and Elaine J. Sorensen. 1998. "Deadbeats and Turnips in Child Support Reform." *Journal of Policy Analysis and Management* 17(1): 44–51.

Mink, Gwendolyn. 2002. *Welfare's End*. Ithaca: Cornell University Press.

Modell, Judith S. 1994. *Kinship with Strangers: Adoption and Interpretations of Kinship in America Culture*. Berkeley: University of California Press.

———. 2002. *A Sealed and Secret Kinship: The Culture of Policies and Practices in American Adoption*. New York: Berghahn Books.

Monette, Paul. 1988. *Borrowed Time: An AIDS Memoir*. San Diego: Harcourt, Brace, Jovanovich.

Mundy, Liza. 2007. *Everything Conceivable: How Assisted Reproduction Is Changing Men, Women, and the World*. New York: Knopf.

Murphy, Sheigla, and Marsha Rosenbaum. 1999. *Pregnant Women on Drugs: Combating Stereotypes and Stigma*. New Brunswick: Rutgers University Press.

Murray, Stephen O. 1979. "The Institution of a Quasi-Ethnic Community." *International Review of Modern Sociology* 9:155–75.

Nardi, Peter. 1999. *Gay Men's Friendship: Invincible Communities*. Chicago: University of Chicago Press.

Nelkin, Dorothy, and M. Susan Lindee. 1996. *The DNA Mystique: The Gene as a Cultural Icon*. New York: WH Freeman.

Nelson, Margaret K. 1991. *Negotiated Care: The Experience of Family Day Care Providers*. Philadelphia: Temple University Press.

Newman, Andy. 2007. "Journey from a Chinese Orphanage to a Jewish Rite of Passage." *New York Times*, March 8.

Newton, Esther. 1979 (1972). *Mother Camp: Female Impersonators in America*. Chicago: University of Chicago Press.

———. 1993. *Cherry Grove, Fire Island: Sixty Years in America's First Gay and Lesbian Town*. Boston: Beacon Press.

Oaks, Laury. 2000. *Smoking and Pregnancy: The Politics of Fetal Protection*. New Brunswick: Rutgers University Press.

O'Brien, Mary. 1981. *The Politics of Reproduction*. Boston: Routledge & Kegan Paul.

O'Halloran, Kerry. 2006. *The Politics of Adoption: International Perspectives on Law, Policy, and Practice*. Dordrecht, The Netherlands: Springer.

Orenstein, Peggy. 2007. *Waiting for Daisy: A Tale of Two Continents, Three Religions, Five Infertility Doctors, an Oscar, an Atomic Bomb, a Romantic Night, and One Woman's Quest to Become a Mother*. New York: Bloomsbury.

Ortner, Sherry B. 1974. "Is Female to Male as Nature Is to Culture?" In *Woman, Culture, and Society*, ed. M. Z. Rosaldo and L. Lamphere, 67–88. Stanford: Stanford University Press.

———. 1995. "Resistance and the Problem of Ethnographic Refusal." *Comparative Studies in Society and History* 37(1): 173–93.

Passet, Joanne E. 2003. *Sex Radicals and the Quest for Women's Equality*. Urbana-Champaign, IL: University of Illinois Press.

Patterson, Charlotte J. 1995. "Lesbian Mothers, Gay Fathers, and Their Children." In *Lesbian, Gay, and Bisexual Identities over the Lifespan*, ed. A. R. D'Augelli and C. J. Patterson, 262–90. New York: Oxford University Press.

Patton, Sandra. 2000. *Birth Marks: Transracial Adoption in Contemporary America*. New York: New York University Press.

Peacock, Ben. 2006. *"But I Want That One": Consumer Citizenship and the Politics of Exclusion, Public Space and Homelessness in the Gay Ghetto*. Berkeley: Institute for the Study of Social Change, University of California.

Peacock, Ben, Stephen L. Eyre, Sandra Crouse Quinn, and Susan Kegeles. 2001. "Delineating Differences: Subcommunities in the San Francisco Gay Community." *Culture, Health, and Sexuality* 3(2): 183–201.

Pelka, Suzanne. 2005. "Lesbian Couples Creating Families Using In Vitro Fertilization to Co-Mother: A Cultural Study of Biological Ties." Ph.D. diss., University of Chicago.

Perry, Troy D. 1972. *The Lord Is My Shepherd and He Knows I'm Gay: The Autobiography of the Reverend Troy D. Perry.* Martinsburg, WV: Nash Publications.

Pertman, Adam. 2000. *Adoption Nation: How the Adoption Revolution Is Transforming America.* New York: Basic Books.

Peskowitz, Miriam. 2005. *The Truth behind the Mommy Wars: Who Decides What Makes a Good Mother?* Emeryville, CA: Seal Press.

Petchesky, Rosalind Pollack. 1987. "Fetal Images: The Power of Visual Culture in the Politics of Reproduction." *Feminist Studies* 13(2): 264–92.

Pinto-Correia, Clara. 1998. *The Ovary of Eve: Egg and Sperm and Preformation.* Chicago: University of Chicago Press.

Plummer, Ken. 1995. *Telling Sexual Stories: Power, Change, and Social Worlds.* London: Routledge.

Polikoff, Nancy D. 1993. "We Will Get What We Ask For: Why Legalizing Gay and Lesbian Marriage Will Not 'Dismantle the Legal Structure of Gender in Every Marriage.'" *Virginia Law Review* 79(7): 1535–50.

———. 2008. *Beyond (Straight and Gay) Marriage: Valuing All Families under the Law.* Boston: Beacon Press.

Pollan, Michael. 2007. *The Omnivore's Dilemma: A Natural History of Four Meals.* New York: Penguin.

Povinelli, Elizabeth A. 2001. "Radical Worlds: The Anthropology of Incommensurability and Inconceivability." *Annual Review of Anthropology* 30:319–34.

Quadagno, Jill. 1996. *The Color of Welfare: How Racism Undermined the War on Poverty.* Oxford: Oxford University Press.

Ragoné, Helena. 1994. *Surrogate Motherhood: Conception in the Heart.* Boulder: Westview.

———. 1998. "Incontestable Motivations." In *Reproducing Reproduction: Kinship, Power, and Technological Innovation,* ed. S. Franklin and H. Ragoné, 118–31. Philadelphia: University of Pennsylvania Press.

Ransel, David L. 2005. *Village Mothers: Three Generations of Change in Russia and Tataria.* Bloomington, IN: Indiana University Press.

Reardon, Jenny. 2004. *Race to the Finish: Identity and Governance in an Age of Genomics.* Princeton: Princeton University Press.

Reese, Ellen. 2005. *Backlash against Welfare Mothers: Past and Present.* Berkeley: University of California Press.

Register, Cheri. 1990. *Are Those Kids Yours? American Families with Children Adopted from Other Countries.* New York: Free Press.

Rich, Adrienne. 1976. *Of Woman Born: Motherhood as Experience and Institution.* New York: W.W. Norton.

Risman, Barbara J. 1986. "Can Men 'Mother'? Life as a Single Father." *Family Relations* 35(1): 95–102.

———. 1998. *Gender Vertigo: American Families in Transition*. New Haven: Yale University Press.

Roberts, Dorothy. 1998. *Killing the Black Body: Race, Reproduction, and the Meaning of Liberty*. New York: Vintage.

———. 2002. *Shattered Bonds: The Color of Child Welfare*. New York: Basic Books.

Robinson, Paul. 2002. *Opera, Sex, and Other Vital Matters*. Chicago: University of Chicago Press.

Robson, Ruthann. 1994. "Resisting the Family: Repositioning Lesbians in Legal Theory." *Signs* 19(4): 975–96.

Rosaldo, Michelle Zimbalist. 1974. "Woman, Culture, and Society: A Theoretical Overview." In *Woman, Culture, and Society*, ed. M. Z. Rosaldo and L. Lamphere, 17–42. Stanford: Stanford University Press.

Rosaldo, Renato. 1986. "Ilongot Hunting as Story and Experience." In *The Anthropology of Experience*, ed. V. W. Turner and E. M. Bruner, 97–138. Urbana-Champaign, IL: University of Illinois Press.

Rose, Nikolas. 2007. *The Politics of Life Itself: Biomedicine, Power, and Subjectivity in the Twenty-First Century*. Princeton: Princeton University Press.

Rothman, Barbara Katz. 2005. *Weaving a Family: Untangling Race and Adoption*. Boston: Beacon Press.

Rotundo, E. Anthony. 1993. *American Manhood: Transformations in Masculinity from the Revolution to the Modern Era*. New York: Basic Books.

Ruby, Jay, ed. 1982. *A Crack in the Mirror: Reflexive Perspectives in Anthropology*. Philadelphia: University of Pennsylvania Press.

Ruddick, Sara. 1989. *Maternal Thinking: Toward a Politics of Peace*. Boston: Beacon Press.

Salzman, Philip Carl. 2002. "On Reflexivity." *American Anthropologist* 104(3): 805–11.

Sandelowski, Margarete. 1993. *With Child in Mind: Studies of the Personal Encounter with Infertility*. Philadelphia: University of Pennsylvania Press.

Savage, Dan. 1999. *The Kid (What Happened after My Boyfriend and I Decided to Go Get Pregnant): An Adoption Story*. New York: Dutton.

Scheper-Hughes, Nancy. 1992. *Death Without Weeping: The Violence of Everyday Life in Brazil*. Berkeley: University of California Press.

Schneider, David N. 1968. *American Kinship: A Cultural Account*. Englewood Cliffs, NJ: Prentice-Hall.

———. 1984. *A Critique of the Study of Kinship*. Ann Arbor: University of Michigan Press.

Schwartz, F. N. 1989. "Management Women and the New Facts of Life." *Harvard Business Review* 67(1): 65–76.

Segal, Lynne. 1990. *Slow Motion: Changing Masculinities, Changing Men*. New Brunswick: Rutgers University Press.

Seiter, Ellen. 1995. *Sold Separately: Parents and Children in Consumer Culture*. New Brunswick: Rutgers University Press.

Selman, Peter. 2000. "The Demographic History of Intercountry Adoption." In *Intercountry Adoption: Developments, Trends, and Perspectives*, ed. P. Selman, 15–39. London: British Agencies for Adoption and Fostering.

Sember, Brette McWhorter. 2006. *Gay & Lesbian Parenting Choices: From Adopting or Using a Surrogate to Choosing the Perfect Father*. Franklin Lakes, NJ: Career Press.

Sender, Katherine. 2004. *Business, Not Politics: The Making of the Gay Market*. New York: Columbia University Press.

Shallenberger, David. 1998. *Reclaiming the Spirit: Gay Men and Lesbians Come to Terms with Religion*. New Brunswick: Rutgers University Press.

Share, Jessica Ann. 2006. "Getting Away from Gay: The Construction of Lesbian and Gay Anti-Community at the Dinah Shore and White Parties in Palm Springs." Ph.D. diss., University of Iowa.

Shilts, Randy. 1987. *And the Band Played On: Politics, People and the AIDS Epidemic*. New York: St. Martin's Press.

Shokeid, Moshe. 2002. *A Gay Synagogue in New York*. Philadelphia: University of Pennsylvania Press.

Shorter, Edward. 1975. *The Making of the Modern Family*. New York: Basic Books.

Siker, Jeffrey S. 1994. *Homosexuality in the Church: Both Sides of the Debate*. Louisville: Westminster John Knox Press.

Silber, Kathleen, and Phyllis Speedlin. 1991. *Dear Birthmother*. San Antonio: Corona Publishing Company.

Simmons, Tavia, and Martin O'Connell. 2003. "Married Couples and Unmarried Partner Households: 2000." U.S. Bureau of the Census.

Simon, Rita J., and Howard Altstein. 2000. *Adoption across Borders: Serving the Children in Transracial and Intercountry Adoptions*. Lanham, MD: Rowman & Littlefield.

Slotkin, Richard. 1973. *Regeneration through Violence: The Mythology of the American Frontier, 1600–1860*. Norman, OK: University of Oklahoma Press.

Smith, Dorothy E. 1993. "The Standard North American Family: SNAF as an Ideological Code." *Journal of Family Issues* 14:50–65.

Solinger, Rickie. 1994. *Wake Up Little Susie: Single Pregnancy and Race Before Roe v. Wade*. New York: Routledge.

———. 2001. *Beggars and Choosers: How the Politics of Choice Shapes Adoption, Abortion, and Welfare in the United States*. New York: Hill & Wang.

Spallone, Patricia, and Deborah Lynn Steinberg. 1992. *Made to Order*. New York: Teachers College Press.

Spar, Deborah L. 2006. *The Baby Business: How Money, Science, and Politics Drive the Commerce of Conception*. Boston: Harvard Business School Press.

Spears, Valarie Honeycutt. 2004. "Gay Parents of Quads Have Separated; Court Records Show Dispute." *Lexington Herald-Leader*, June 20.

Stacey, Judith. 2006. "Gay Parenthood and the Decline of Paternity as We Knew It." *Sexualities* 9(1): 27–55.

Stacey, Judith, and Timothy J. Biblarz. 2001. "(How) Does the Sexual Orientation of Parents Matter?" *American Sociological Review* 66(2): 159–83.

Stanworth, Michelle. 1990. "Birth Pangs: Conceptive Technologies and the Threat to Motherhood." In *Conflicts in Feminism*, ed. M. Hirsch and E. F. Keller, 288–304. New York: Routledge.

Steckel, Ailsa. 1985. "Separation-Individuation in Children of Lesbian and Heterosexual Couples." Ph.D. diss., The Wright Institute Graduate School.

Steiner, Leslie Morgan. 2006. *Mommy Wars: Stay-at-Home and Career Moms Face Off on Their Choices, Their Lives, Their Families*. New York: Random House.

Stone, Pamela. 2007. *Opting Out: Why Women Really Quit Careers and Head Home*. Berkeley: University of California Press.

Strathern, Marilyn. 1992. *After Nature: English Kinship in the Late Twentieth Century*. Cambridge: Cambridge University Press.

Sullivan, Maureen. 2004. *The Family of Woman: Lesbian Mothers, Their Children, and the Undoing of Gender*. Berkeley: University of California Press.

Symons, Johnny. 2002. *Daddy and Papa*. DVD. New Day Films.

———. 2006. *Beyond Conception: Men Having Babies*. DVD. Persistent Visions.

Takezawa, Yasuko I. 1995. *Breaking the Silence: Redress and Japanese American Ethnicity*. Ithaca: Cornell University Press.

Taylor, Janelle S. 2004. Introd. to *Consuming Motherhood*, ed. J. S. Taylor, L. L. Layne, and D. F. Wozniak, 1–18. New Brunswick: Rutgers University Press.

Taylor, Janelle S., Linda L. Layne, and Danielle F. Wozniak, eds. 2004. *Consuming Motherhood*. New Brunswick: Rutgers University Press.

Taylor, Verta. 1996. *Rock-a-by Baby: Feminism, Self-Help, and Postpartum Depression*. New York: Routledge.

Terry, Jennifer. 1999. *An American Obsession: Science, Medicine, and Homosexuality in Modern Society*. Chicago: University of Chicago Press.

Thompson, Charis. 2001. "Strategic Naturalizing: Kinship in an Infertility Clinic." In *Relative Values: Reconfiguring Kinship Studies*, ed. S. Franklin and S. McKinnon, 175–202. Durham: Duke University Press.

———. 2005. *Making Parents: The Ontological Choreography of Reproductive Technologies*. Cambridge, MA: MIT Press.

Thompson, Julie M. 2002. *Mommy Queerest: Contemporary Rhetorics of Lesbian Maternal Identity*. Amherst: University of Massachusetts Press.

Thumma, Scott, and Edward R Gray. 2005. *Gay Religion*. Lanham, MD: AltaMira Press.

Tober, Diane M. 2001. "Semen as Gift, Semen as Goods: Reproductive Workers and the Market in Altruism." *Body & Society* 7(2–3): 137–60.

Townsend, Nicholas W. 2002. *The Package Deal: Marriage, Work and Fatherhood in Men's Lives*. Philadelphia: Temple University Press.

Triseliotis, John. 1999. "Inter-Country Adoption: Global Trade or Global Gift?" In *Mine—Yours—Ours—and Theirs: Adoption, Changing Kinship and Family Patterns*, ed. A.-L. Rygvold, M. Dalen, and B. Saetersdal, 14–31. Oslo: University of Oslo.

Tsing, Anna Lowenhaupt. 1990. "Monster Stories: Women Charged with Perinatal Endangerment." In *Uncertain Terms: Negotiating Gender in American Culture*, ed. F. Ginsburg and A. L. Tsing, 282–99. Boston: Beacon Press.

Turner, Victor W., and Edward M. Bruner, eds. 1986. *The Anthropology of Experience*. Urbana-Champaign, IL: University of Illinois Press.

Umansky, Lauri. 1996. *Motherhood Reconceived: Feminism and the Legacies of the Sixties*. New York: New York University Press.

Vaid, Urvashi. 1995. *Virtual Equality: The Mainstreaming of Gay and Lesbian Liberation*. New York: Doubleday.

Valentine, David. 2007. *Imagining Transgender: An Ethnography of a Category*. Durham: Duke University Press.

Waite, Linda J. 2000. *The Case for Marriage: Why Married People Are Happier, Healthier, and Better Off Financially*. New York: Broadway Books.

Walters, Suzanna Danuta. 2001. "Take My Domestic Partner, Please: Gays and Marriage in the Era of the Visible." In *Queer Families, Queer Politics: Challenging Culture and the State*, ed. M. Bernstein and R. Reimann, 338–57. New York: Columbia University Press.

Warner, Judith. 2005. *Perfect Madness: Motherhood in the Age of Anxiety*. New York: Riverhead Books.

Warner, Michael. 1999. *The Trouble with Normal: Sex, Politics, and the Ethics of Queer Life*. New York: Free Press.

Weeks, Jeffrey, Brian Heaphy, and Catherine Donovan. 2001. *Same Sex Intimacies: Families of Choice and Other Life Experiments*. London: Routledge.

Weitzman, Lenore. 1985. *The Divorce Revolution: The Unexpected Social and Economic Consequences for Women and Children in America*. New York: Free Press.

Weston, Kath. 1991. *Families We Choose: Lesbians, Gays, Kinship*. New York: Columbia University Press.

———. 1998. "Theory, Theory, Who's Got the Theory?" In *Long Slow Burn: Sexuality and Social Science*, 143–46. New York: Routledge.

Wiegman, Robyn. 2003. "Intimate Publics: Race, Property, and Personhood." In *Race, Nature, and the Politics of Difference*, ed. D. S. Moore, A. Pandian, and J. Kosek, 296–320. Durham: Duke University Press.

Wink, Walter. 1999. *Homosexuality and Christian Faith: Questions of Conscience for the Churches*. Minneapolis: Augsburg Fortress Publishers.

Wolfson, Evan. 2004. *Why Marriage Matters: America, Equality, and Gay People's Right to Marry*. New York: Simon & Schuster.

Wolkomir, Michelle. 2006. *Be Not Deceived: The Sacred and Sexual Struggles of Gay and Ex-Gay Christian Men*. New Brunswick: Rutgers University Press.

Woodhull, Victoria. 2005. *Free Lover: Sex, Marriage And Eugenics in the Early Speeches of Victoria Woodhull*. Seattle: Inkling Books.

Yanagisako, Sylvia, and Carol Delaney, eds. 1995. *Naturalizing Power: Essays in Feminist Cultural Analysis*. New York: Routledge.

Yngvesson, Barbara. 2005. "Going 'Home': Adoption, Loss of Bearings, and the Mythology of Roots." In *Cultures of Transnational Adoption*, ed. T. A. Volkman, 25–48. Durham: Duke University Press.

Zaslow, Robert D. 1994. "Child Custody, Visitation, and the HIV Virus: Revisiting the Best Interests Doctrine to Ensure Impartial Parental Rights Determinations for HIV-Infected Parents." *Journal of Pharmacy and Law* 3:61.

Zelizer, Viviana. 1985. *Pricing the Priceless Child: The Changing Social Value of Children*. Princeton: Princeton University Press.

Zimmerman, Bonnie. 1984. "The Politics of Transliteration: Lesbian First-Person Narratives." *Signs* 9(4): 663–82.

Index